# STAR WARS

## MACE WINDU

### JEDI OF THE REPUBLIC

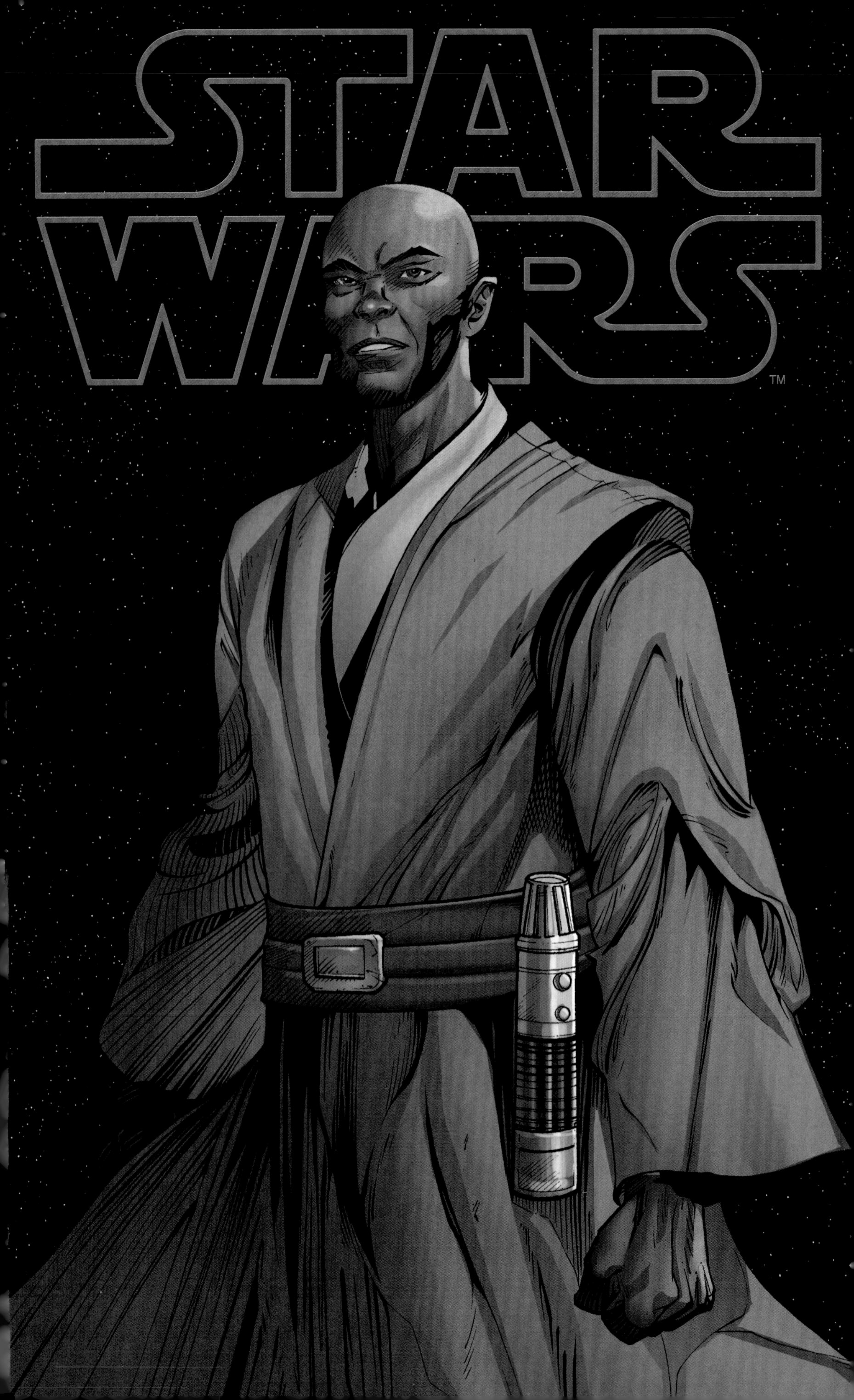
STAR WARS™

# MACE WINDU

## JEDI OF THE REPUBLIC

Writer MATT OWENS
Pencilers DENYS COWAN
WITH EDGAR SALAZAR (#4)
Inkers ROBERTO POGGI
WITH SCOTT HANNA (#4)
Color Artist GURU-eFX
Letterer VC's JOE CARAMAGNA
Cover Art JESÚS SAIZ (#1-4) & ROD REIS (#5)
Assistant Editors HEATHER ANTOS &
CHARLES BEACHAM
Editor JORDAN D. WHITE

Editor in Chief C.B CEBULSKI
Chief Creative Officer JOE QUESADA
President DAN BUCKLEY

**For Lucasfilm:**

Senior Editor FRANK PARISI
Creative Director MICHAEL SIGLAIN
Lucasfilm Story Group JAMES WAUGH, LELAND CHEE,
MATT MARTIN


Collection Editor JENNIFER GRÜNWALD
Assistant Editor CAITLIN O'CONNELL
Associate Managing Editor KATERI WOODY
Editor, Special Projects MARK D. BEAZLEY
VP Production & Special Projects JEFF YOUNGQUIST
SVP Print, Sales & Marketing DAVID GABRIEL
Book Designer ADAM DEL RE

**STAR WARS: JEDI OF THE REPUBLIC — MACE WINDU.** Contains material originally published in magazine form as STAR WARS: JEDI OF THE REPUBLIC — MACE WINDU #1-5. First printing 2018. ISBN 978-1-302-90941-3. Published by MARVEL WORLDWIDE, INC., a subsidiary of MARVEL ENTERTAINMENT, LLC. OFFICE OF PUBLICATION: 135 West 50th Street, New York, NY 10020.



**Printed in Canada.** DAN BUCKLEY, President, Marvel Entertainment; JOE QUESADA, Chief Creative Officer; TOM BREVOORT, SVP of Publishing; DAVID BOGART, SVP of Business Affairs & Operations, Publishing & Partnership; DAVID GABRIEL, SVP of Sales & Marketing, Publishing; JEFF YOUNGQUIST, VP of Production & Special Projects; DAN CARR, Executive Director of Publishing Technology; ALEX MORALES, Director of Publishing Operations; SUSAN CRESPI, Production Manager; STAN LEE, Chairman Emeritus. For information regarding advertising in Marvel Comics or on Marvel.com, please contact Vit DeBellis, Custom Solutions & Integrated Advertising Manager, at vdebellis@marvel.com. For Marvel subscription inquiries, please call 888-511-5480.

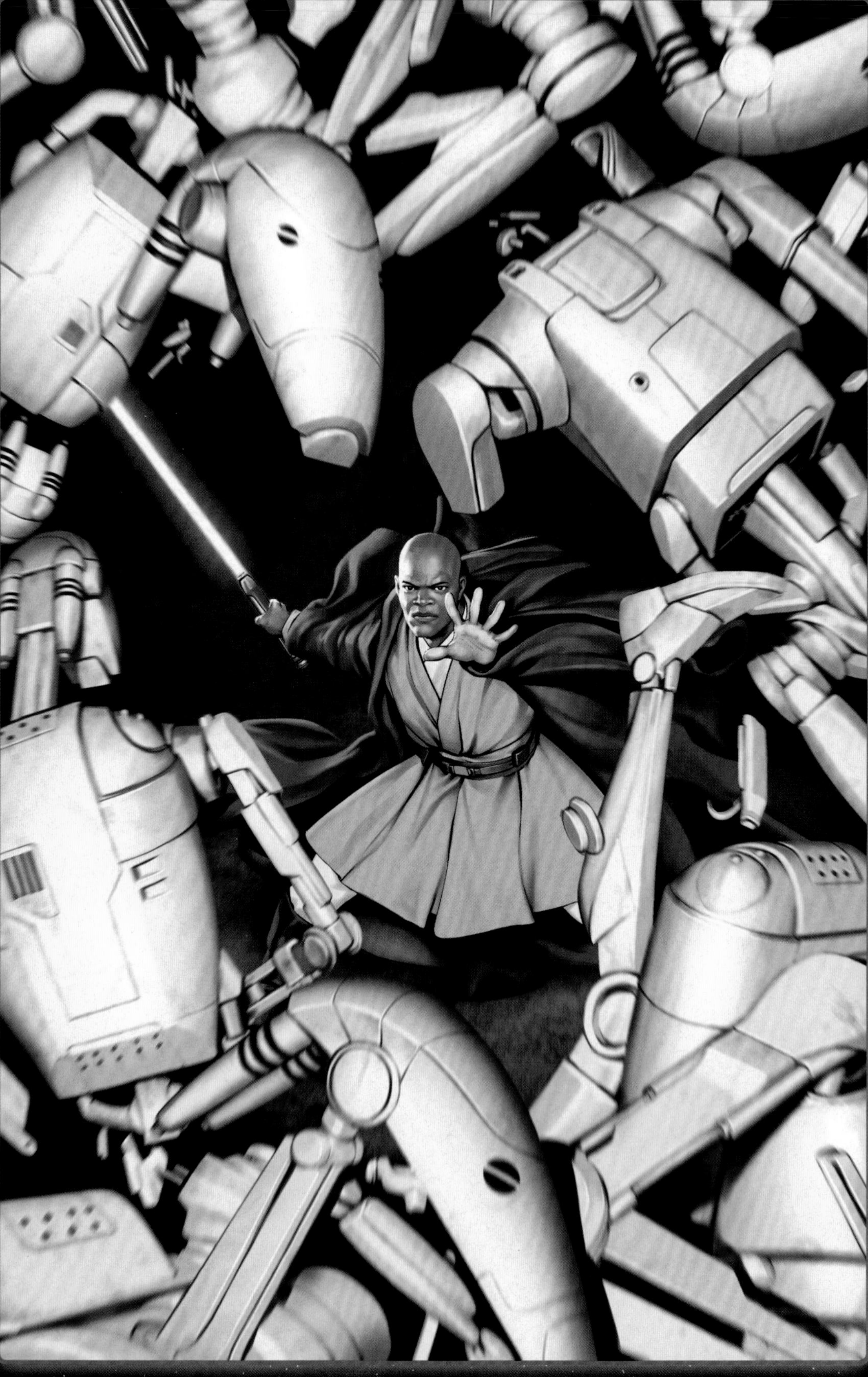

1

# MACE WINDU

*It is a time of war! The Separatist plot to build a massive droid army on Geonosis was interrupted when the Republic activated an army of clone troopers secretly commissioned by a late Jedi Master years earlier. To lead this newly-formed Grand Army of the Republic, Jedi Knights have been made military Generals.*

*Jedi Master Mace Windu fought on the front lines of the Battle of Geonosis, helping to secure a victory for the Republic, but not without loss—many Jedi fell.*

*Now, as the Clone Wars rage on, Windu and his fellow Jedi find themselves pulled away from their roles as peace keepers to become warriors for the Republic....*

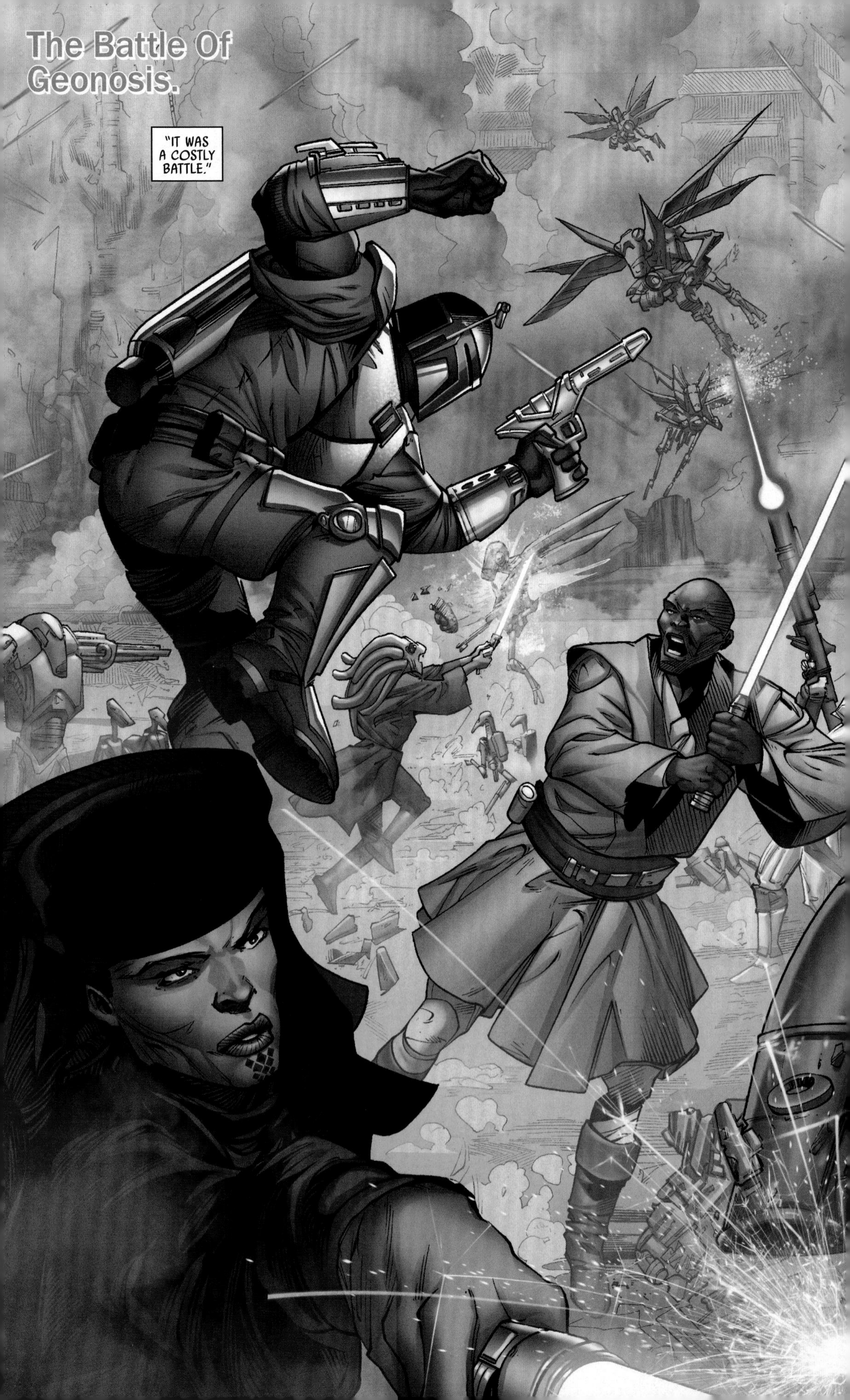
The Battle Of Geonosis.
"IT WAS A COSTLY BATTLE."

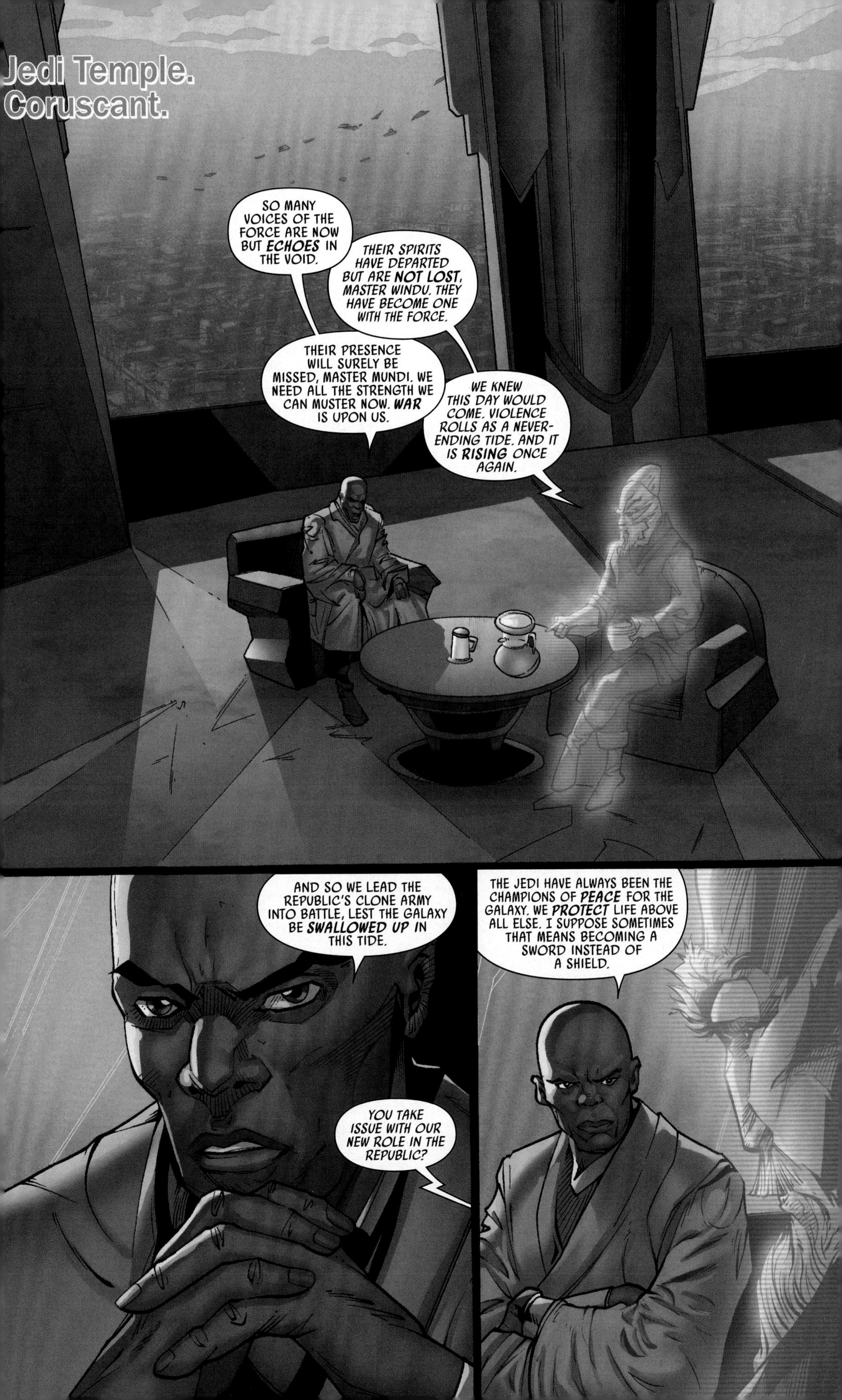
Jedi Temple. Coruscant.
SO MANY VOICES OF THE FORCE ARE NOW BUT ECHOES IN THE VOID.
THEIR SPIRITS HAVE DEPARTED BUT ARE NOT LOST, MASTER WINDU. THEY HAVE BECOME ONE WITH THE FORCE.
THEIR PRESENCE WILL SURELY BE MISSED, MASTER MUNDI. WE NEED ALL THE STRENGTH WE CAN MUSTER NOW. WAR IS UPON US.
WE KNEW THIS DAY WOULD COME. VIOLENCE ROLLS AS A NEVER-ENDING TIDE. AND IT IS RISING ONCE AGAIN.
AND SO WE LEAD THE REPUBLIC'S CLONE ARMY INTO BATTLE, LEST THE GALAXY BE SWALLOWED UP IN THIS TIDE.
YOU TAKE ISSUE WITH OUR NEW ROLE IN THE REPUBLIC?
THE JEDI HAVE ALWAYS BEEN THE CHAMPIONS OF PEACE FOR THE GALAXY. WE PROTECT LIFE ABOVE ALL ELSE. I SUPPOSE SOMETIMES THAT MEANS BECOMING A SWORD INSTEAD OF A SHIELD.

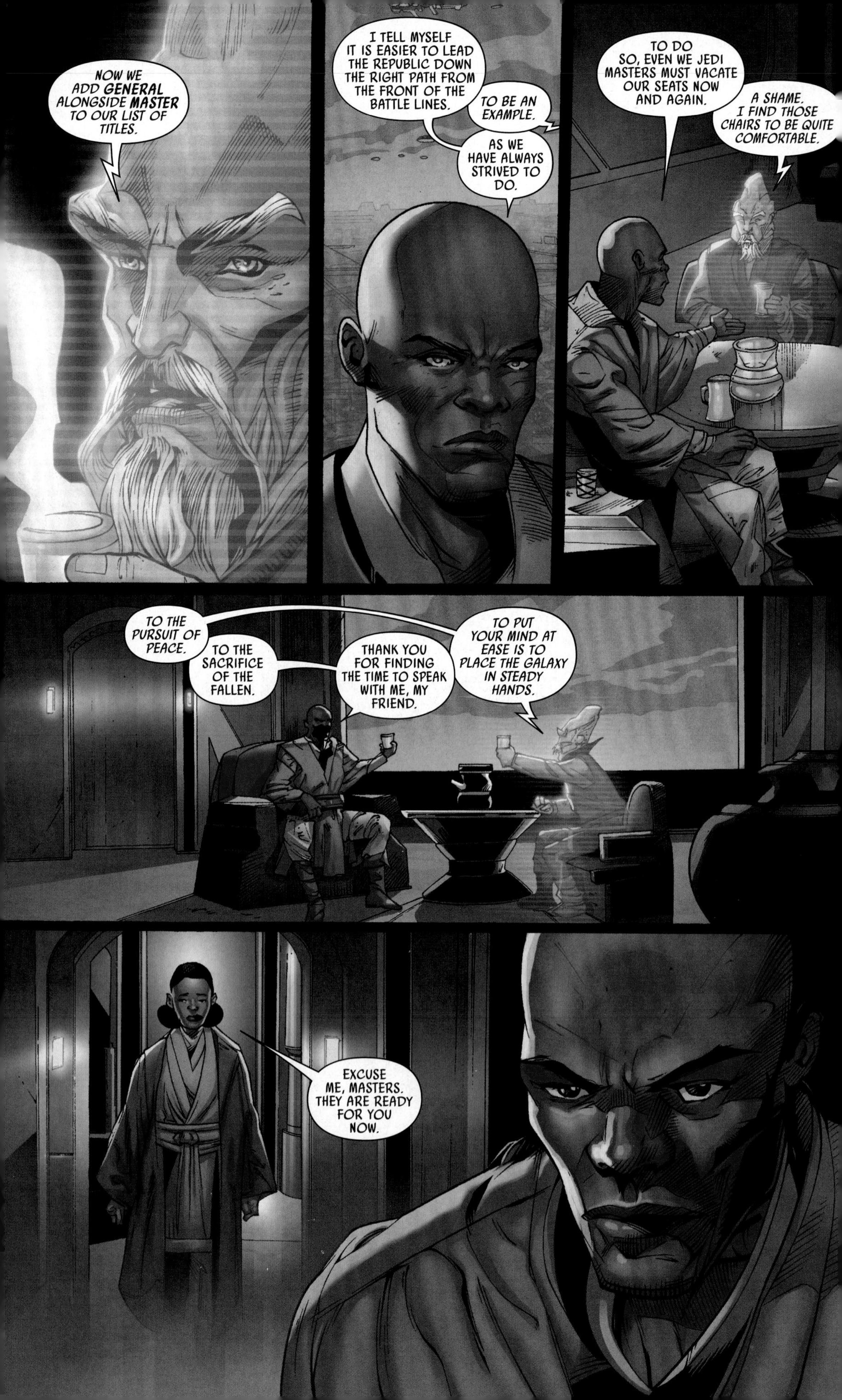
NOW WE ADD GENERAL ALONGSIDE MASTER TO OUR LIST OF TITLES.
I TELL MYSELF IT IS EASIER TO LEAD THE REPUBLIC DOWN THE RIGHT PATH FROM THE FRONT OF THE BATTLE LINES.
TO BE AN EXAMPLE.
AS WE HAVE ALWAYS STRIVED TO DO.
TO DO SO, EVEN WE JEDI MASTERS MUST VACATE OUR SEATS NOW AND AGAIN.
A SHAME. I FIND THOSE CHAIRS TO BE QUITE COMFORTABLE.
THANK YOU FOR FINDING THE TIME TO SPEAK WITH ME, MY FRIEND.
TO PUT YOUR MIND AT EASE IS TO PLACE THE GALAXY IN STEADY HANDS.
TO THE SACRIFICE OF THE FALLEN.
TO THE PURSUIT OF PEACE.
EXCUSE ME, MASTERS. THEY ARE READY FOR YOU NOW.

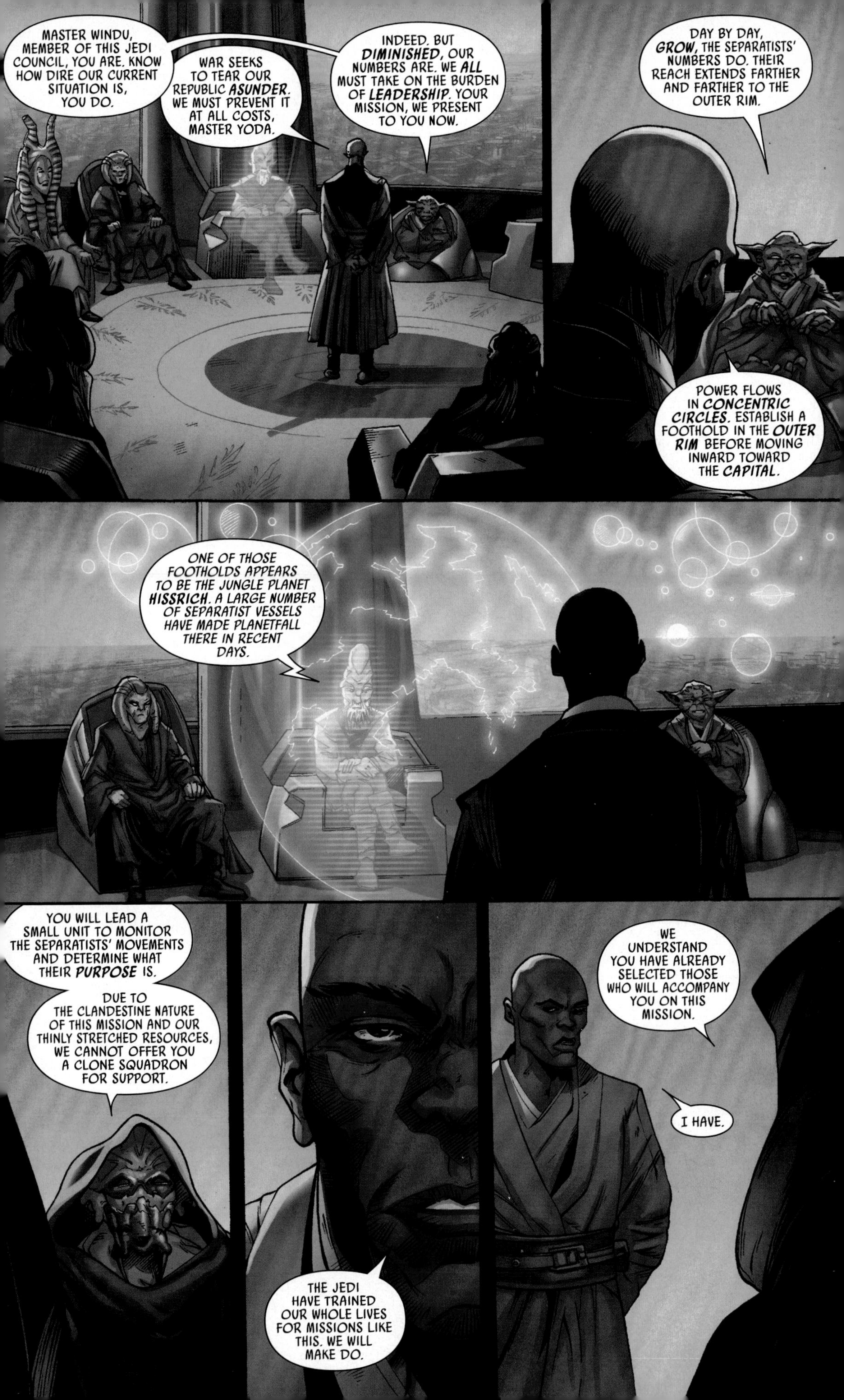
MASTER WINDU, MEMBER OF THIS JEDI COUNCIL, YOU ARE. KNOW HOW DIRE OUR CURRENT SITUATION IS, YOU DO.
WAR SEEKS TO TEAR OUR REPUBLIC ASUNDER. WE MUST PREVENT IT AT ALL COSTS, MASTER YODA.
INDEED. BUT DIMINISHED, OUR NUMBERS ARE. WE ALL MUST TAKE ON THE BURDEN OF LEADERSHIP. YOUR MISSION, WE PRESENT TO YOU NOW.
DAY BY DAY, GROW, THE SEPARATISTS' NUMBERS DO. THEIR REACH EXTENDS FARTHER AND FARTHER TO THE OUTER RIM.
POWER FLOWS IN CONCENTRIC CIRCLES. ESTABLISH A FOOTHOLD IN THE OUTER RIM BEFORE MOVING INWARD TOWARD THE CAPITAL.
ONE OF THOSE FOOTHOLDS APPEARS TO BE THE JUNGLE PLANET HISSRICH. A LARGE NUMBER OF SEPARATIST VESSELS HAVE MADE PLANETFALL THERE IN RECENT DAYS.
YOU WILL LEAD A SMALL UNIT TO MONITOR THE SEPARATISTS' MOVEMENTS AND DETERMINE WHAT THEIR PURPOSE IS.
DUE TO THE CLANDESTINE NATURE OF THIS MISSION AND OUR THINLY STRETCHED RESOURCES, WE CANNOT OFFER YOU A CLONE SQUADRON FOR SUPPORT.
THE JEDI HAVE TRAINED OUR WHOLE LIVES FOR MISSIONS LIKE THIS. WE WILL MAKE DO.
WE UNDERSTAND YOU HAVE ALREADY SELECTED THOSE WHO WILL ACCOMPANY YOU ON THIS MISSION.
I HAVE.

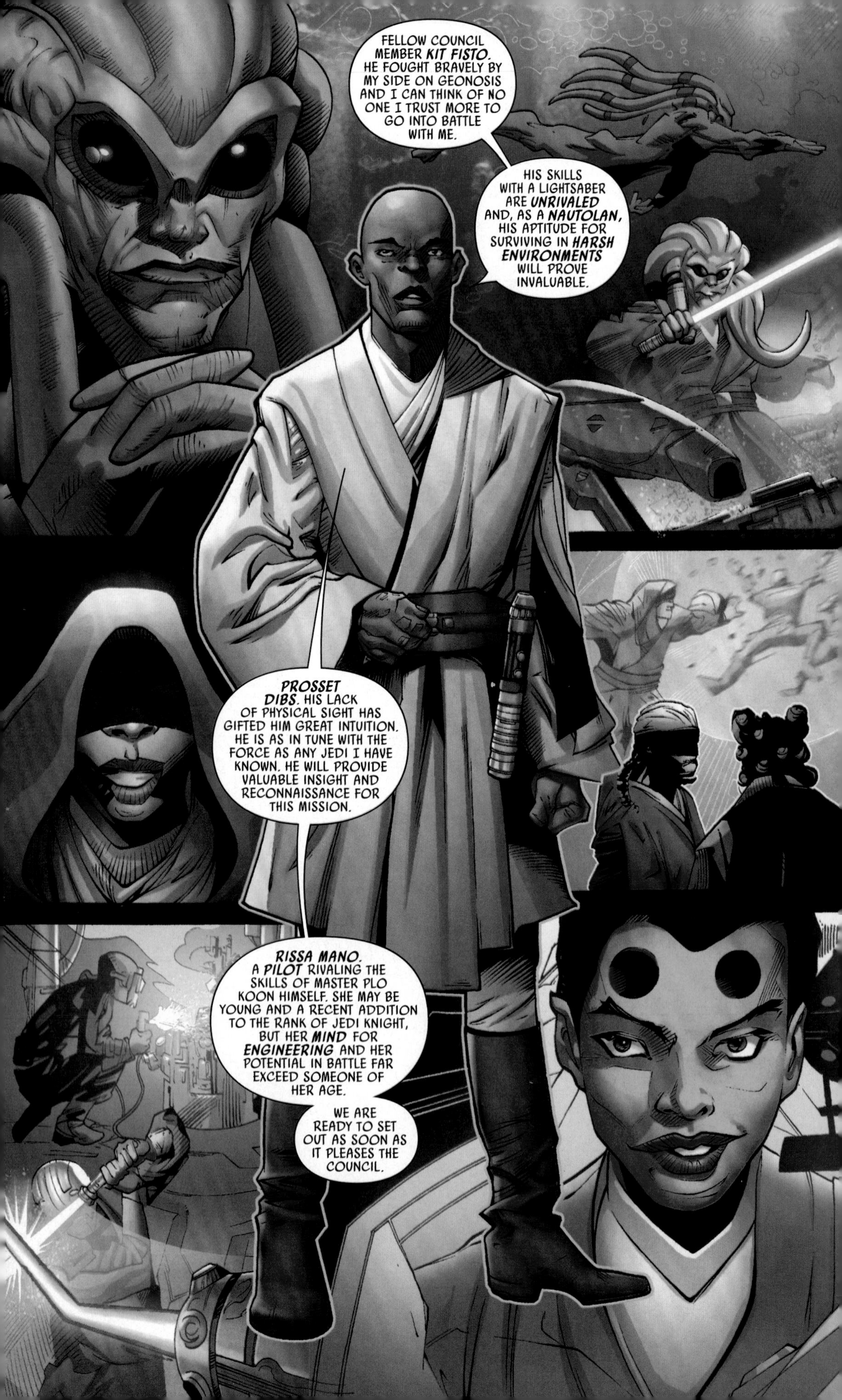
FELLOW COUNCIL MEMBER KIT FISTO. HE FOUGHT BRAVELY BY MY SIDE ON GEONOSIS AND I CAN THINK OF NO ONE I TRUST MORE TO GO INTO BATTLE WITH ME.
HIS SKILLS WITH A LIGHTSABER ARE UNRIVALED AND, AS A NAUTOLAN, HIS APTITUDE FOR SURVIVING IN HARSH ENVIRONMENTS WILL PROVE INVALUABLE.
PROSSET DIBS. HIS LACK OF PHYSICAL SIGHT HAS GIFTED HIM GREAT INTUITION. HE IS AS IN TUNE WITH THE FORCE AS ANY JEDI I HAVE KNOWN. HE WILL PROVIDE VALUABLE INSIGHT AND RECONNAISSANCE FOR THIS MISSION.
RISSA MANO. A PILOT RIVALING THE SKILLS OF MASTER PLO KOON HIMSELF. SHE MAY BE YOUNG AND A RECENT ADDITION TO THE RANK OF JEDI KNIGHT, BUT HER MIND FOR ENGINEERING AND HER POTENTIAL IN BATTLE FAR EXCEED SOMEONE OF HER AGE.
WE ARE READY TO SET OUT AS SOON AS IT PLEASES THE COUNCIL.

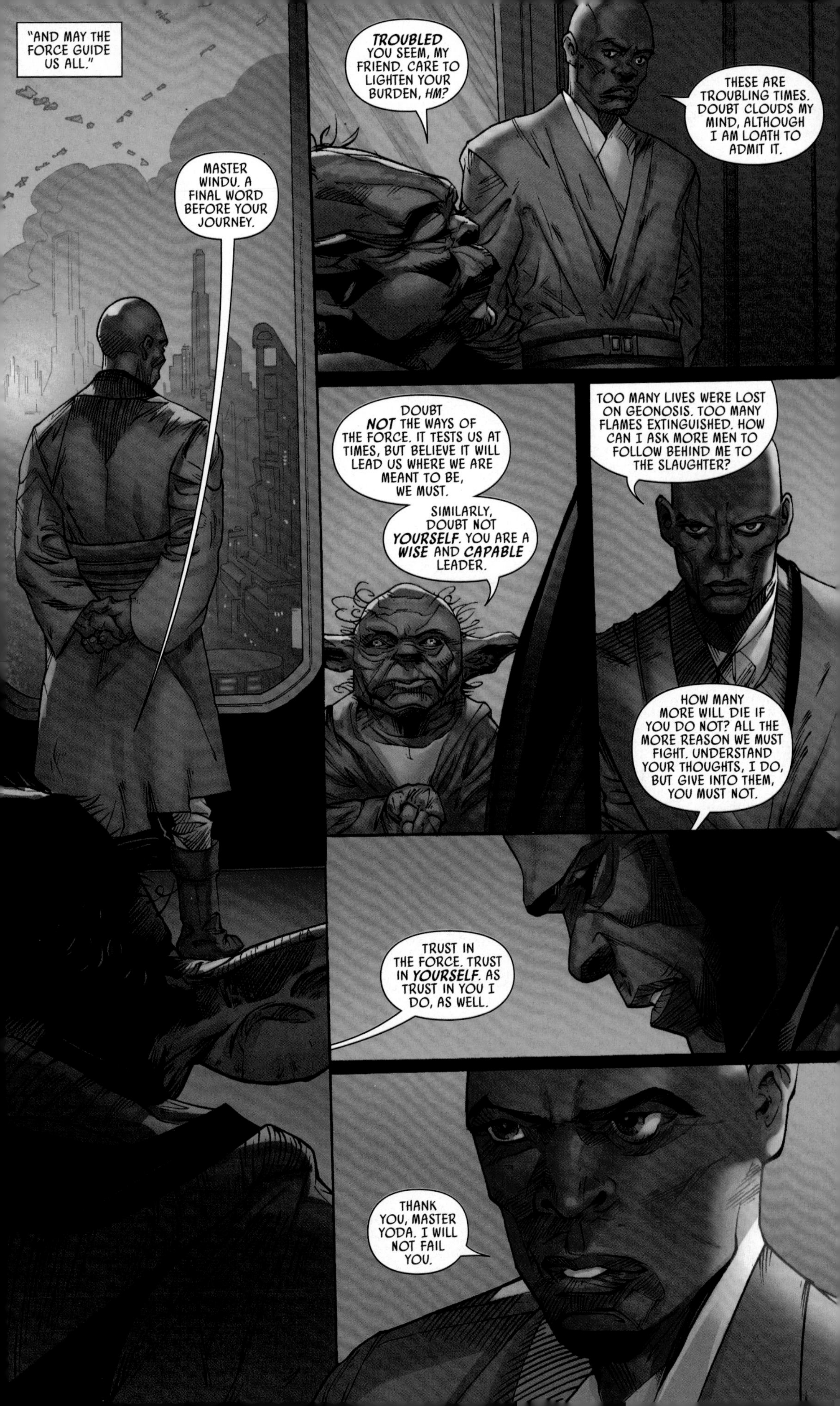
"AND MAY THE FORCE GUIDE US ALL."
MASTER WINDU. A FINAL WORD BEFORE YOUR JOURNEY.
TROUBLED YOU SEEM, MY FRIEND. CARE TO LIGHTEN YOUR BURDEN, HM?
THESE ARE TROUBLING TIMES. DOUBT CLOUDS MY MIND, ALTHOUGH I AM LOATH TO ADMIT IT.
DOUBT NOT THE WAYS OF THE FORCE. IT TESTS US AT TIMES, BUT BELIEVE IT WILL LEAD US WHERE WE ARE MEANT TO BE, WE MUST.
SIMILARLY, DOUBT NOT YOURSELF. YOU ARE A WISE AND CAPABLE LEADER.
TOO MANY LIVES WERE LOST ON GEONOSIS. TOO MANY FLAMES EXTINGUISHED. HOW CAN I ASK MORE MEN TO FOLLOW BEHIND ME TO THE SLAUGHTER?
HOW MANY MORE WILL DIE IF YOU DO NOT? ALL THE MORE REASON WE MUST FIGHT. UNDERSTAND YOUR THOUGHTS, I DO, BUT GIVE INTO THEM, YOU MUST NOT.
TRUST IN THE FORCE. TRUST IN YOURSELF. AS TRUST IN YOU I DO, AS WELL.
THANK YOU, MASTER YODA. I WILL NOT FAIL YOU.

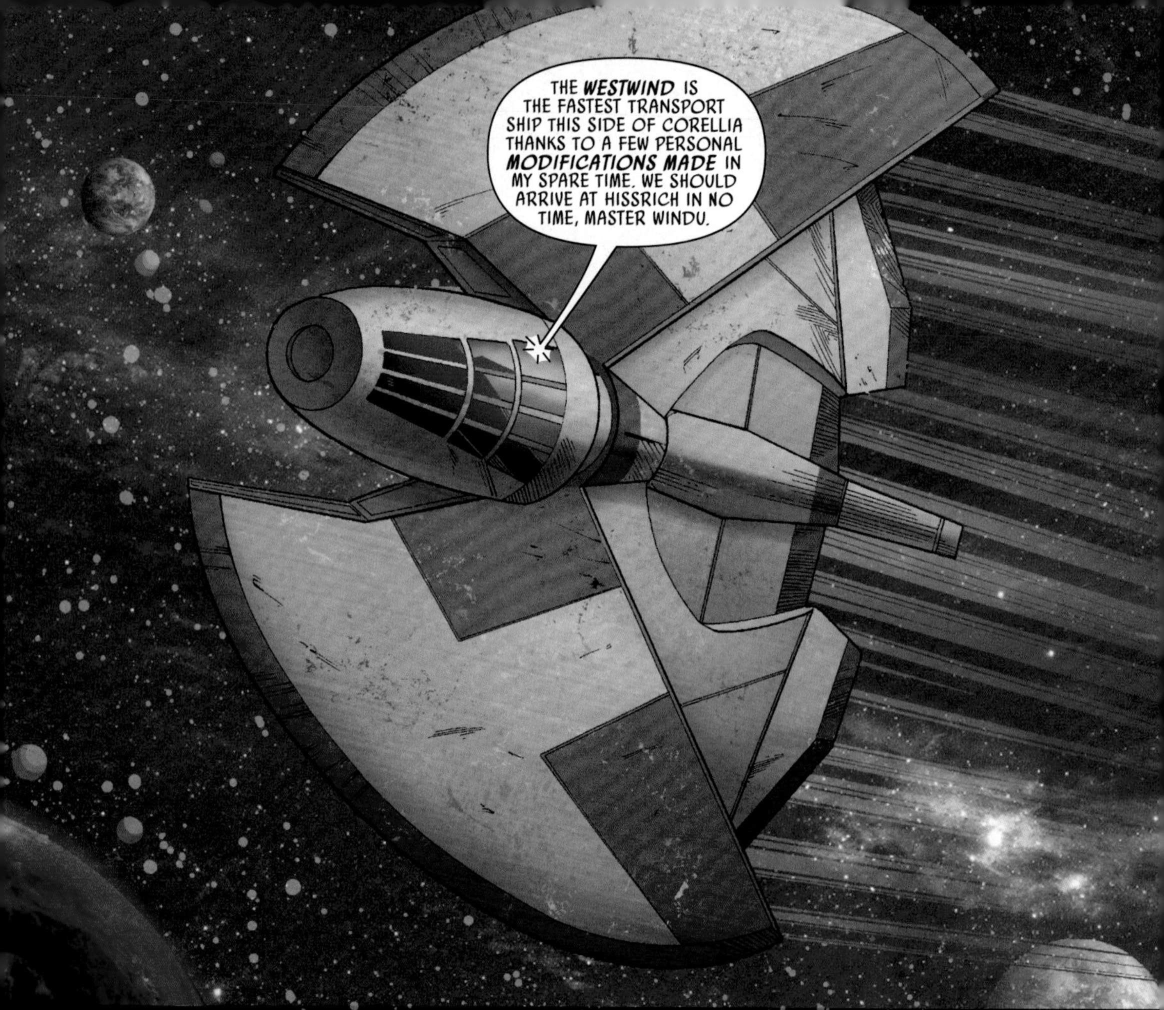
THE WESTWIND IS THE FASTEST TRANSPORT SHIP THIS SIDE OF CORELLIA THANKS TO A FEW PERSONAL MODIFICATIONS MADE IN MY SPARE TIME. WE SHOULD ARRIVE AT HISSRICH IN NO TIME, MASTER WINDU.

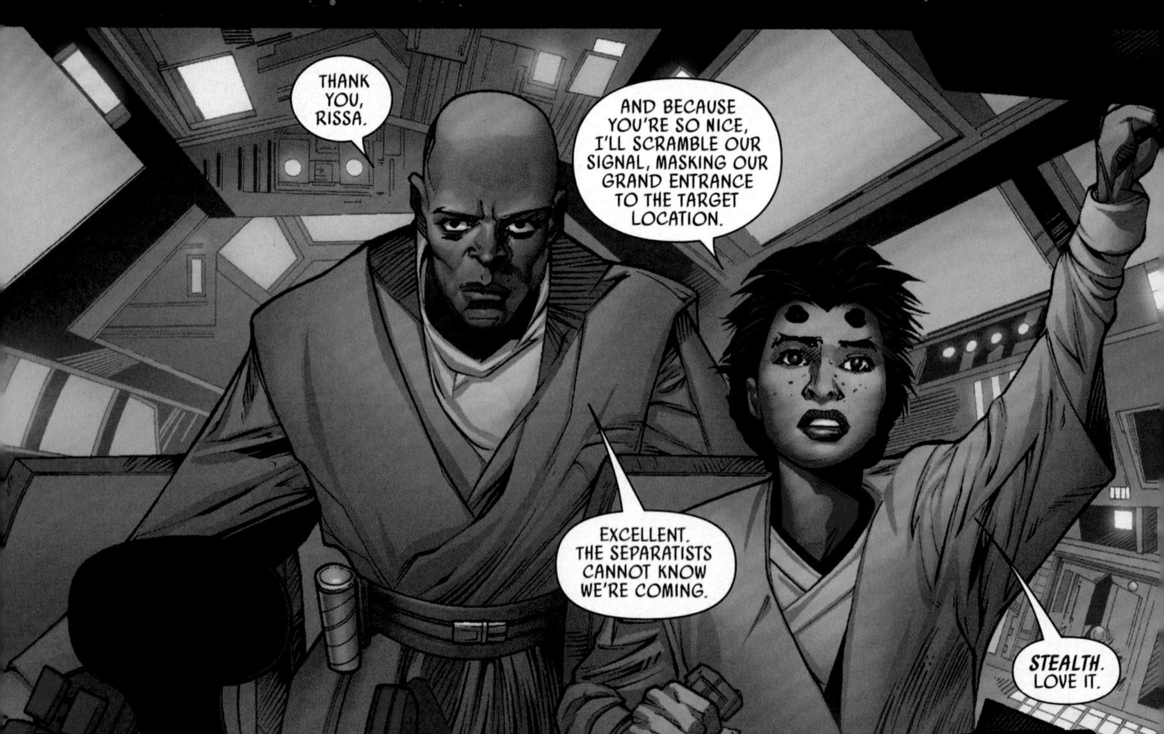
THANK YOU, RISSA.
AND BECAUSE YOU'RE SO NICE, I'LL SCRAMBLE OUR SIGNAL, MASKING OUR GRAND ENTRANCE TO THE TARGET LOCATION.
EXCELLENT. THE SEPARATISTS CANNOT KNOW WE'RE COMING.
STEALTH. LOVE IT.

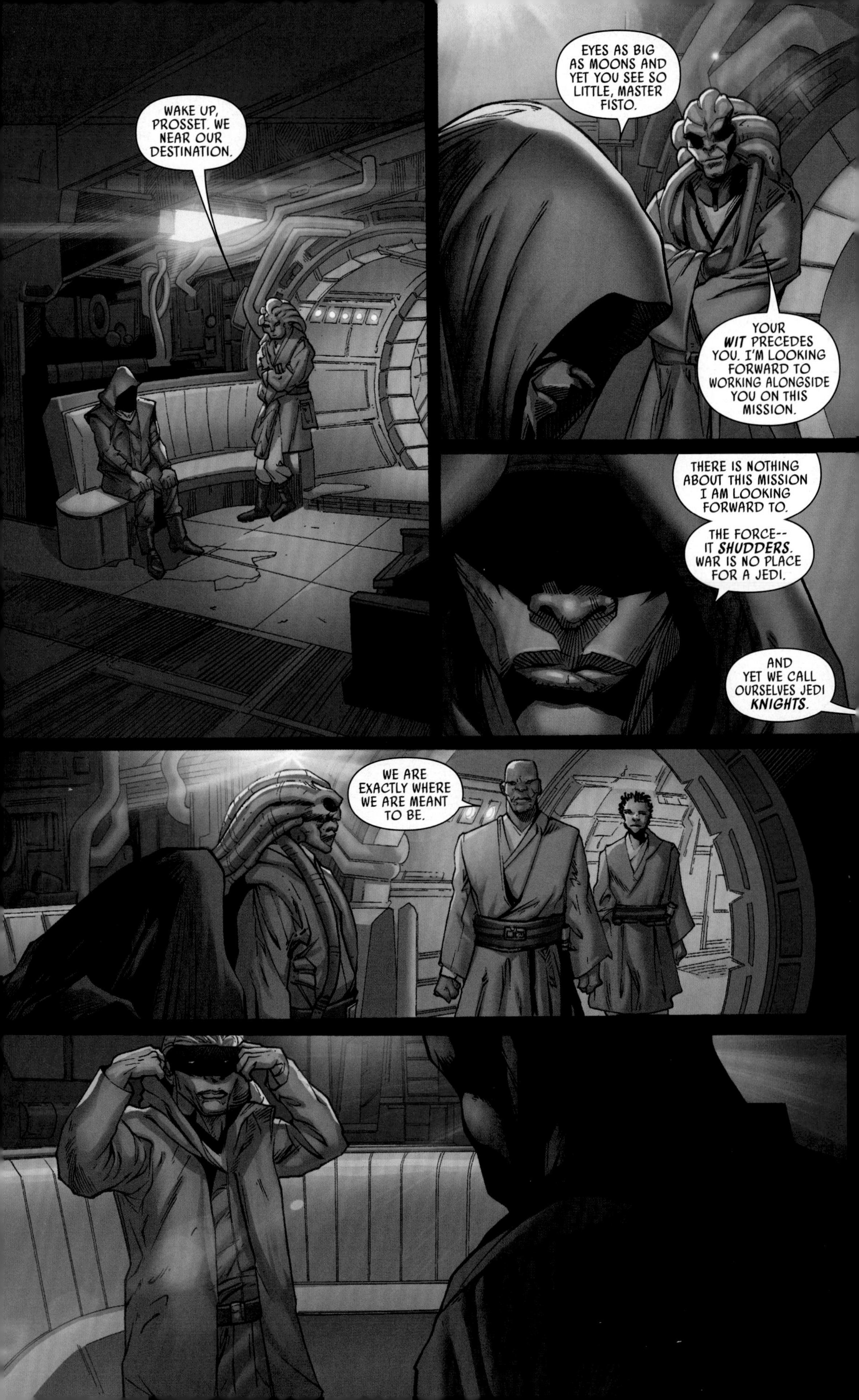
WAKE UP, PROSSET. WE NEAR OUR DESTINATION.
EYES AS BIG AS MOONS AND YET YOU SEE SO LITTLE, MASTER FISTO.
YOUR WIT PRECEDES YOU. I'M LOOKING FORWARD TO WORKING ALONGSIDE YOU ON THIS MISSION.
THERE IS NOTHING ABOUT THIS MISSION I AM LOOKING FORWARD TO.
THE FORCE-- IT SHUDDERS. WAR IS NO PLACE FOR A JEDI.
AND YET WE CALL OURSELVES JEDI KNIGHTS.
WE ARE EXACTLY WHERE WE ARE MEANT TO BE.

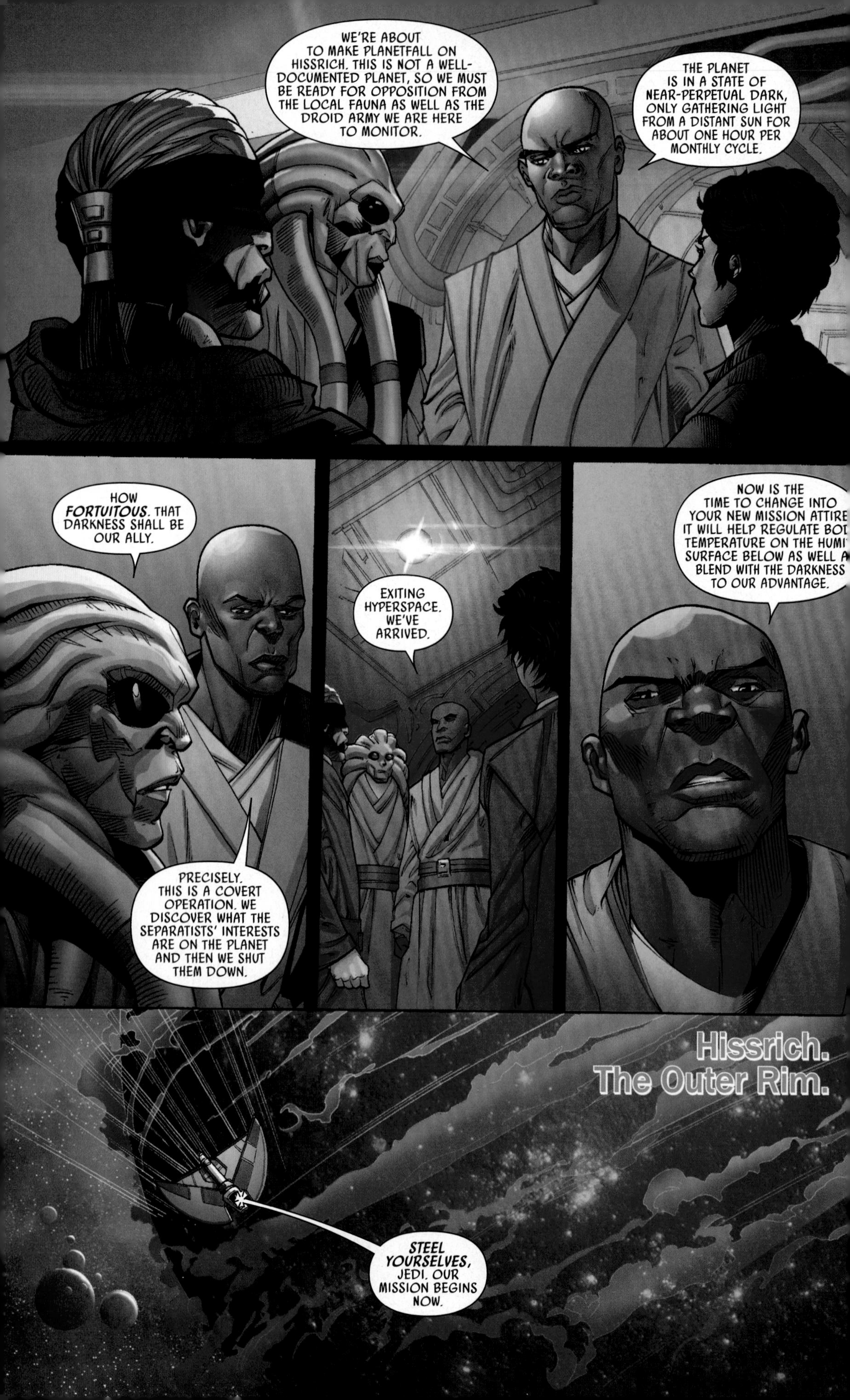

WE'RE ABOUT TO MAKE PLANETFALL ON HISSRICH. THIS IS NOT A WELL-DOCUMENTED PLANET, SO WE MUST BE READY FOR OPPOSITION FROM THE LOCAL FAUNA AS WELL AS THE DROID ARMY WE ARE HERE TO MONITOR.
THE PLANET IS IN A STATE OF NEAR-PERPETUAL DARK, ONLY GATHERING LIGHT FROM A DISTANT SUN FOR ABOUT ONE HOUR PER MONTHLY CYCLE.
HOW *FORTUITOUS*. THAT DARKNESS SHALL BE OUR ALLY.
PRECISELY. THIS IS A COVERT OPERATION. WE DISCOVER WHAT THE SEPARATISTS' INTERESTS ARE ON THE PLANET AND THEN WE SHUT THEM DOWN.
EXITING HYPERSPACE. WE'VE ARRIVED.
NOW IS THE TIME TO CHANGE INTO YOUR NEW MISSION ATTIRE IT WILL HELP REGULATE BOD TEMPERATURE ON THE HUMI SURFACE BELOW AS WELL A BLEND WITH THE DARKNESS TO OUR ADVANTAGE.
Hissrich. The Outer Rim.
*STEEL YOURSELVES,* JEDI. OUR MISSION BEGINS NOW.

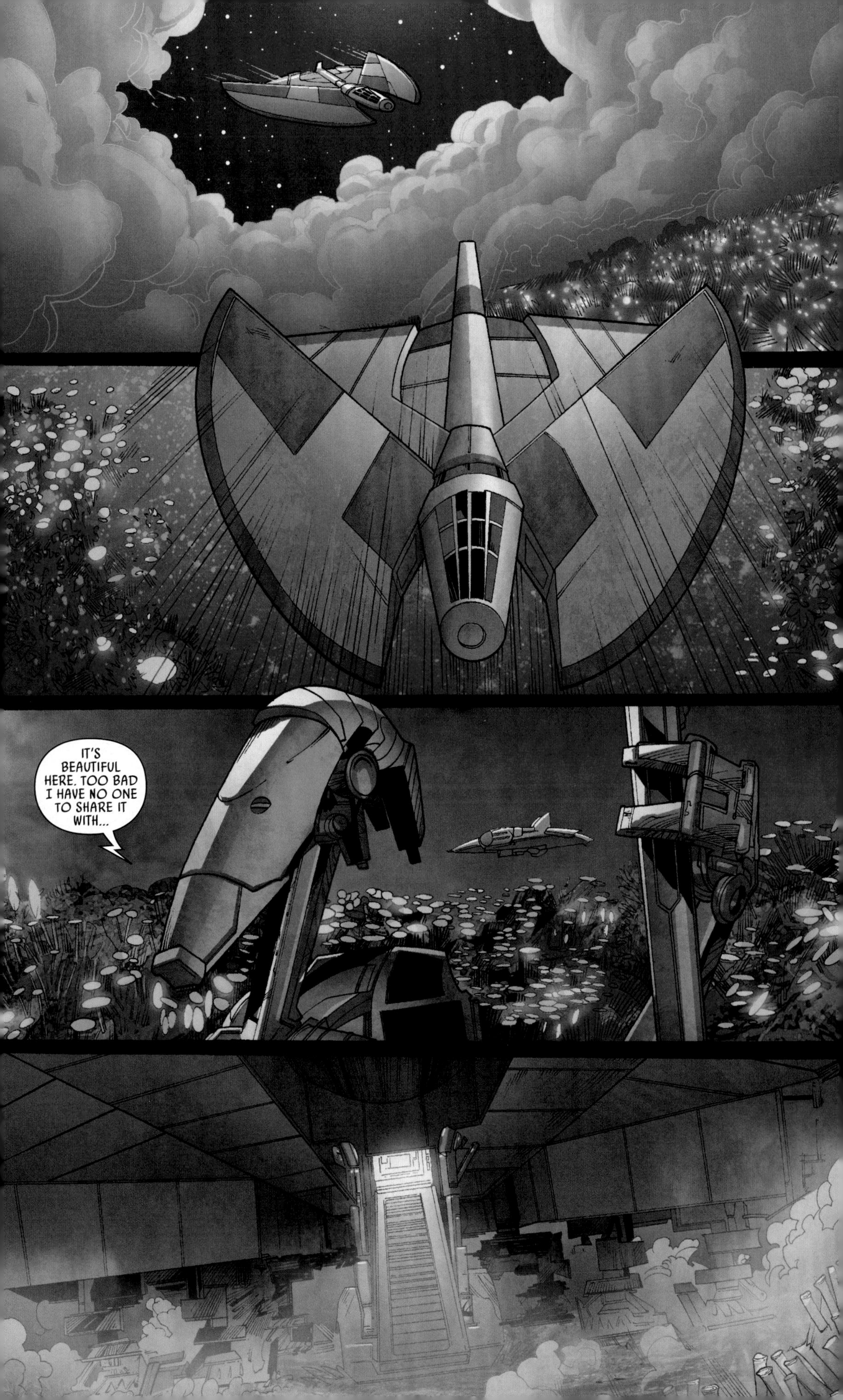
IT'S BEAUTIFUL HERE. TOO BAD I HAVE NO ONE TO SHARE IT WITH...

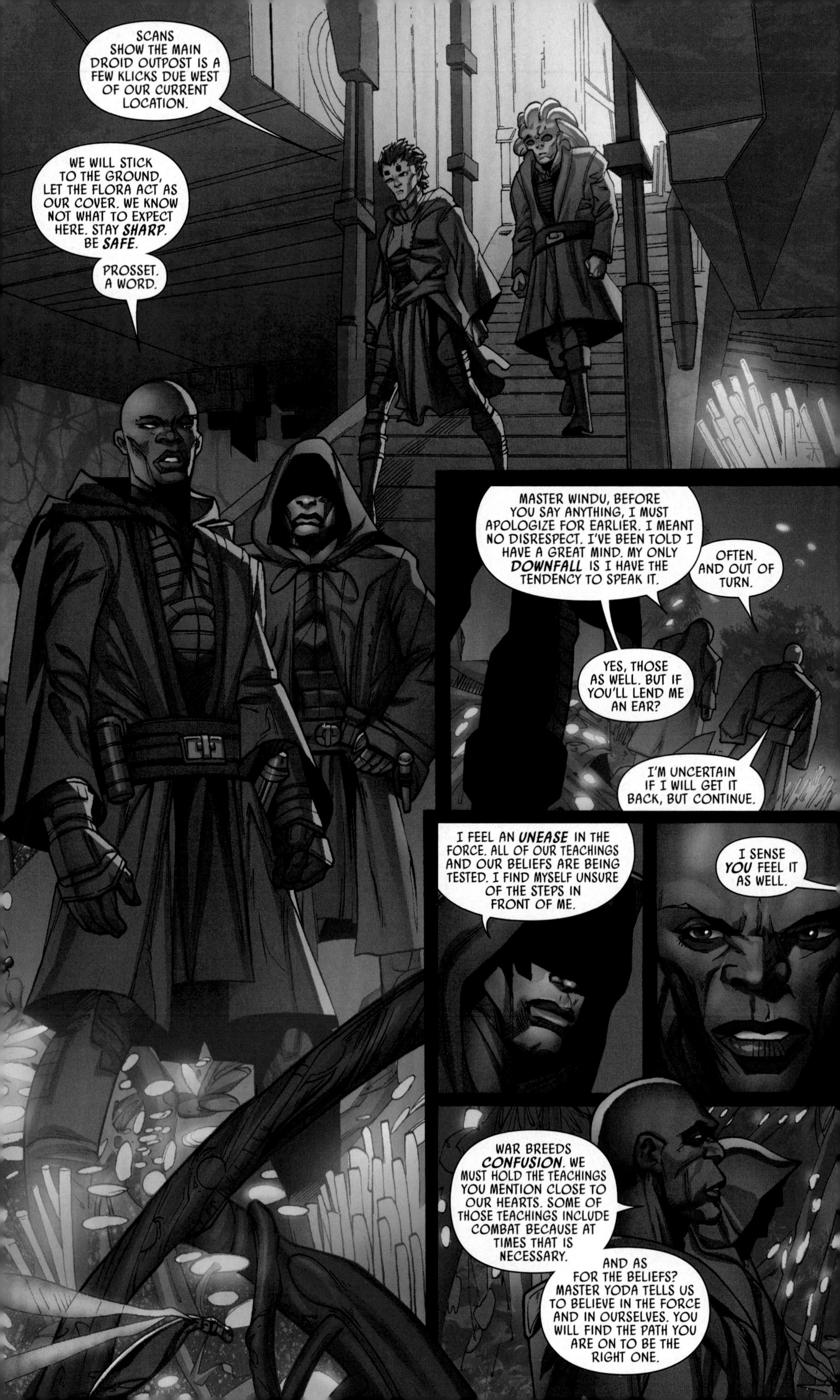

SCANS SHOW THE MAIN DROID OUTPOST IS A FEW KLICKS DUE WEST OF OUR CURRENT LOCATION.
WE WILL STICK TO THE GROUND, LET THE FLORA ACT AS OUR COVER. WE KNOW NOT WHAT TO EXPECT HERE. STAY SHARP. BE SAFE.
PROSSET. A WORD.
MASTER WINDU, BEFORE YOU SAY ANYTHING, I MUST APOLOGIZE FOR EARLIER. I MEANT NO DISRESPECT. I'VE BEEN TOLD I HAVE A GREAT MIND. MY ONLY DOWNFALL IS I HAVE THE TENDENCY TO SPEAK IT.
OFTEN. AND OUT OF TURN.
YES, THOSE AS WELL. BUT IF YOU'LL LEND ME AN EAR?
I'M UNCERTAIN IF I WILL GET IT BACK, BUT CONTINUE.
I FEEL AN UNEASE IN THE FORCE. ALL OF OUR TEACHINGS AND OUR BELIEFS ARE BEING TESTED. I FIND MYSELF UNSURE OF THE STEPS IN FRONT OF ME.
I SENSE YOU FEEL IT AS WELL.
WAR BREEDS CONFUSION. WE MUST HOLD THE TEACHINGS YOU MENTION CLOSE TO OUR HEARTS. SOME OF THOSE TEACHINGS INCLUDE COMBAT BECAUSE AT TIMES THAT IS NECESSARY.
AND AS FOR THE BELIEFS? MASTER YODA TELLS US TO BELIEVE IN THE FORCE AND IN OURSELVES. YOU WILL FIND THE PATH YOU ARE ON TO BE THE RIGHT ONE.

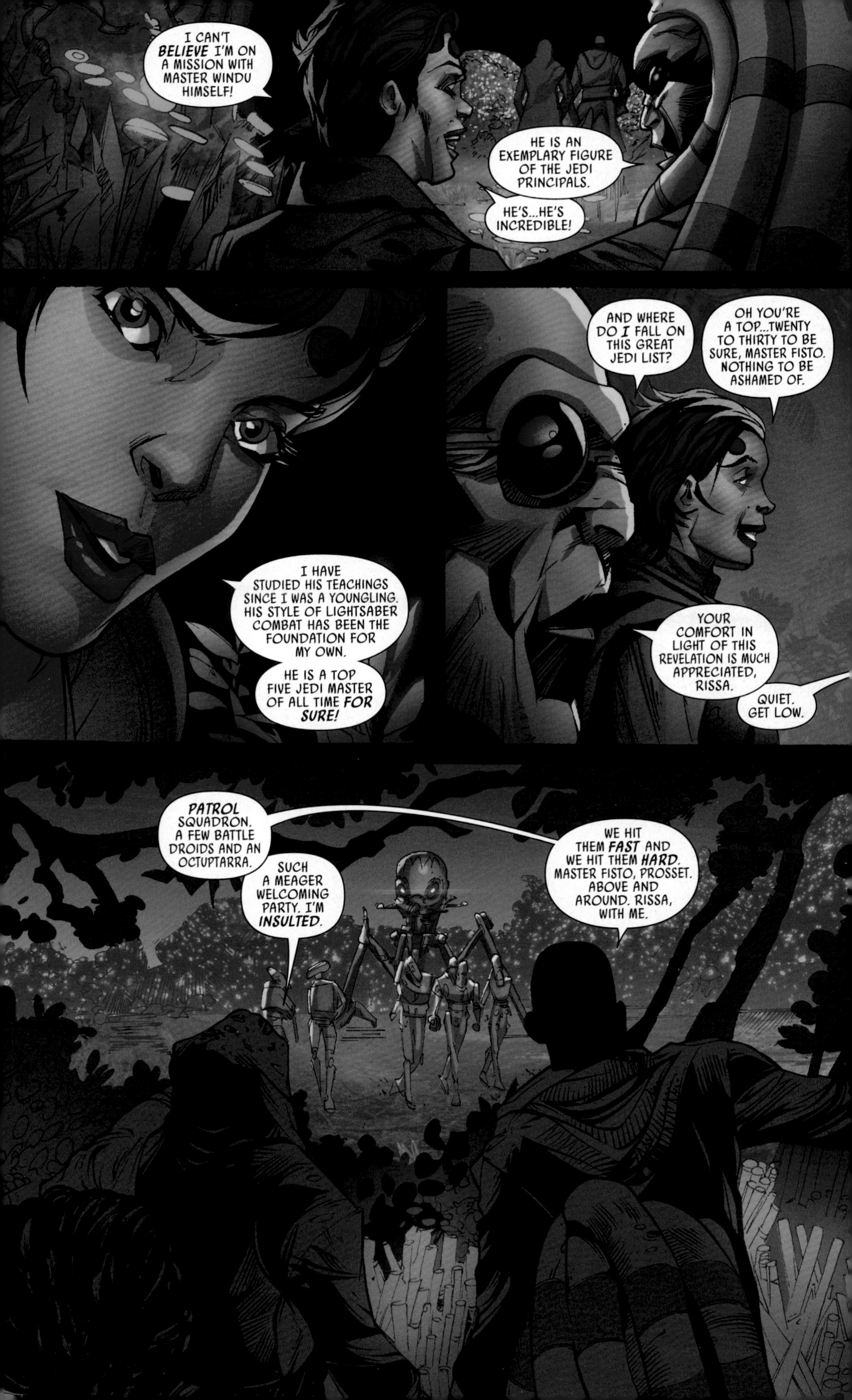
I CAN'T BELIEVE I'M ON A MISSION WITH MASTER WINDU HIMSELF!
HE IS AN EXEMPLARY FIGURE OF THE JEDI PRINCIPALS.
HE'S...HE'S INCREDIBLE!
I HAVE STUDIED HIS TEACHINGS SINCE I WAS A YOUNGLING. HIS STYLE OF LIGHTSABER COMBAT HAS BEEN THE FOUNDATION FOR MY OWN.
HE IS A TOP FIVE JEDI MASTER OF ALL TIME FOR SURE!
AND WHERE DO I FALL ON THIS GREAT JEDI LIST?
OH YOU'RE A TOP...TWENTY TO THIRTY TO BE SURE, MASTER FISTO. NOTHING TO BE ASHAMED OF.
YOUR COMFORT IN LIGHT OF THIS REVELATION IS MUCH APPRECIATED, RISSA.
QUIET. GET LOW.
PATROL SQUADRON. A FEW BATTLE DROIDS AND AN OCTUPTARRA.
SUCH A MEAGER WELCOMING PARTY. I'M INSULTED.
WE HIT THEM FAST AND WE HIT THEM HARD. MASTER FISTO, PROSSET. ABOVE AND AROUND. RISSA, WITH ME.

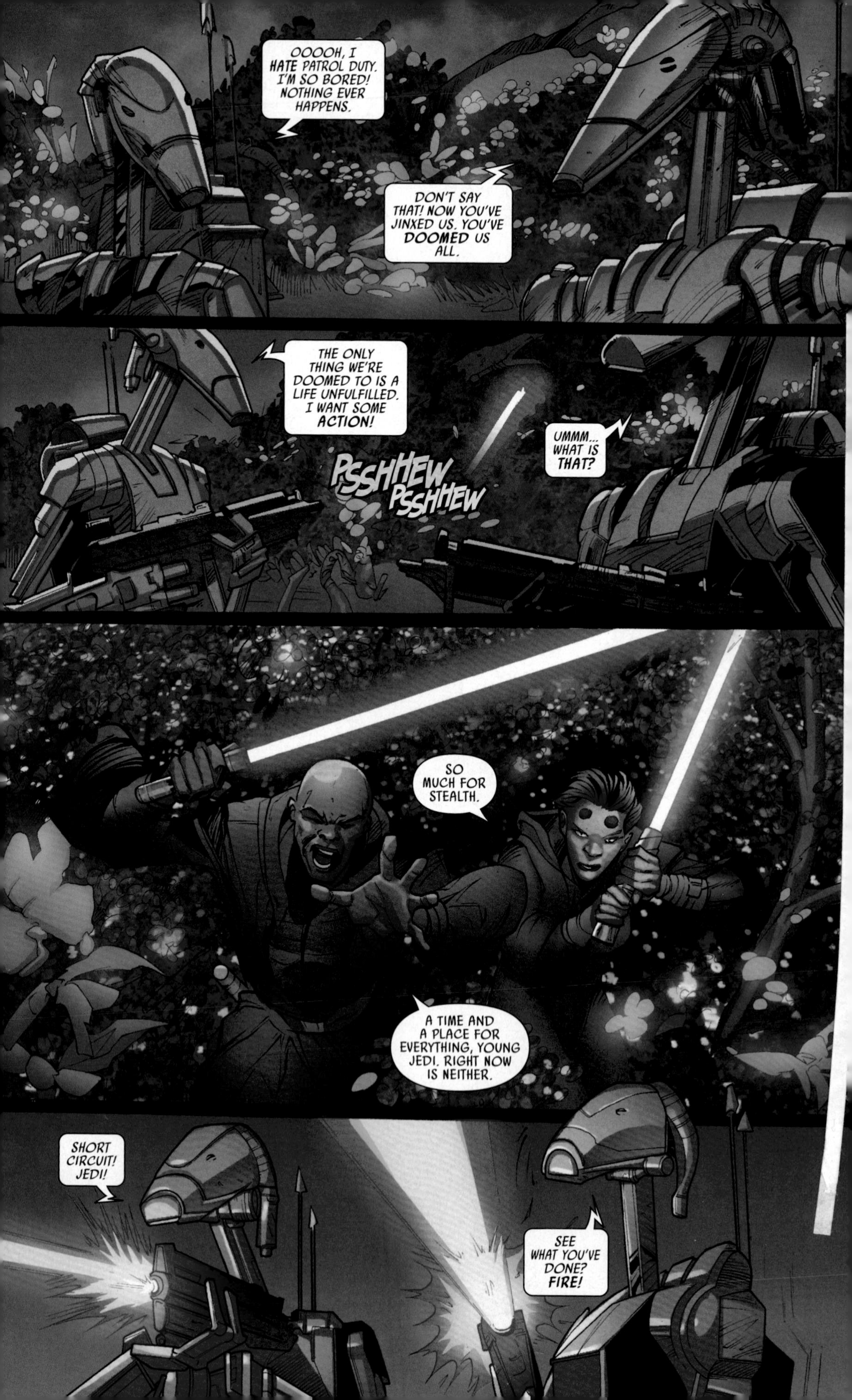
OOOOH, I HATE PATROL DUTY. I'M SO BORED! NOTHING EVER HAPPENS.
DON'T SAY THAT! NOW YOU'VE JINXED US. YOU'VE DOOMED US ALL.
THE ONLY THING WE'RE DOOMED TO IS A LIFE UNFULFILLED. I WANT SOME ACTION!
UMMM... WHAT IS THAT?
PSSHHEW PSSHHEW
SO MUCH FOR STEALTH.
A TIME AND A PLACE FOR EVERYTHING, YOUNG JEDI. RIGHT NOW IS NEITHER.
SHORT CIRCUIT! JEDI!
SEE WHAT YOU'VE DONE? FIRE!

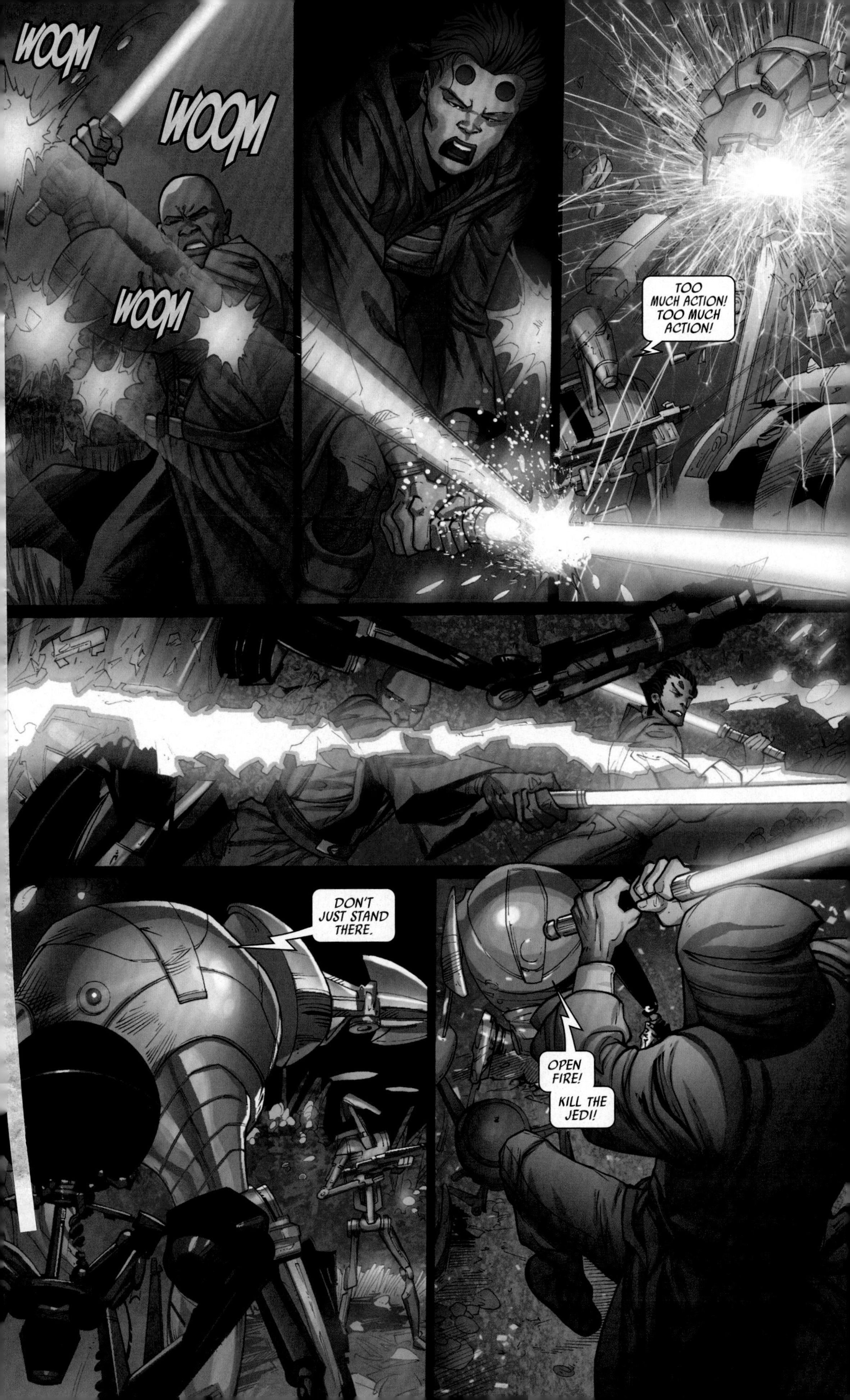
WOOM
WOOM
WOOM
TOO MUCH ACTION! TOO MUCH ACTION!
DON'T JUST STAND THERE.
OPEN FIRE!
KILL THE JEDI!

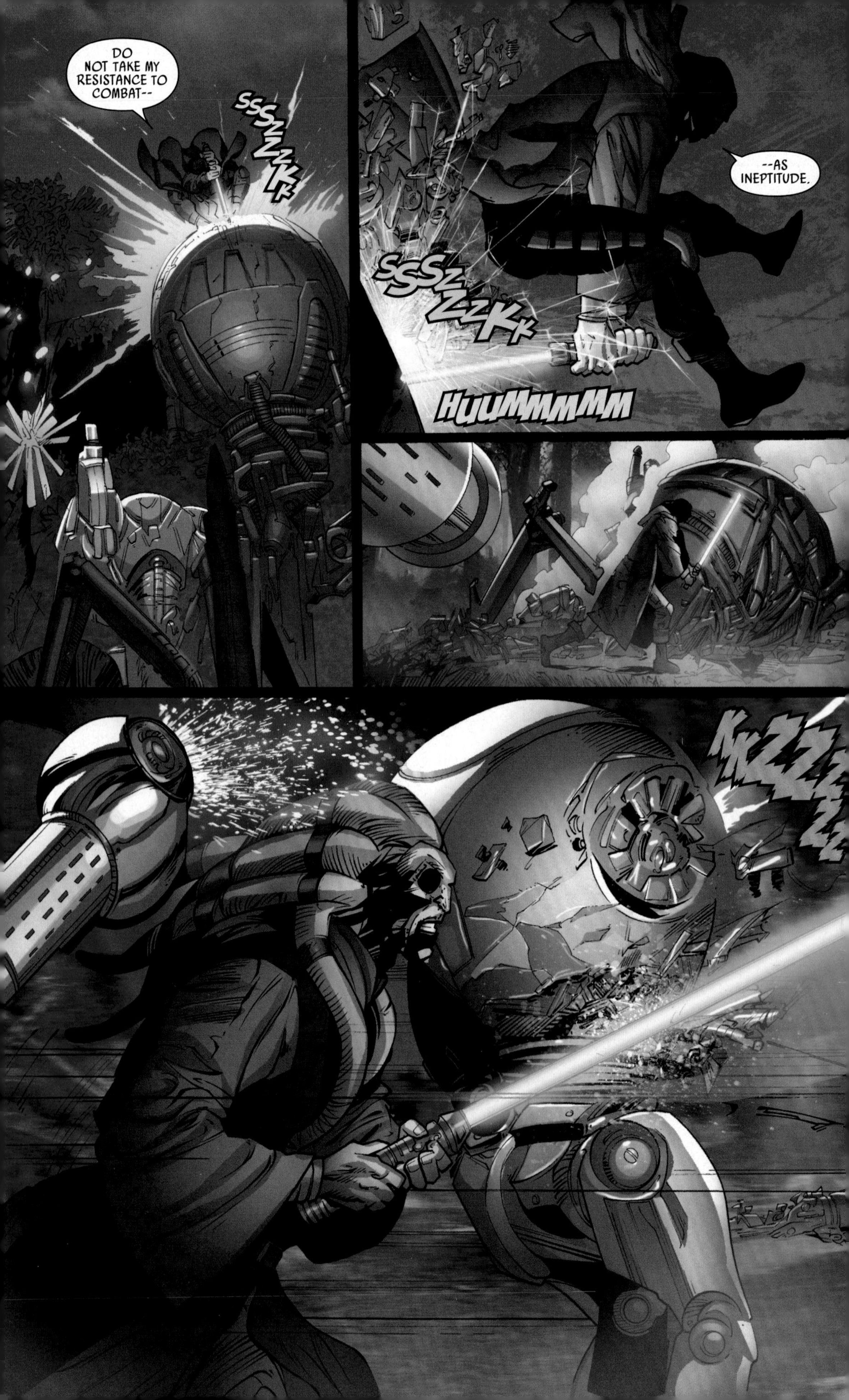
DO NOT TAKE MY RESISTANCE TO COMBAT--
SSSZZZKK
--AS INEPTITUDE.
SSSZZZKK
HUUMMMMM

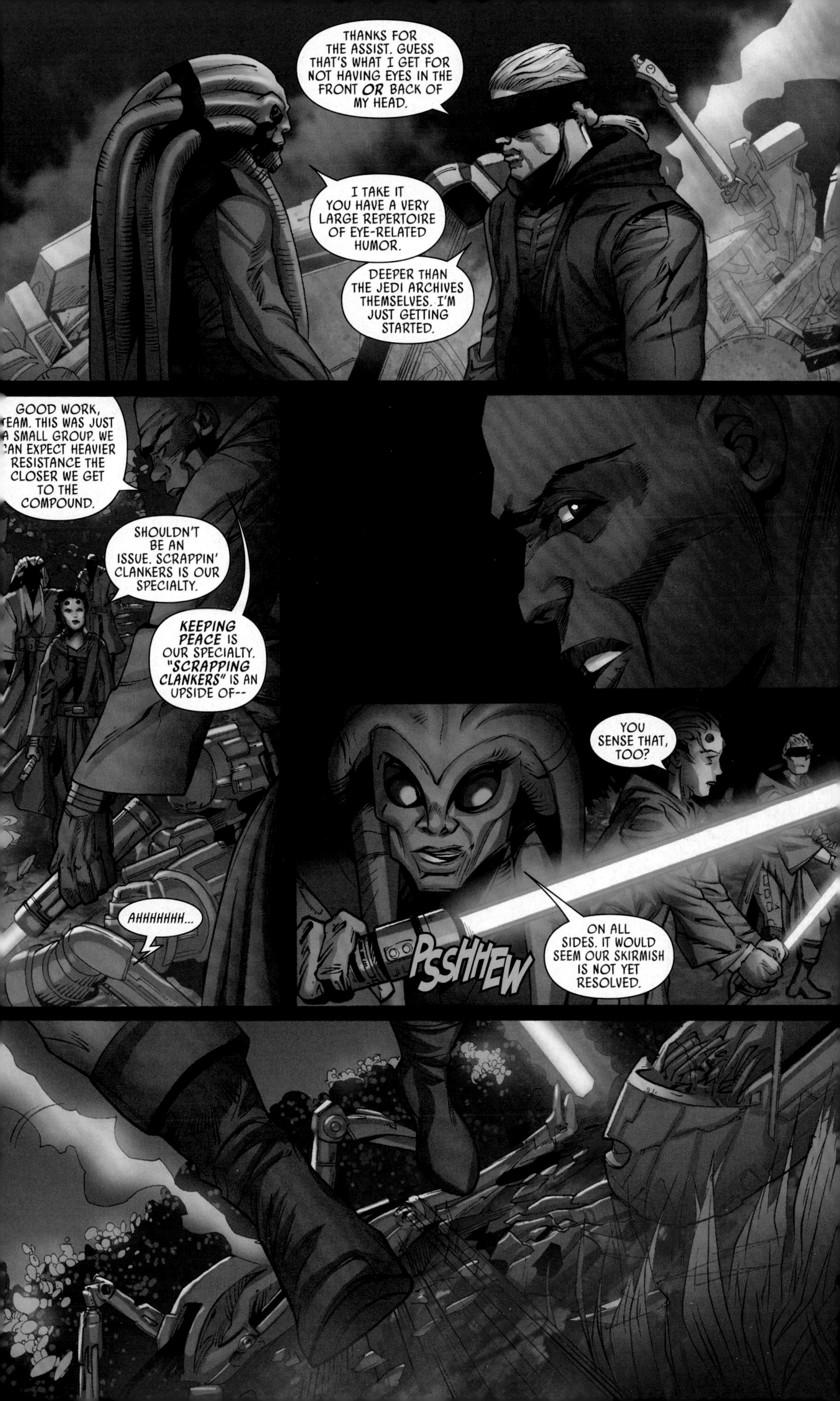

THANKS FOR THE ASSIST. GUESS THAT'S WHAT I GET FOR NOT HAVING EYES IN THE FRONT *OR* BACK OF MY HEAD.
I TAKE IT YOU HAVE A VERY LARGE REPERTOIRE OF EYE-RELATED HUMOR.
DEEPER THAN THE JEDI ARCHIVES THEMSELVES. I'M JUST GETTING STARTED.
GOOD WORK, TEAM. THIS WAS JUST A SMALL GROUP. WE CAN EXPECT HEAVIER RESISTANCE THE CLOSER WE GET TO THE COMPOUND.
SHOULDN'T BE AN ISSUE. SCRAPPIN' CLANKERS IS OUR SPECIALTY.
*KEEPING PEACE* IS OUR SPECIALTY. *"SCRAPPING CLANKERS"* IS AN UPSIDE OF--
AHHHHHHH...
YOU SENSE THAT, TOO?
PSSHHEW
ON ALL SIDES. IT WOULD SEEM OUR SKIRMISH IS NOT YET RESOLVED.

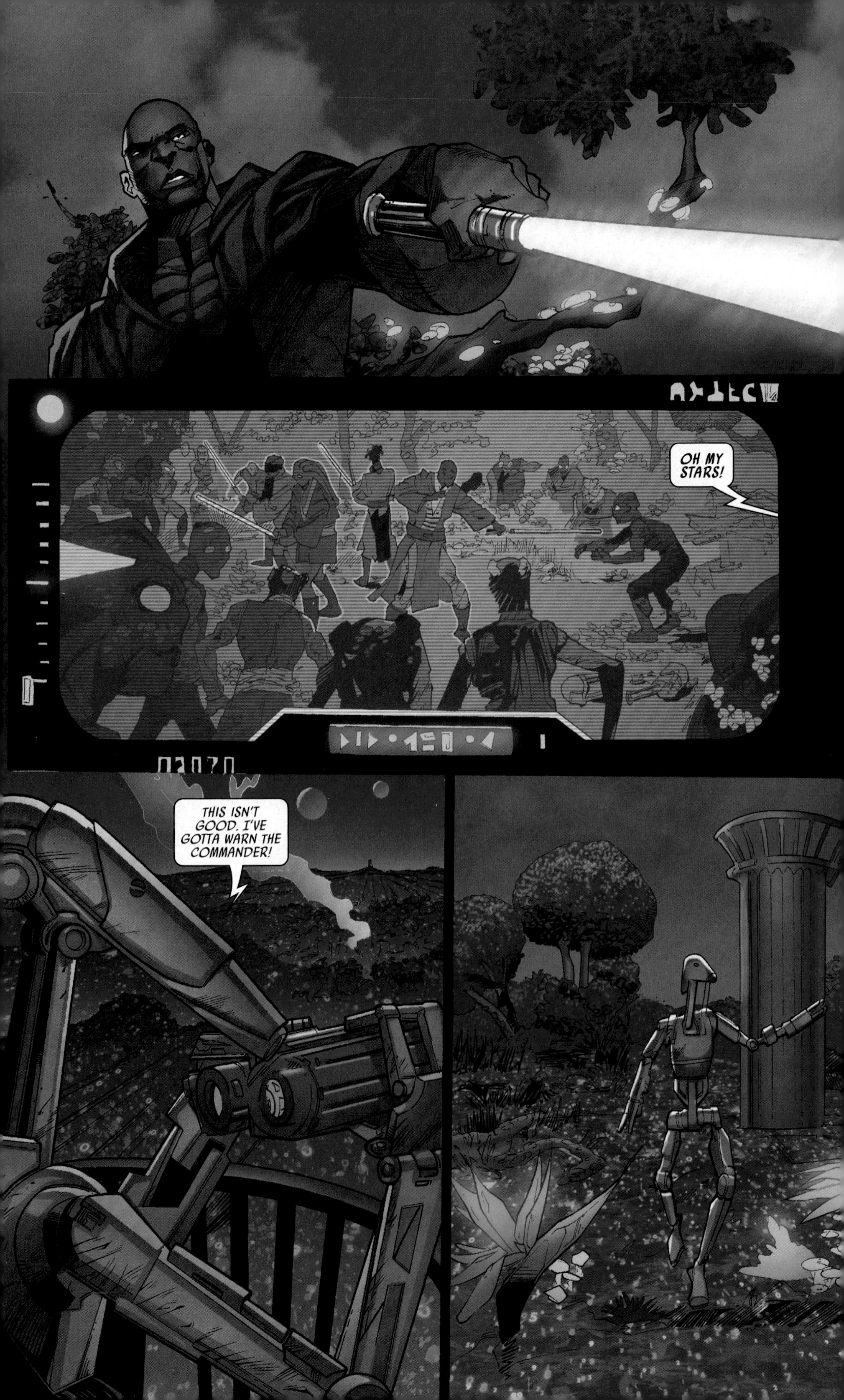
OH MY STARS!
THIS ISN'T GOOD. I'VE GOTTA WARN THE COMMANDER!

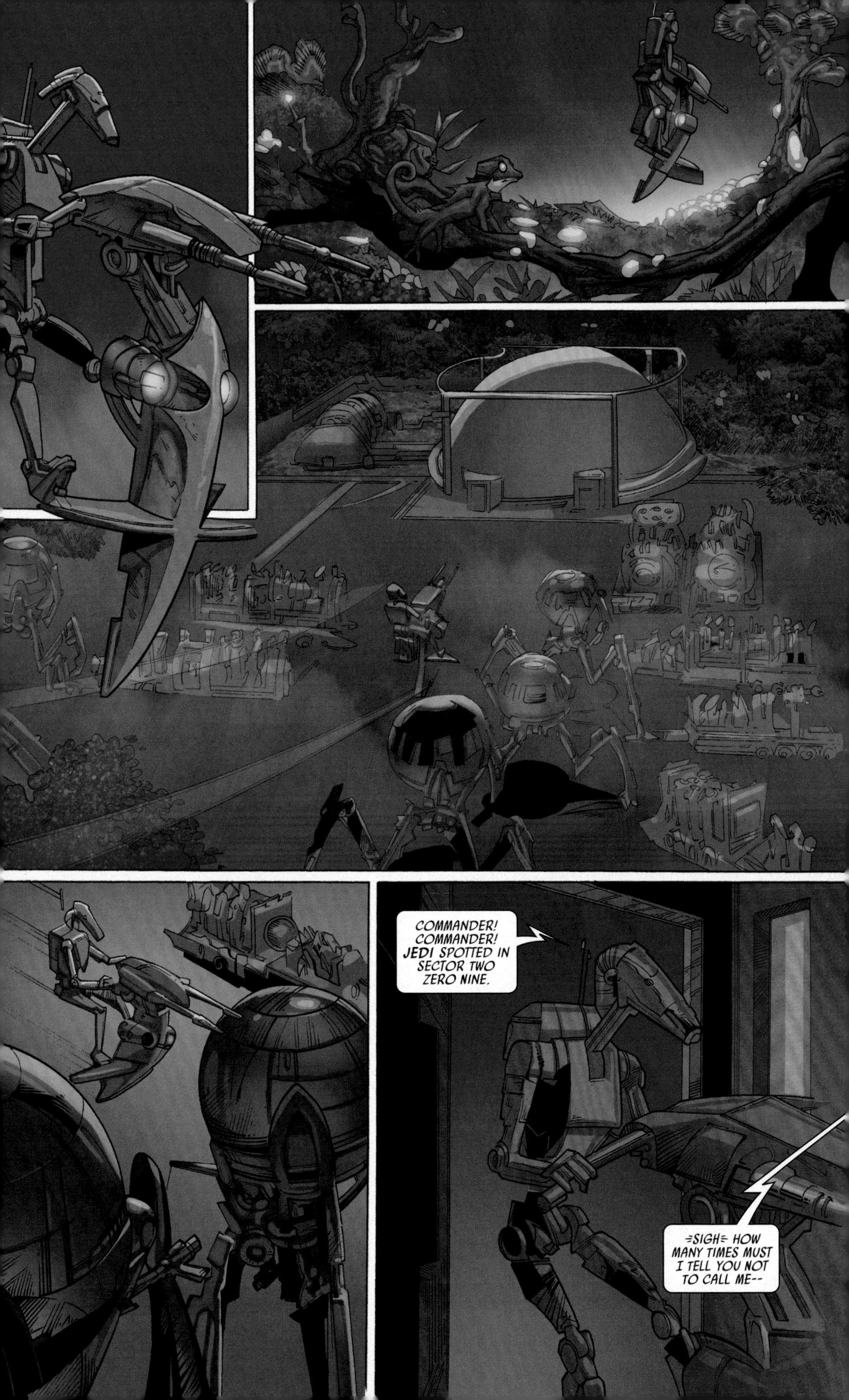
COMMANDER! COMMANDER! JEDI SPOTTED IN SECTOR TWO ZERO NINE.
=SIGH= HOW MANY TIMES MUST I TELL YOU NOT TO CALL ME--

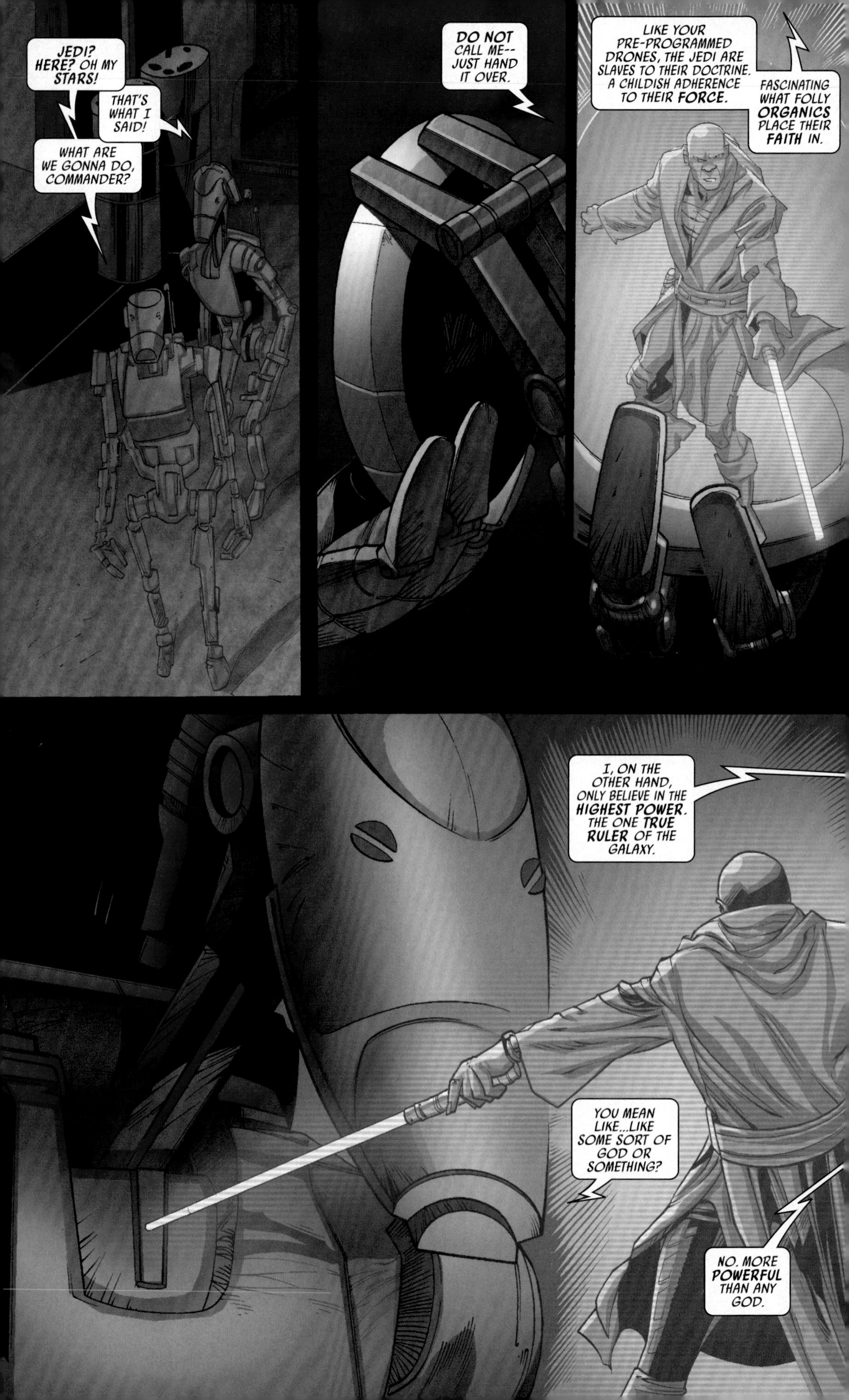
JEDI? HERE? OH MY STARS!
THAT'S WHAT I SAID!
WHAT ARE WE GONNA DO, COMMANDER?
DO NOT CALL ME-- JUST HAND IT OVER.
LIKE YOUR PRE-PROGRAMMED DRONES, THE JEDI ARE SLAVES TO THEIR DOCTRINE. A CHILDISH ADHERENCE TO THEIR FORCE.
FASCINATING WHAT FOLLY ORGANICS PLACE THEIR FAITH IN.
I, ON THE OTHER HAND, ONLY BELIEVE IN THE HIGHEST POWER. THE ONE TRUE RULER OF THE GALAXY.
YOU MEAN LIKE...LIKE SOME SORT OF GOD OR SOMETHING?
NO. MORE POWERFUL THAN ANY GOD.

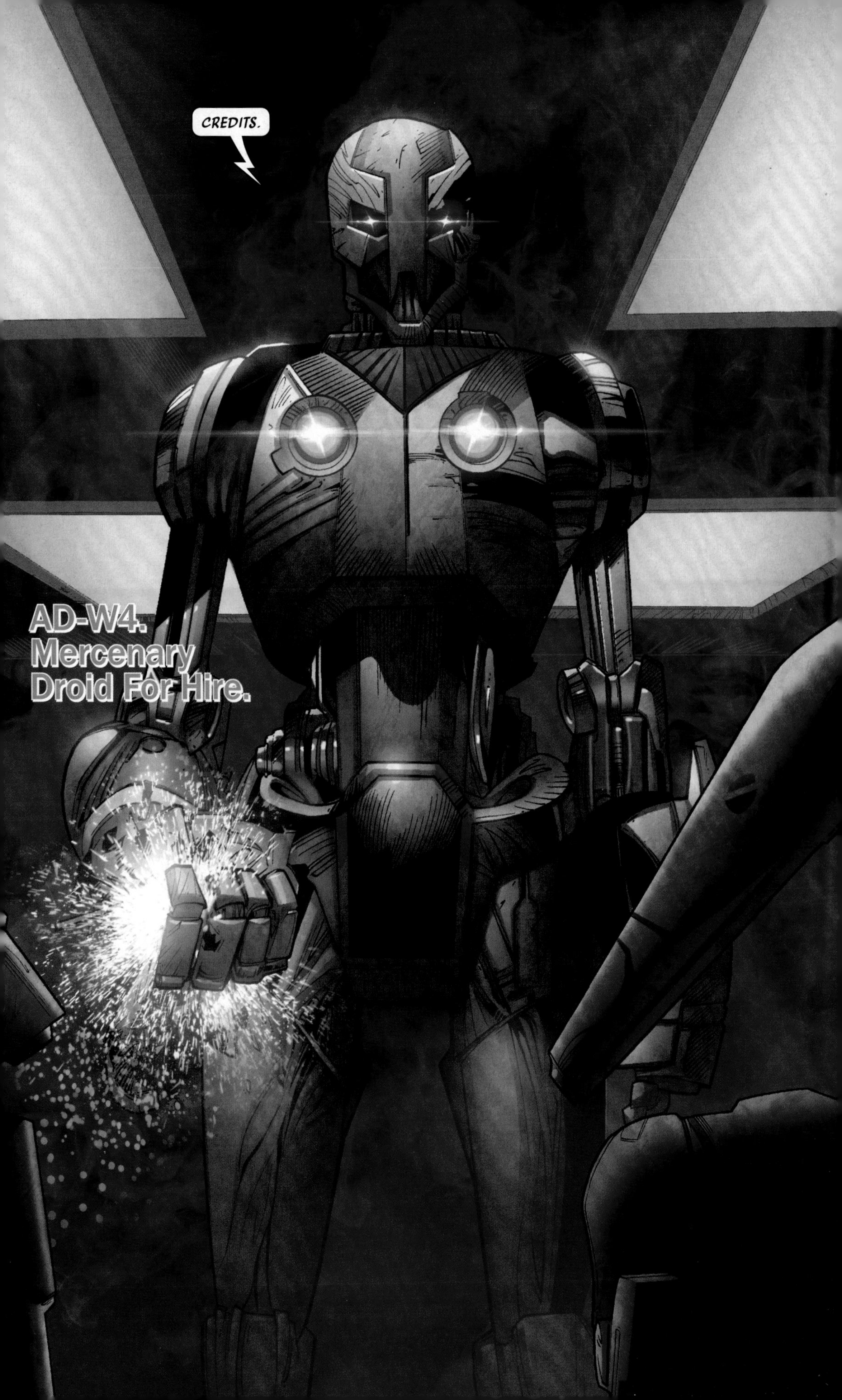
CREDITS.
AD-W4.
Mercenary
Droid For Hire.

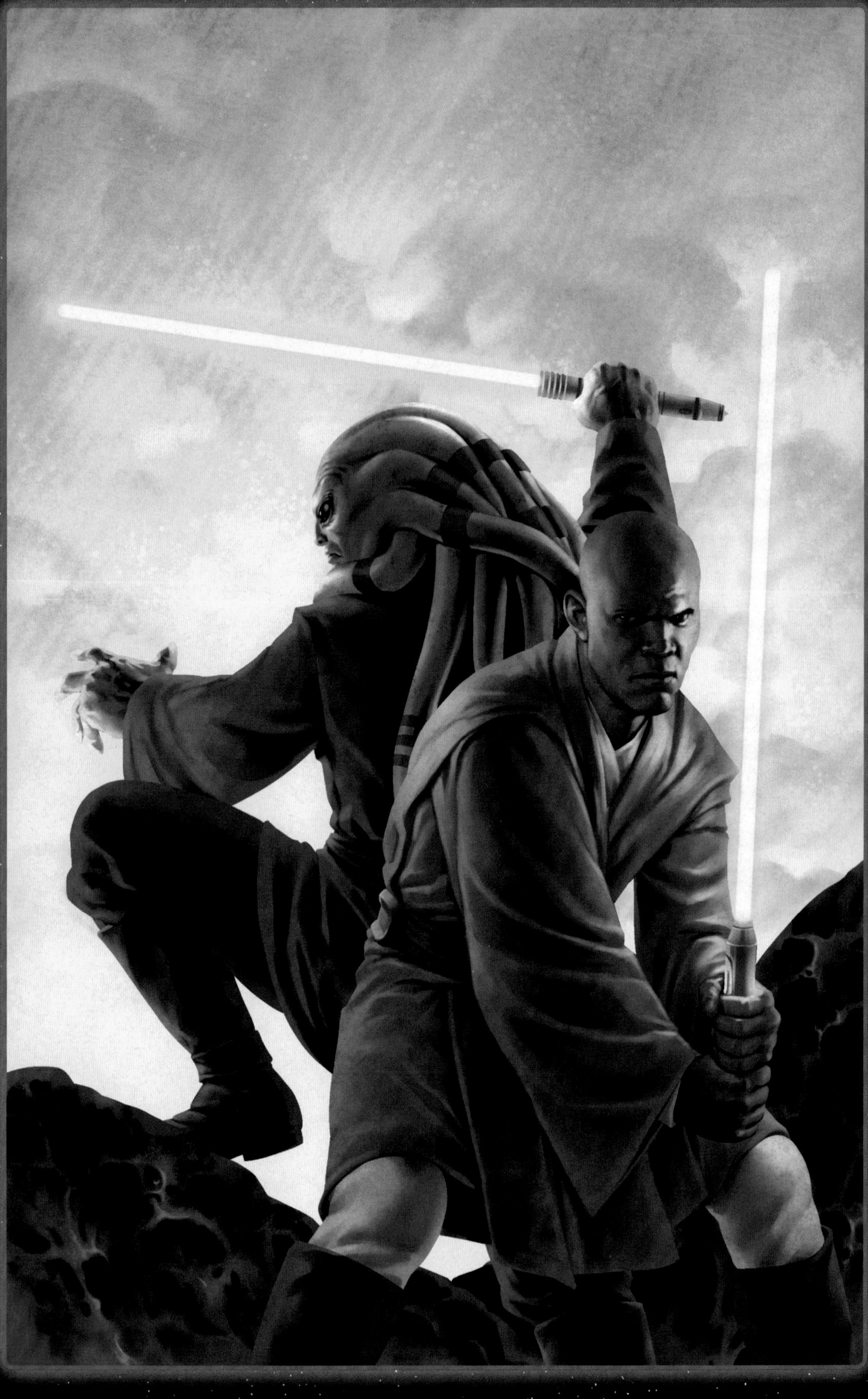

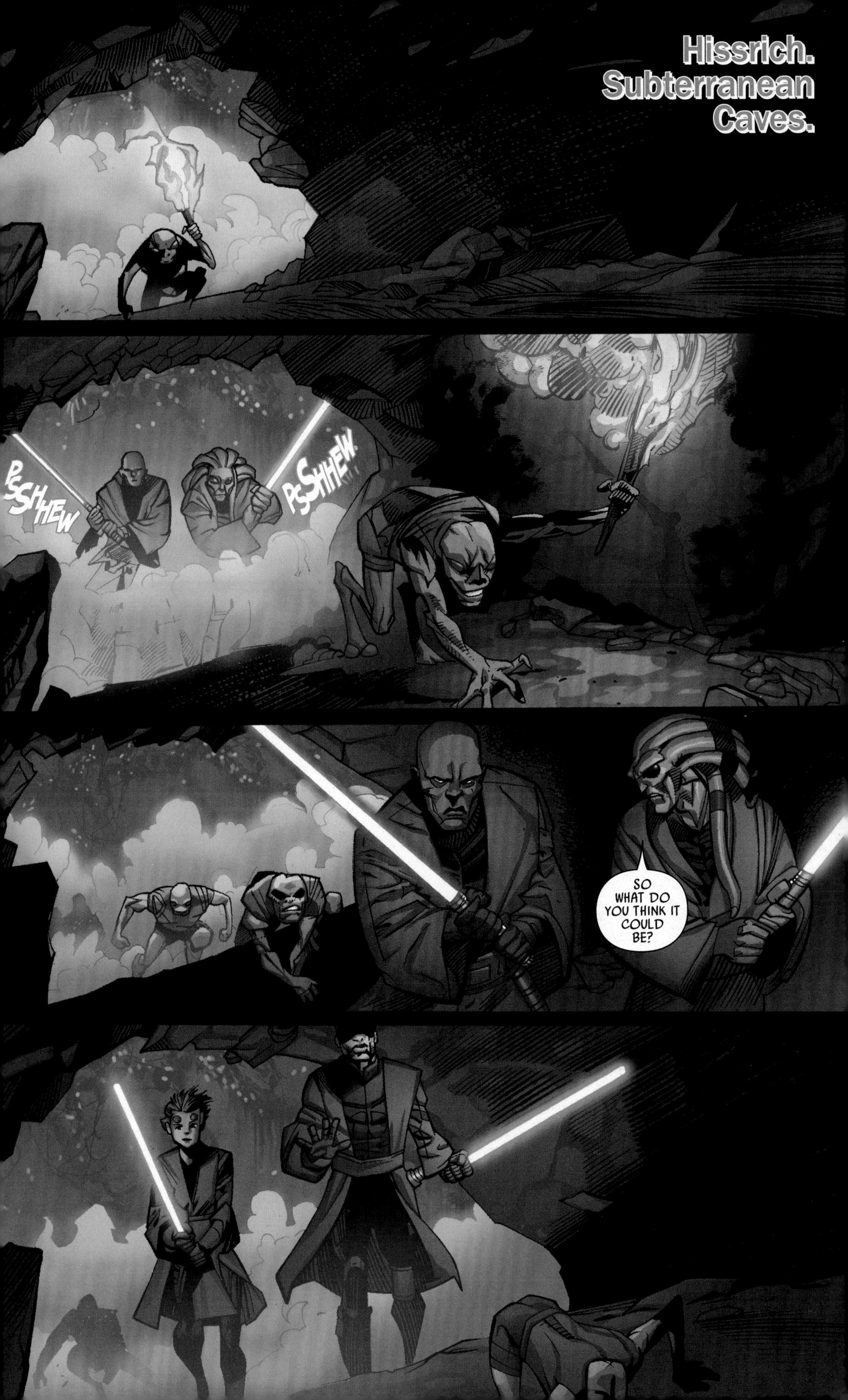
Hissrich.
Subterranean
Caves.
PSSHHEW
PSSHHEW
SO WHAT DO YOU THINK IT COULD BE?

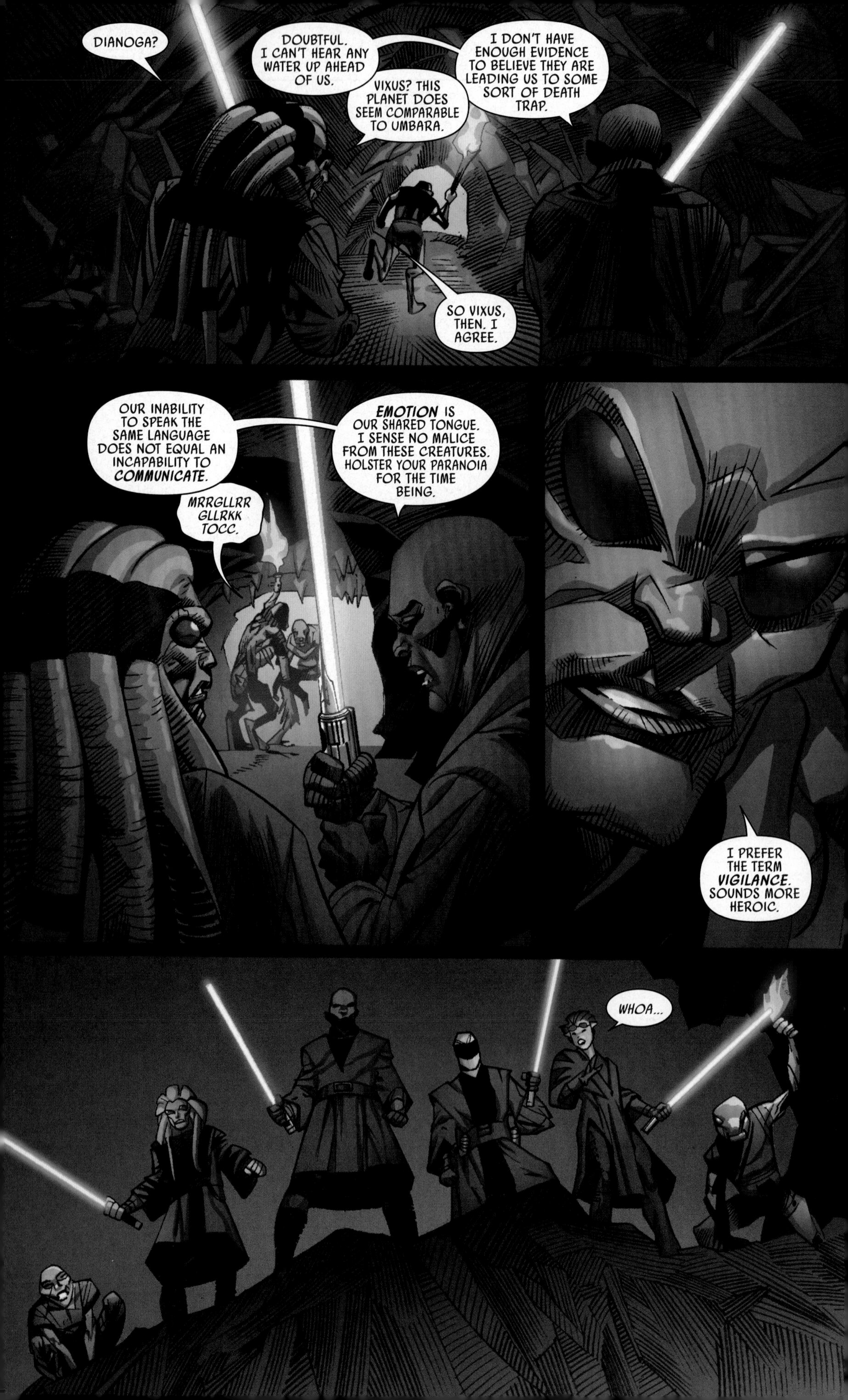

DIANOGA?
DOUBTFUL. I CAN'T HEAR ANY WATER UP AHEAD OF US.
I DON'T HAVE ENOUGH EVIDENCE TO BELIEVE THEY ARE LEADING US TO SOME SORT OF DEATH TRAP.
VIXUS? THIS PLANET DOES SEEM COMPARABLE TO UMBARA.
SO VIXUS, THEN. I AGREE.
OUR INABILITY TO SPEAK THE SAME LANGUAGE DOES NOT EQUAL AN INCAPABILITY TO COMMUNICATE.
EMOTION IS OUR SHARED TONGUE. I SENSE NO MALICE FROM THESE CREATURES. HOLSTER YOUR PARANOIA FOR THE TIME BEING.
MRRGLLRR GLLRKK TOCC.
I PREFER THE TERM VIGILANCE. SOUNDS MORE HEROIC.
WHOA...

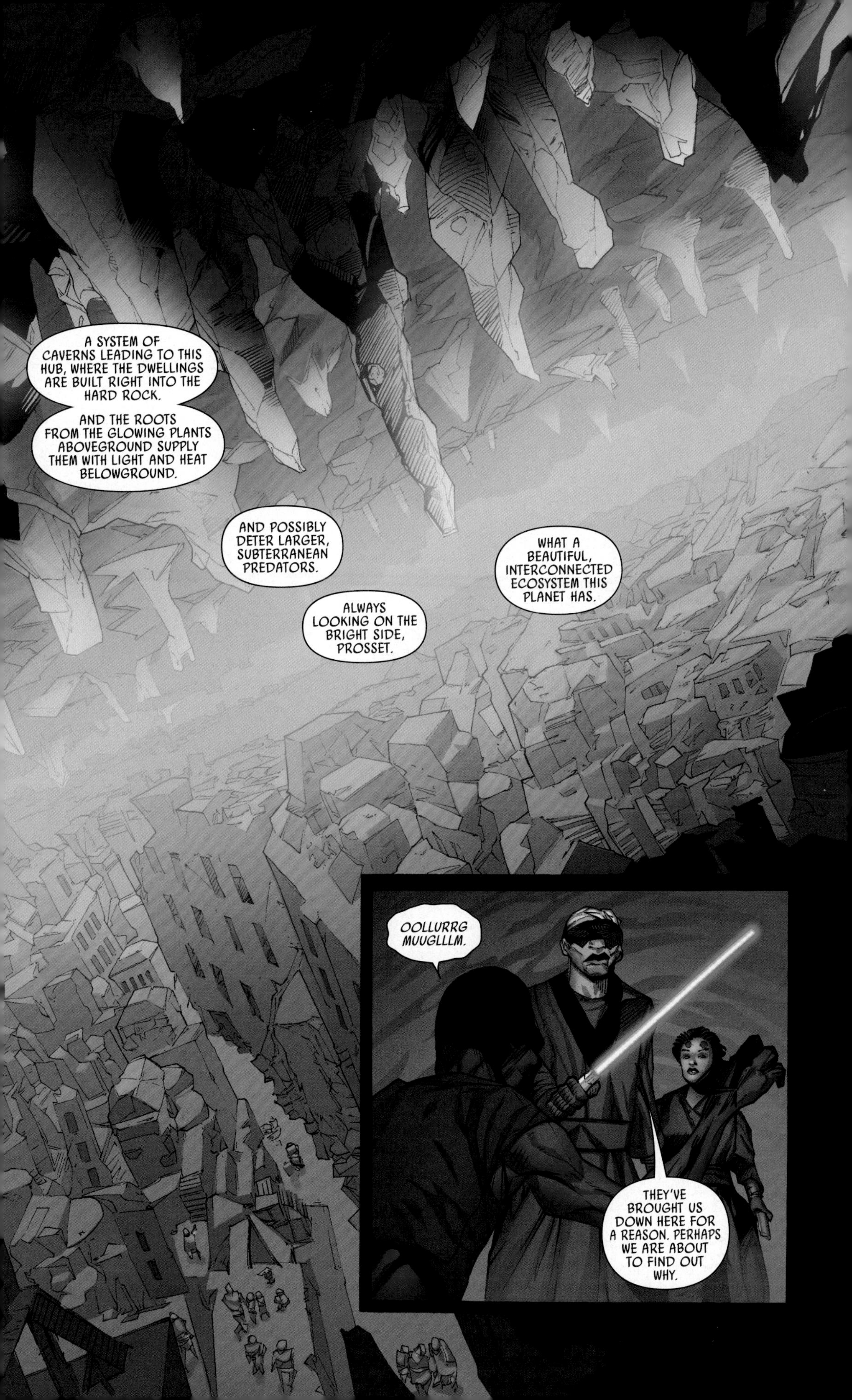
A SYSTEM OF CAVERNS LEADING TO THIS HUB, WHERE THE DWELLINGS ARE BUILT RIGHT INTO THE HARD ROCK.
AND THE ROOTS FROM THE GLOWING PLANTS ABOVEGROUND SUPPLY THEM WITH LIGHT AND HEAT BELOWGROUND.
AND POSSIBLY DETER LARGER, SUBTERRANEAN PREDATORS.
WHAT A BEAUTIFUL, INTERCONNECTED ECOSYSTEM THIS PLANET HAS.
ALWAYS LOOKING ON THE BRIGHT SIDE, PROSSET.
OOLLURRG MUUGLLLM.
THEY'VE BROUGHT US DOWN HERE FOR A REASON. PERHAPS WE ARE ABOUT TO FIND OUT WHY.

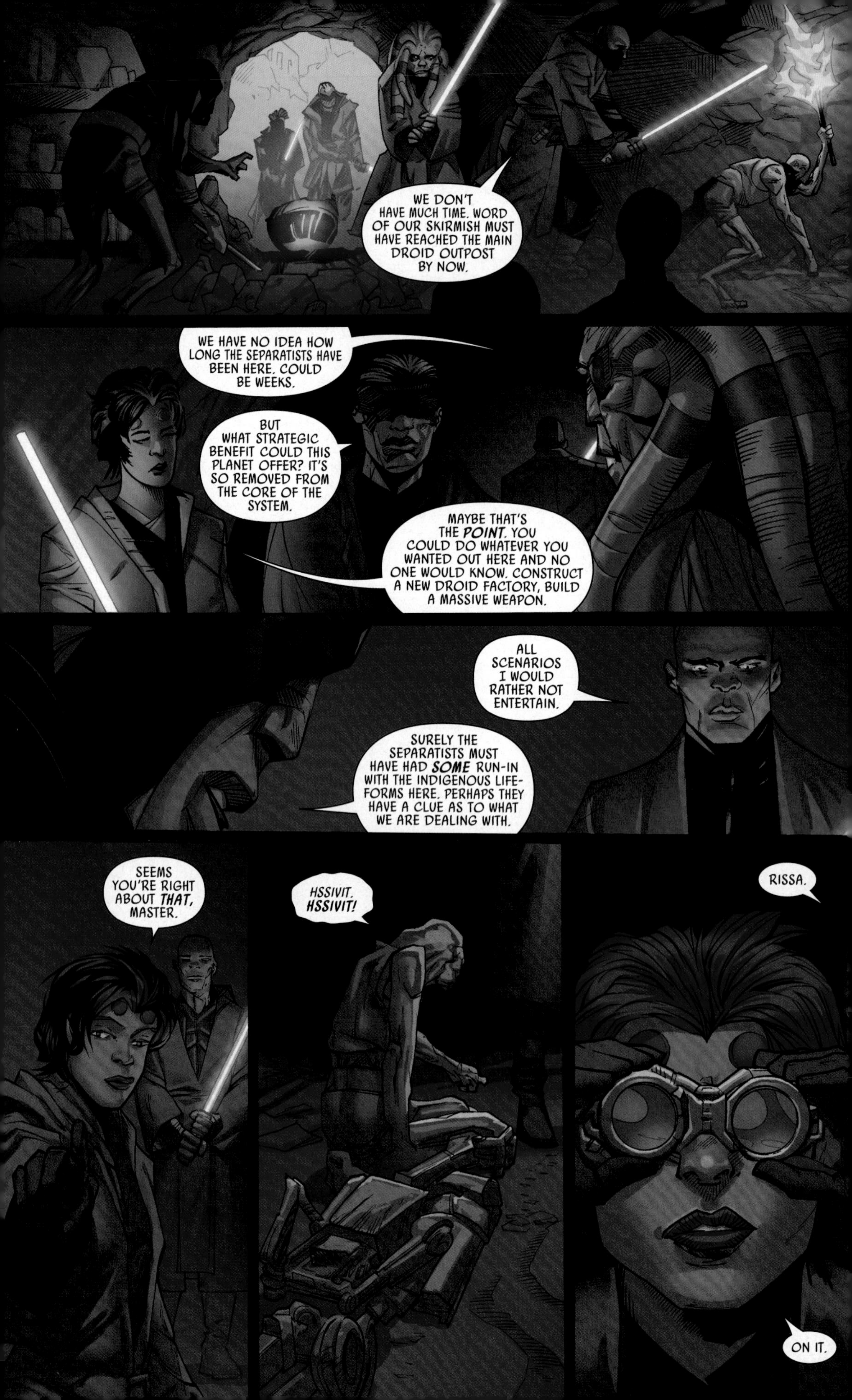

WE DON'T HAVE MUCH TIME. WORD OF OUR SKIRMISH MUST HAVE REACHED THE MAIN DROID OUTPOST BY NOW.
WE HAVE NO IDEA HOW LONG THE SEPARATISTS HAVE BEEN HERE. COULD BE WEEKS.
BUT WHAT STRATEGIC BENEFIT COULD THIS PLANET OFFER? IT'S SO REMOVED FROM THE CORE OF THE SYSTEM.
MAYBE THAT'S THE POINT. YOU COULD DO WHATEVER YOU WANTED OUT HERE AND NO ONE WOULD KNOW. CONSTRUCT A NEW DROID FACTORY, BUILD A MASSIVE WEAPON.
ALL SCENARIOS I WOULD RATHER NOT ENTERTAIN.
SURELY THE SEPARATISTS MUST HAVE HAD SOME RUN-IN WITH THE INDIGENOUS LIFE-FORMS HERE. PERHAPS THEY HAVE A CLUE AS TO WHAT WE ARE DEALING WITH.
SEEMS YOU'RE RIGHT ABOUT THAT, MASTER.
HSSIVIT. HSSIVIT!
RISSA.
ON IT.

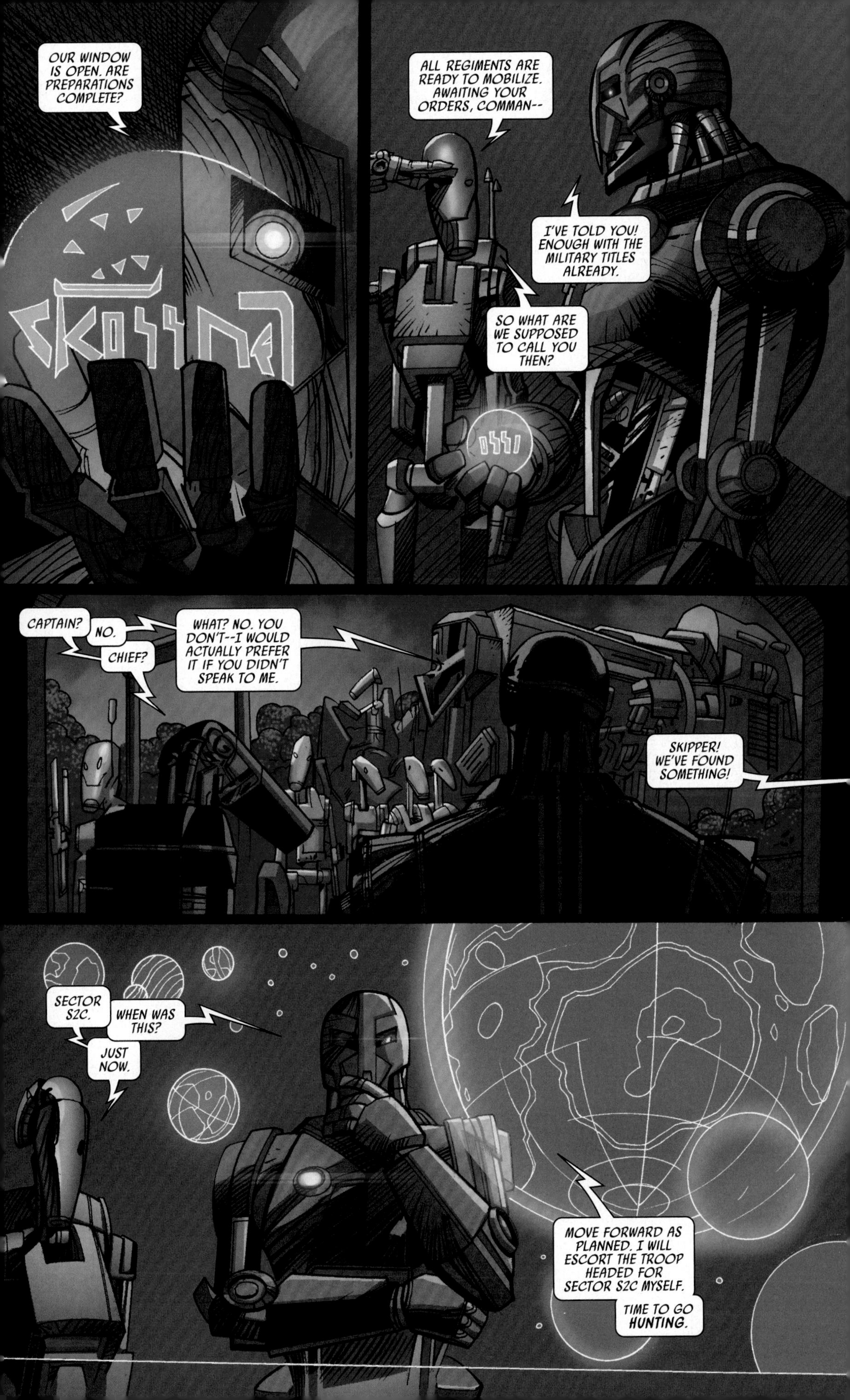

OUR WINDOW IS OPEN. ARE PREPARATIONS COMPLETE?
ALL REGIMENTS ARE READY TO MOBILIZE. AWAITING YOUR ORDERS, COMMAN--
I'VE TOLD YOU! ENOUGH WITH THE MILITARY TITLES ALREADY.
SO WHAT ARE WE SUPPOSED TO CALL YOU THEN?
CAPTAIN?
NO.
CHIEF?
WHAT? NO. YOU DON'T--I WOULD ACTUALLY PREFER IT IF YOU DIDN'T SPEAK TO ME.
SKIPPER! WE'VE FOUND SOMETHING!
SECTOR S2C.
WHEN WAS THIS?
JUST NOW.
MOVE FORWARD AS PLANNED. I WILL ESCORT THE TROOP HEADED FOR SECTOR S2C MYSELF.
TIME TO GO HUNTING.

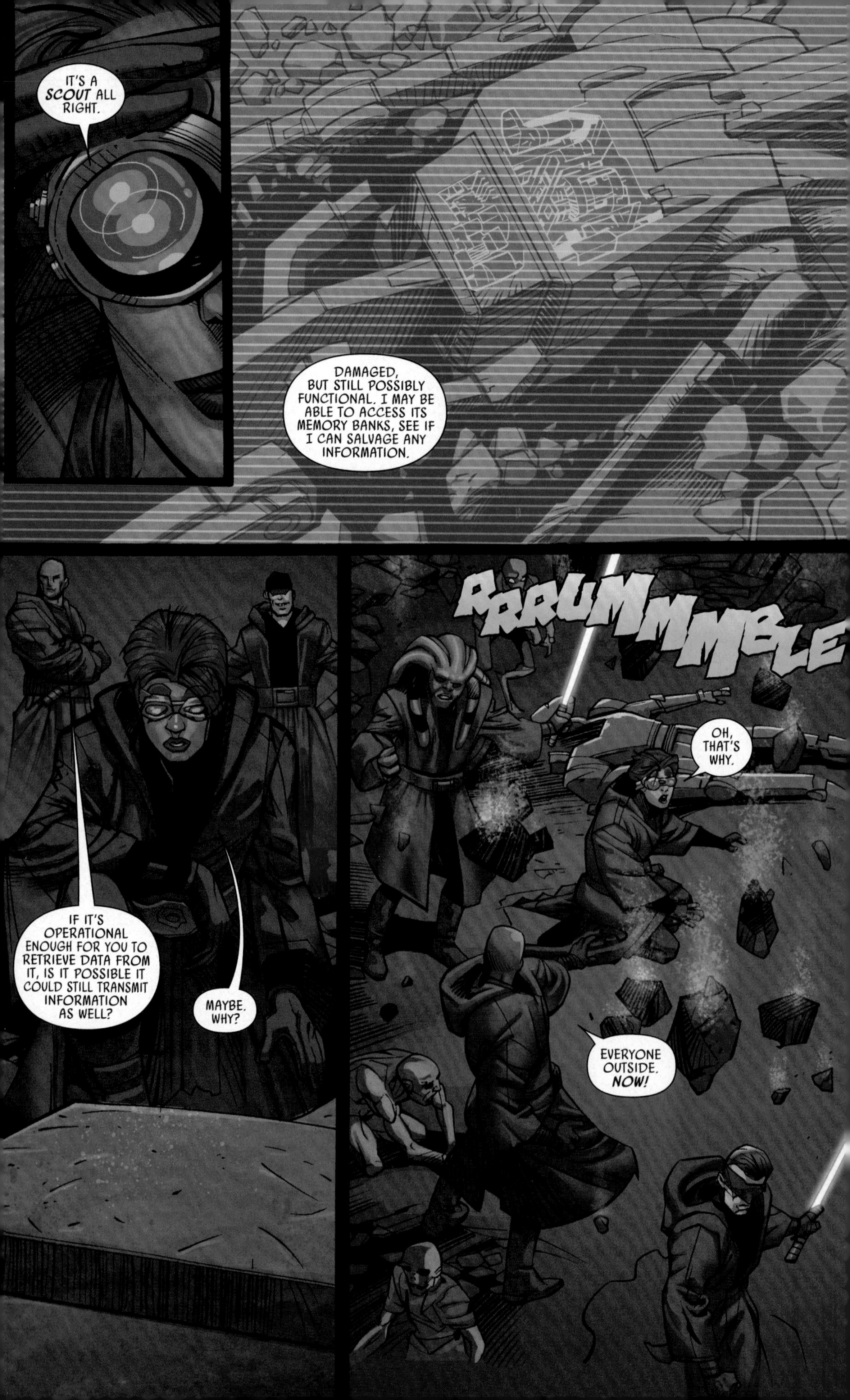
IT'S A SCOUT ALL RIGHT.
DAMAGED, BUT STILL POSSIBLY FUNCTIONAL. I MAY BE ABLE TO ACCESS ITS MEMORY BANKS, SEE IF I CAN SALVAGE ANY INFORMATION.
IF IT'S OPERATIONAL ENOUGH FOR YOU TO RETRIEVE DATA FROM IT, IS IT POSSIBLE IT COULD STILL TRANSMIT INFORMATION AS WELL?
MAYBE. WHY?
RRRUMMMMBLE
OH, THAT'S WHY.
EVERYONE OUTSIDE. NOW!

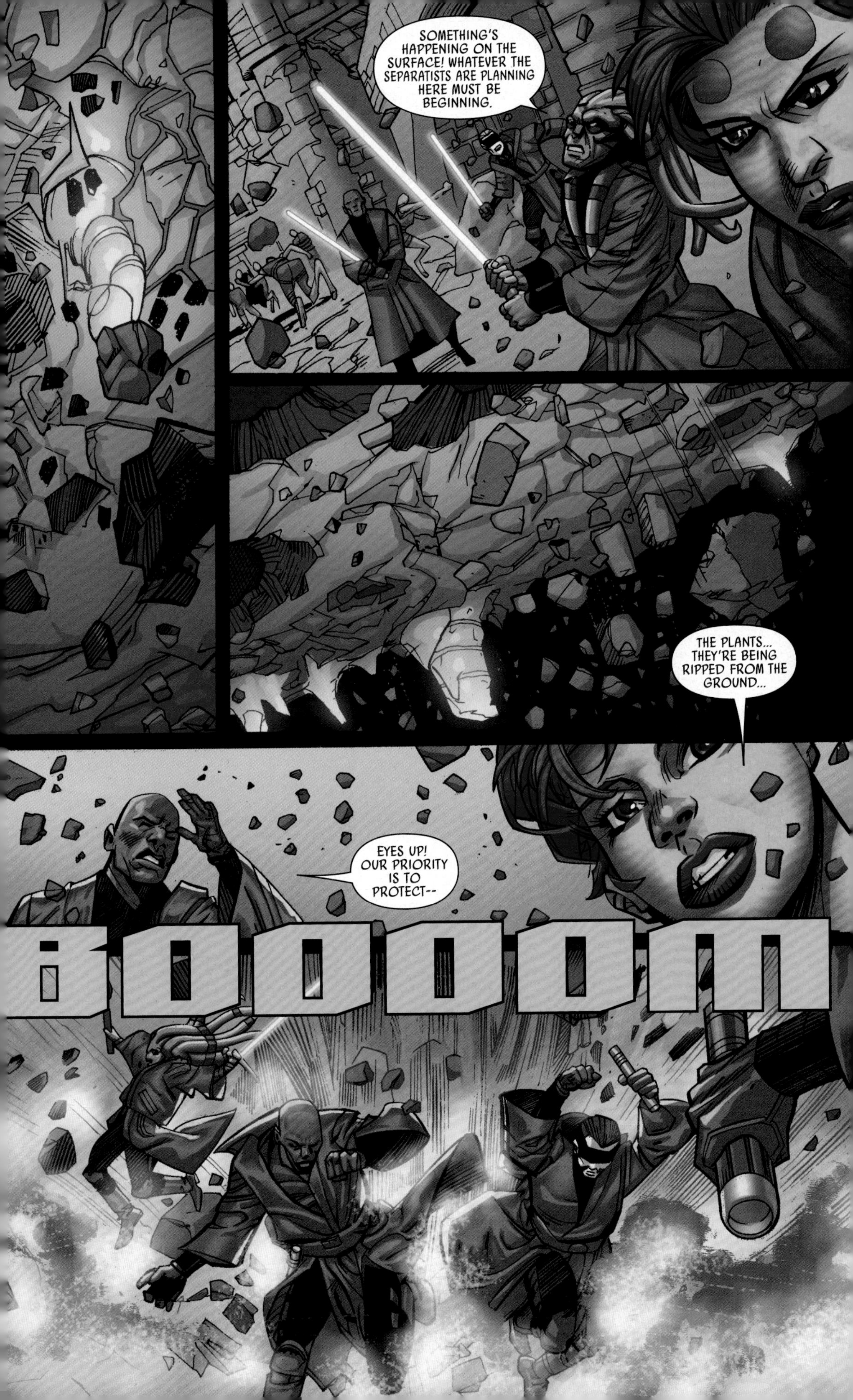
SOMETHING'S HAPPENING ON THE SURFACE! WHATEVER THE SEPARATISTS ARE PLANNING HERE MUST BE BEGINNING.
THE PLANTS... THEY'RE BEING RIPPED FROM THE GROUND...
EYES UP! OUR PRIORITY IS TO PROTECT--
BOOOM

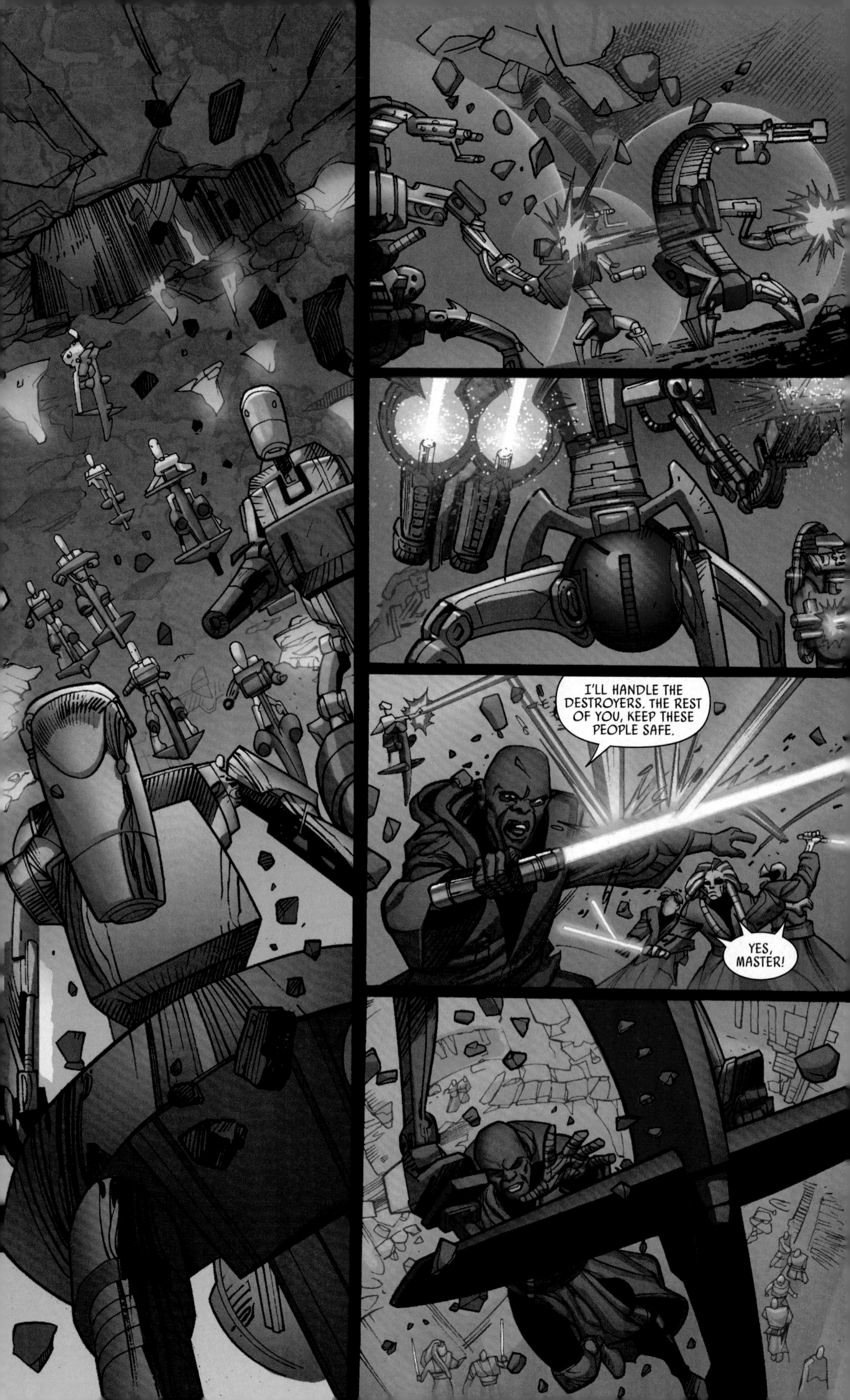
I'LL HANDLE THE DESTROYERS. THE REST OF YOU, KEEP THESE PEOPLE SAFE.
YES, MASTER!

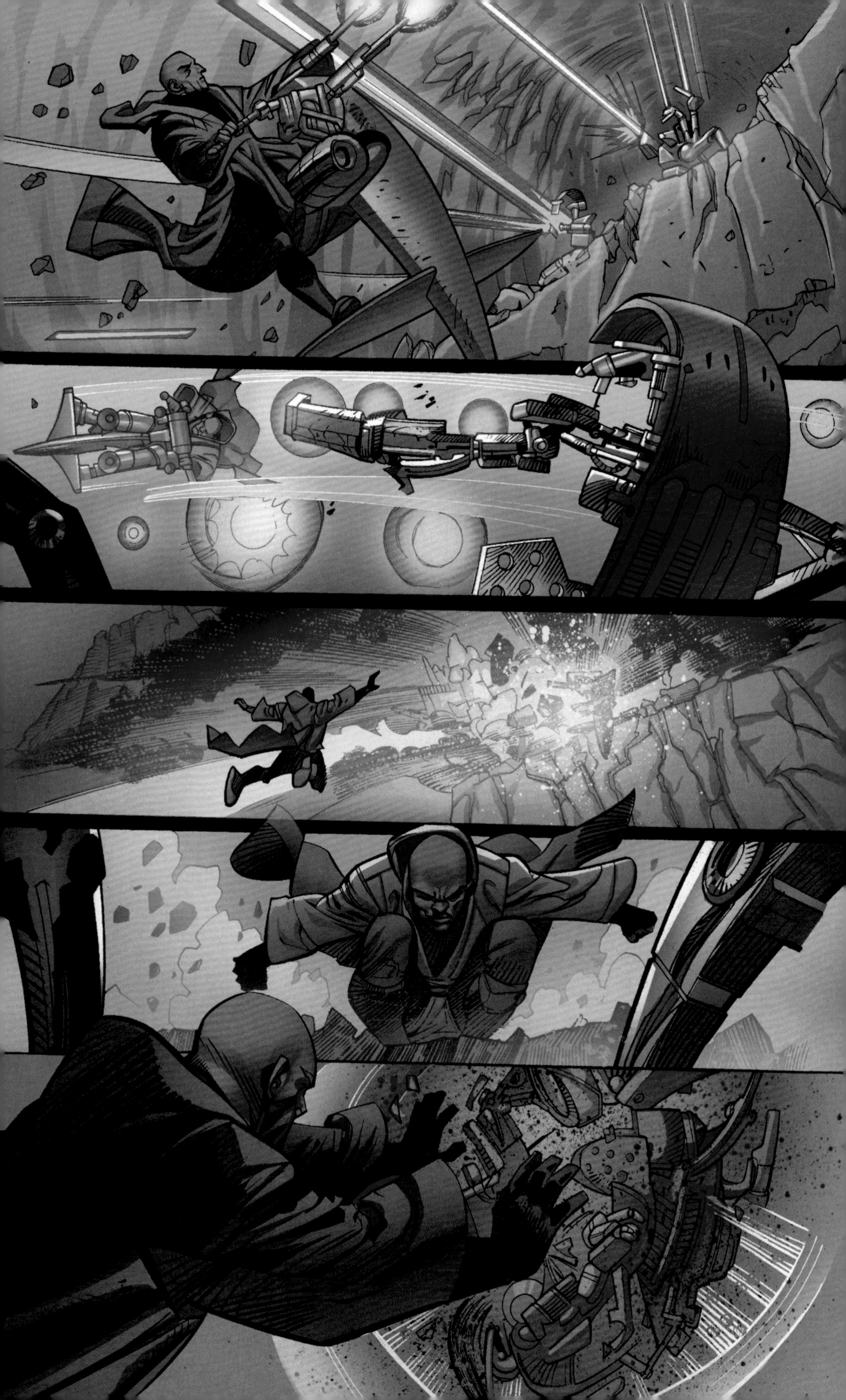

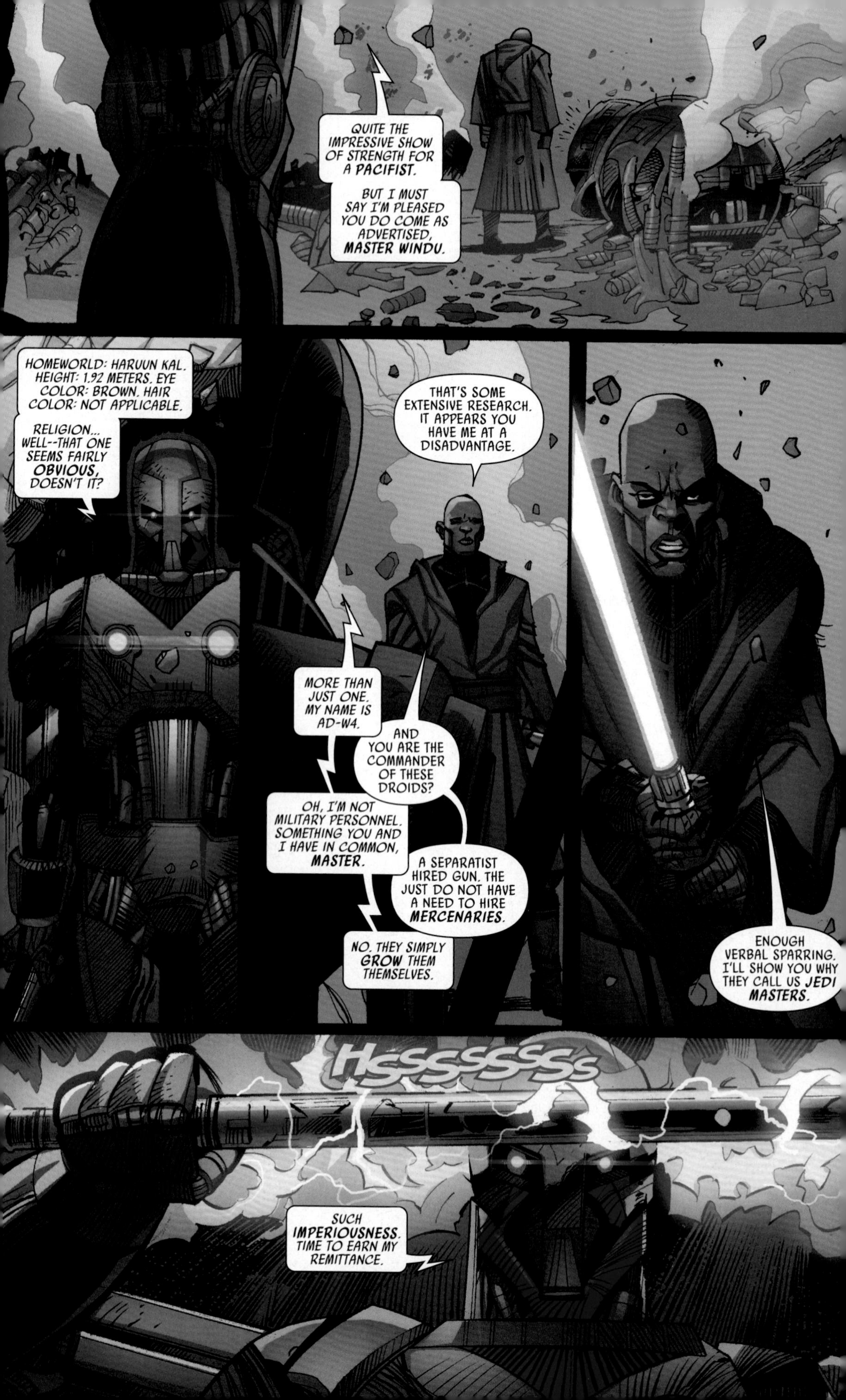
QUITE THE IMPRESSIVE SHOW OF STRENGTH FOR A PACIFIST.
BUT I MUST SAY I'M PLEASED YOU DO COME AS ADVERTISED, MASTER WINDU.
HOMEWORLD: HARUUN KAL. HEIGHT: 1.92 METERS. EYE COLOR: BROWN. HAIR COLOR: NOT APPLICABLE.
RELIGION... WELL--THAT ONE SEEMS FAIRLY OBVIOUS, DOESN'T IT?
THAT'S SOME EXTENSIVE RESEARCH. IT APPEARS YOU HAVE ME AT A DISADVANTAGE.
MORE THAN JUST ONE. MY NAME IS AD-W4.
AND YOU ARE THE COMMANDER OF THESE DROIDS?
OH, I'M NOT MILITARY PERSONNEL. SOMETHING YOU AND I HAVE IN COMMON, MASTER.
A SEPARATIST HIRED GUN. THE JUST DO NOT HAVE A NEED TO HIRE MERCENARIES.
NO. THEY SIMPLY GROW THEM THEMSELVES.
ENOUGH VERBAL SPARRING. I'LL SHOW YOU WHY THEY CALL US JEDI MASTERS.
HSSSSSSSs
SUCH IMPERIOUSNESS. TIME TO EARN MY REMITTANCE.

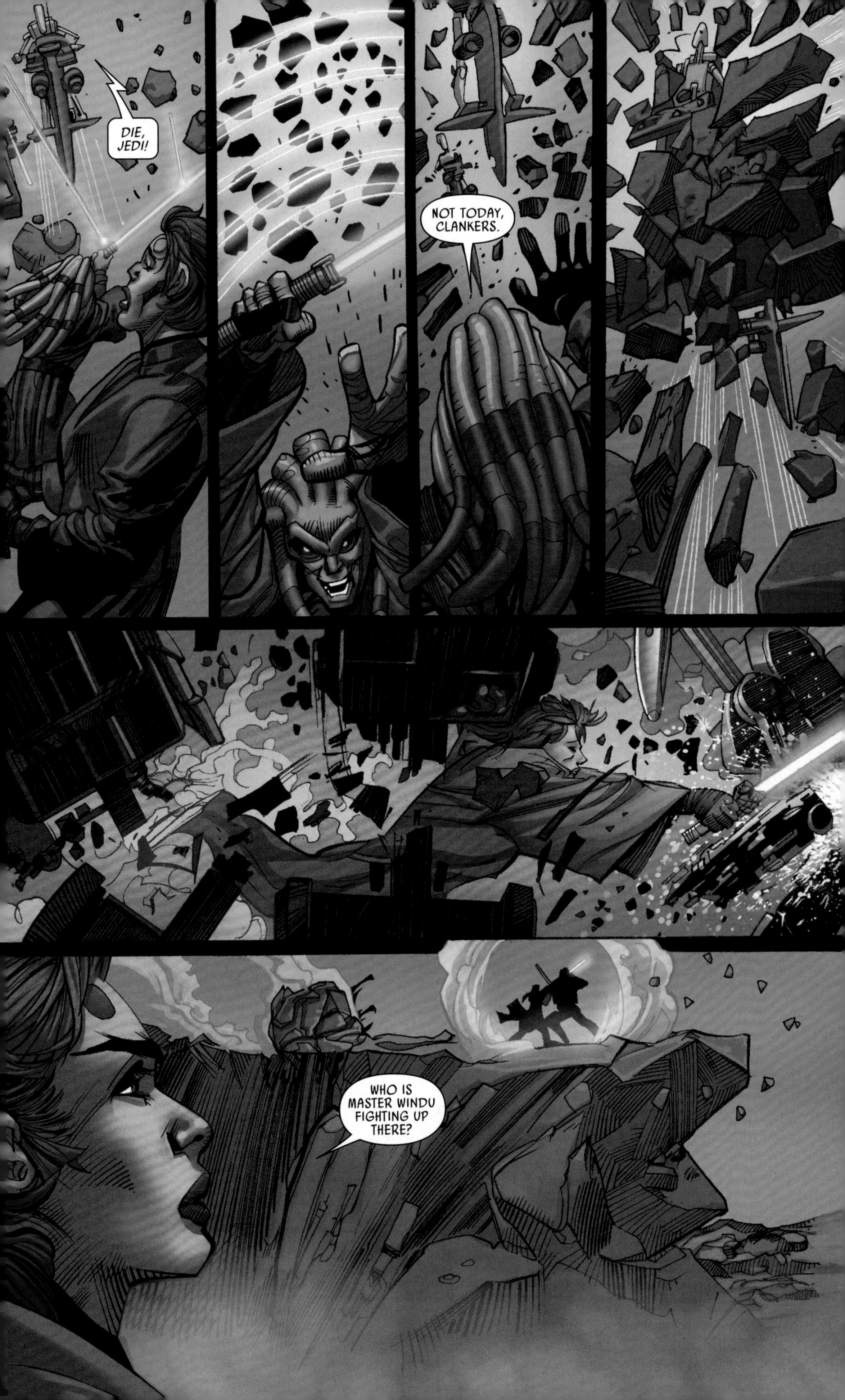
DIE, JEDI!
NOT TODAY, CLANKERS.
WHO IS MASTER WINDU FIGHTING UP THERE?

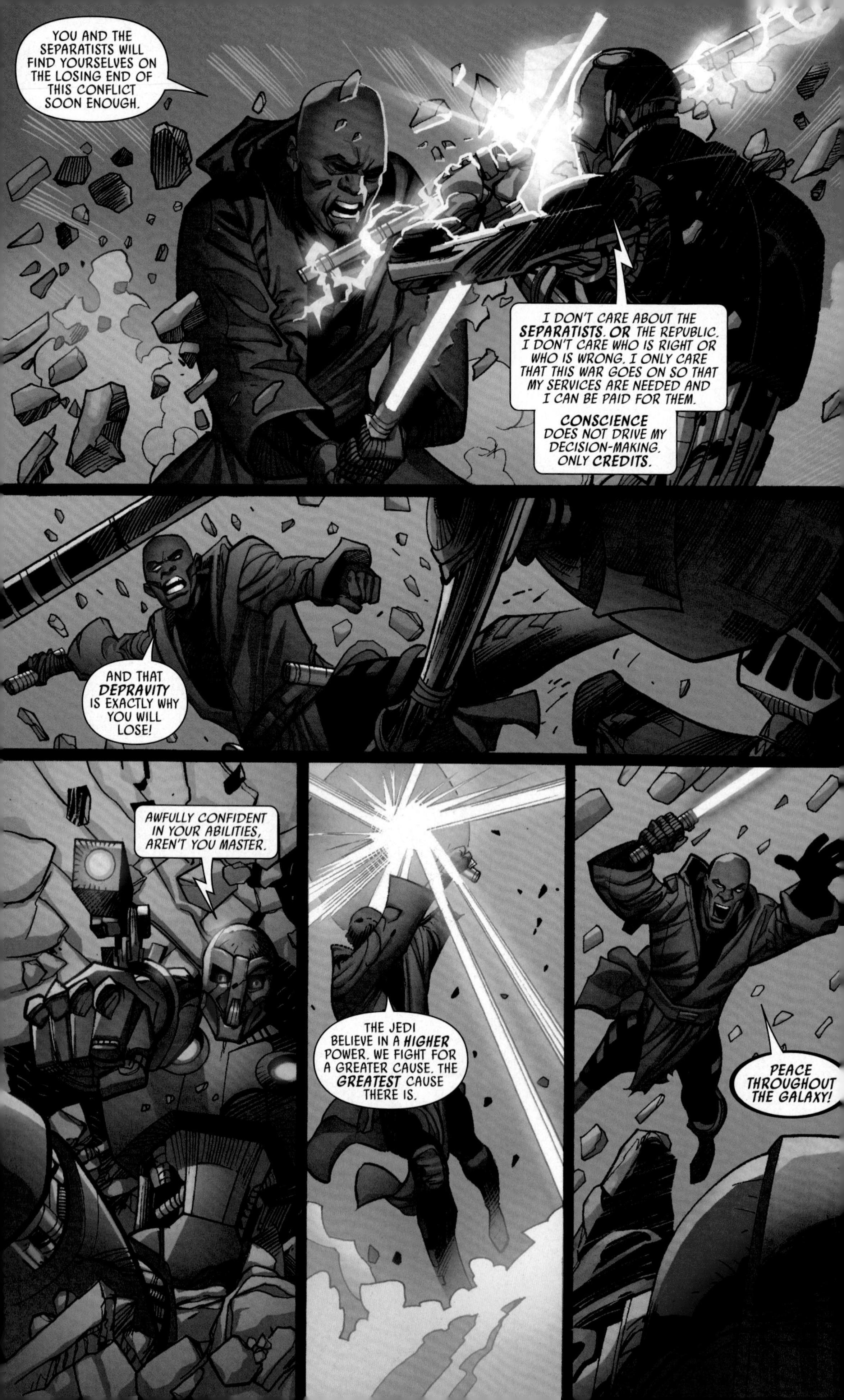
YOU AND THE SEPARATISTS WILL FIND YOURSELVES ON THE LOSING END OF THIS CONFLICT SOON ENOUGH.
I DON'T CARE ABOUT THE SEPARATISTS. OR THE REPUBLIC. I DON'T CARE WHO IS RIGHT OR WHO IS WRONG. I ONLY CARE THAT THIS WAR GOES ON SO THAT MY SERVICES ARE NEEDED AND I CAN BE PAID FOR THEM.
CONSCIENCE DOES NOT DRIVE MY DECISION-MAKING. ONLY CREDITS.
AND THAT DEPRAVITY IS EXACTLY WHY YOU WILL LOSE!
AWFULLY CONFIDENT IN YOUR ABILITIES, AREN'T YOU MASTER.
THE JEDI BELIEVE IN A HIGHER POWER. WE FIGHT FOR A GREATER CAUSE. THE GREATEST CAUSE THERE IS.
PEACE THROUGHOUT THE GALAXY!

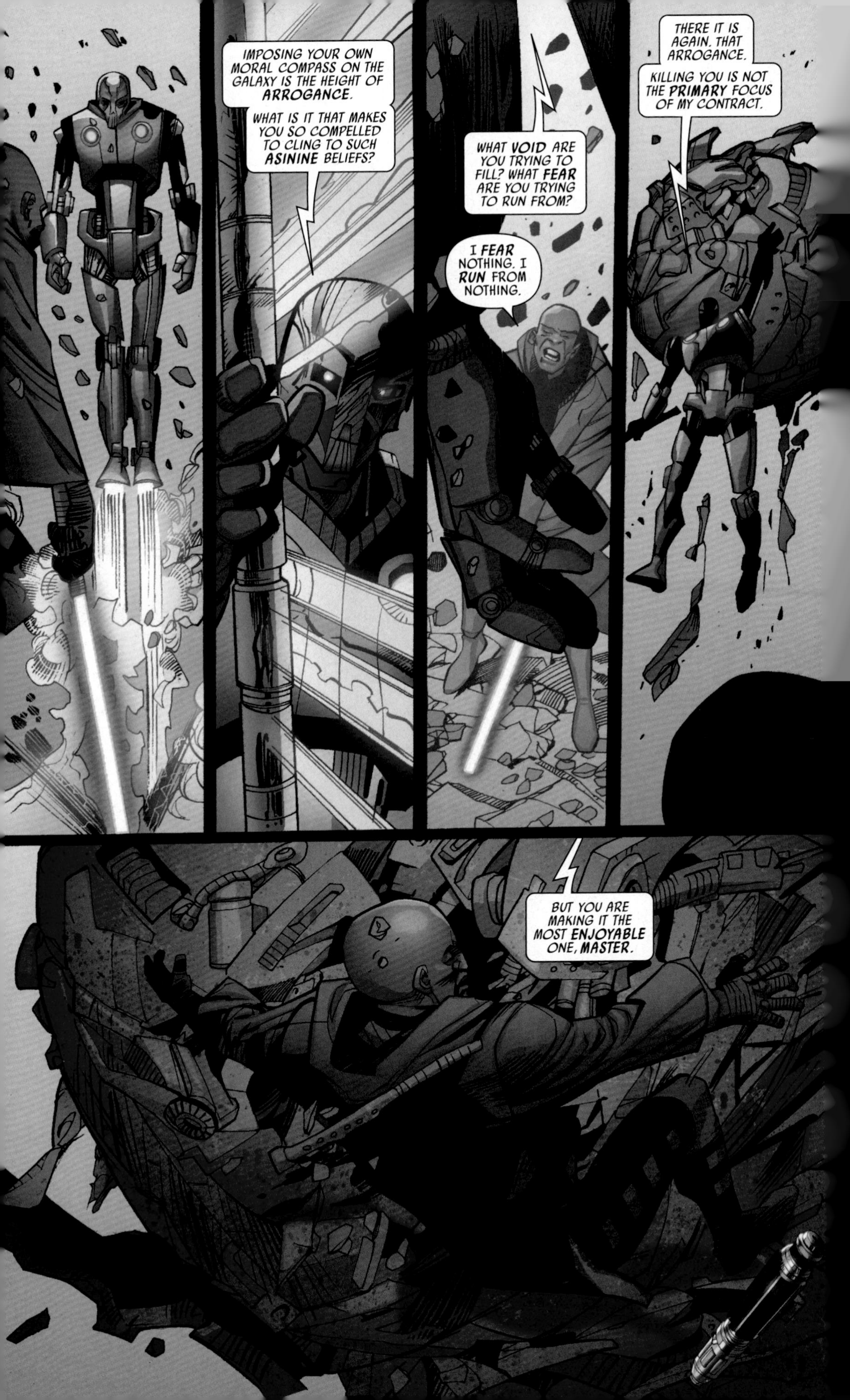

IMPOSING YOUR OWN MORAL COMPASS ON THE GALAXY IS THE HEIGHT OF **ARROGANCE**.
WHAT IS IT THAT MAKES YOU SO COMPELLED TO CLING TO SUCH **ASININE** BELIEFS?
WHAT **VOID** ARE YOU TRYING TO FILL? WHAT **FEAR** ARE YOU TRYING TO RUN FROM?
I **FEAR** NOTHING. I **RUN** FROM NOTHING.
THERE IT IS AGAIN. THAT ARROGANCE.
KILLING YOU IS NOT THE **PRIMARY** FOCUS OF MY CONTRACT.
BUT YOU ARE MAKING IT THE MOST **ENJOYABLE** ONE, **MASTER**.

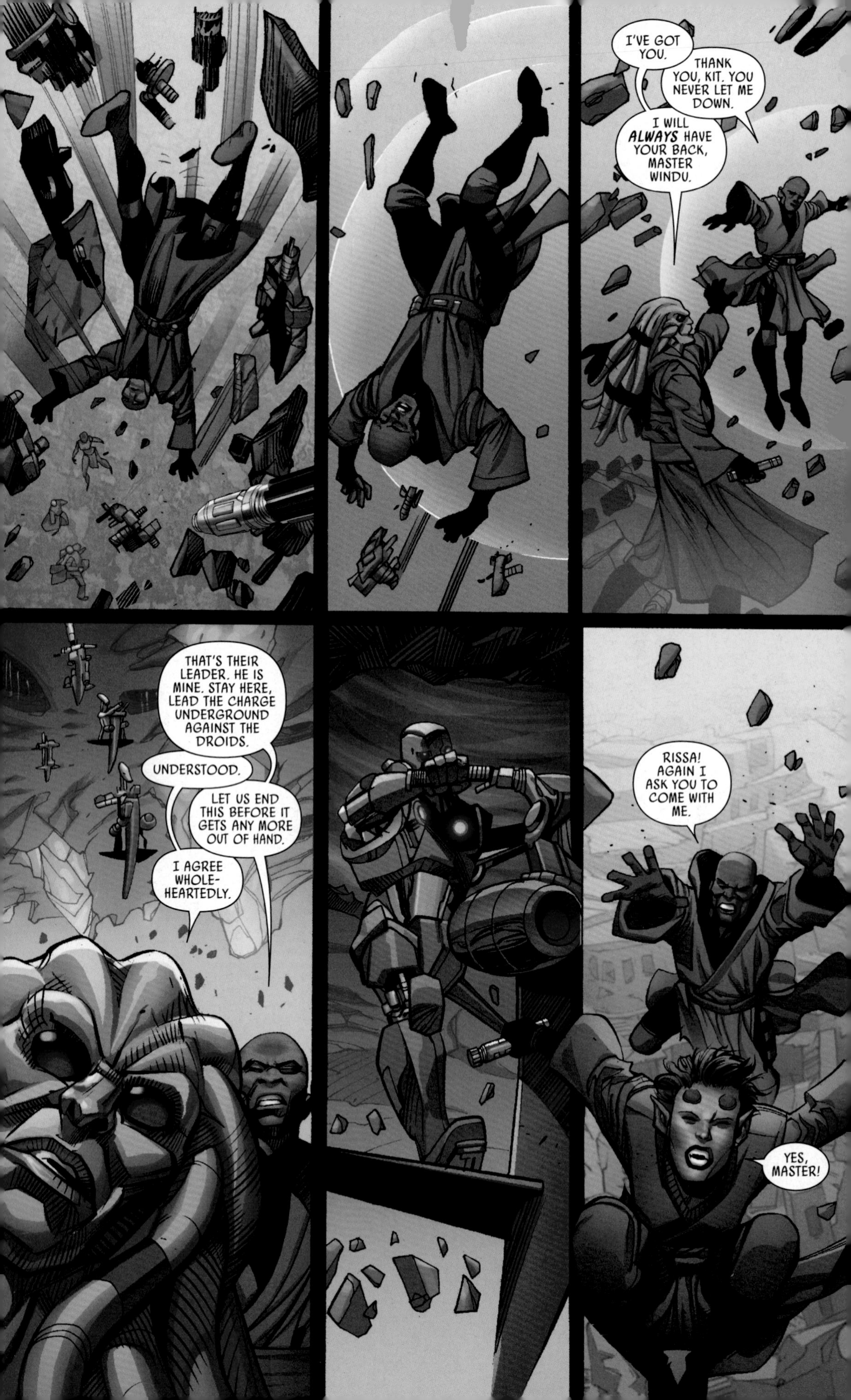
I'VE GOT YOU.
THANK YOU, KIT. YOU NEVER LET ME DOWN.
I WILL ALWAYS HAVE YOUR BACK, MASTER WINDU.
THAT'S THEIR LEADER. HE IS MINE. STAY HERE, LEAD THE CHARGE UNDERGROUND AGAINST THE DROIDS.
UNDERSTOOD.
LET US END THIS BEFORE IT GETS ANY MORE OUT OF HAND.
I AGREE WHOLE-HEARTEDLY.
RISSA! AGAIN I ASK YOU TO COME WITH ME.
YES, MASTER!

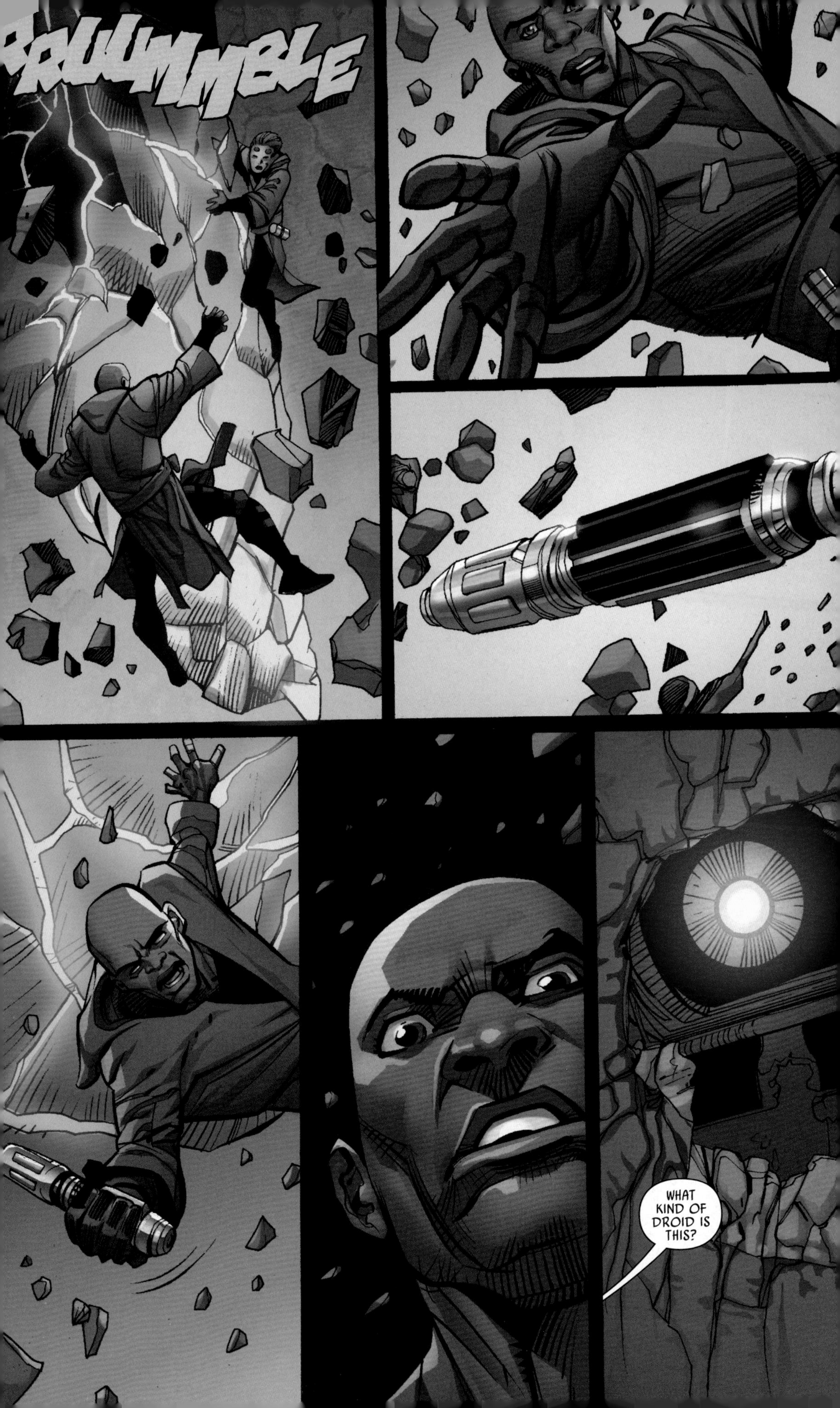
RRUUMMBLE
WHAT KIND OF DROID IS THIS?

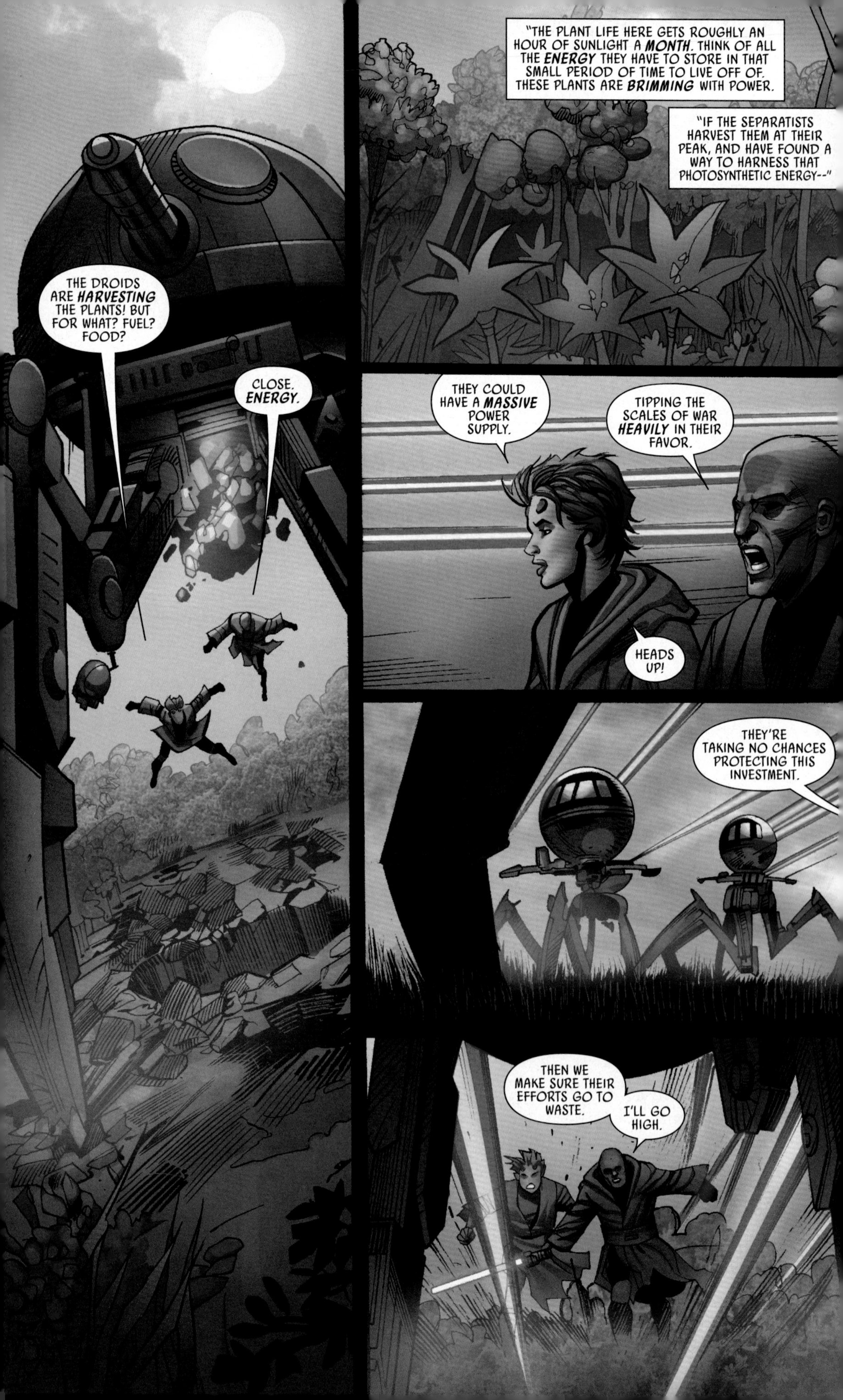
THE DROIDS ARE *HARVESTING* THE PLANTS! BUT FOR WHAT? FUEL? FOOD?
CLOSE. *ENERGY*.
"THE PLANT LIFE HERE GETS ROUGHLY AN HOUR OF SUNLIGHT A *MONTH*. THINK OF ALL THE *ENERGY* THEY HAVE TO STORE IN THAT SMALL PERIOD OF TIME TO LIVE OFF OF. THESE PLANTS ARE *BRIMMING* WITH POWER.
"IF THE SEPARATISTS HARVEST THEM AT THEIR PEAK, AND HAVE FOUND A WAY TO HARNESS THAT PHOTOSYNTHETIC ENERGY--"
THEY COULD HAVE A *MASSIVE* POWER SUPPLY.
TIPPING THE SCALES OF WAR *HEAVILY* IN THEIR FAVOR.
HEADS UP!
THEY'RE TAKING NO CHANCES PROTECTING THIS INVESTMENT.
THEN WE MAKE SURE THEIR EFFORTS GO TO WASTE.
I'LL GO HIGH.

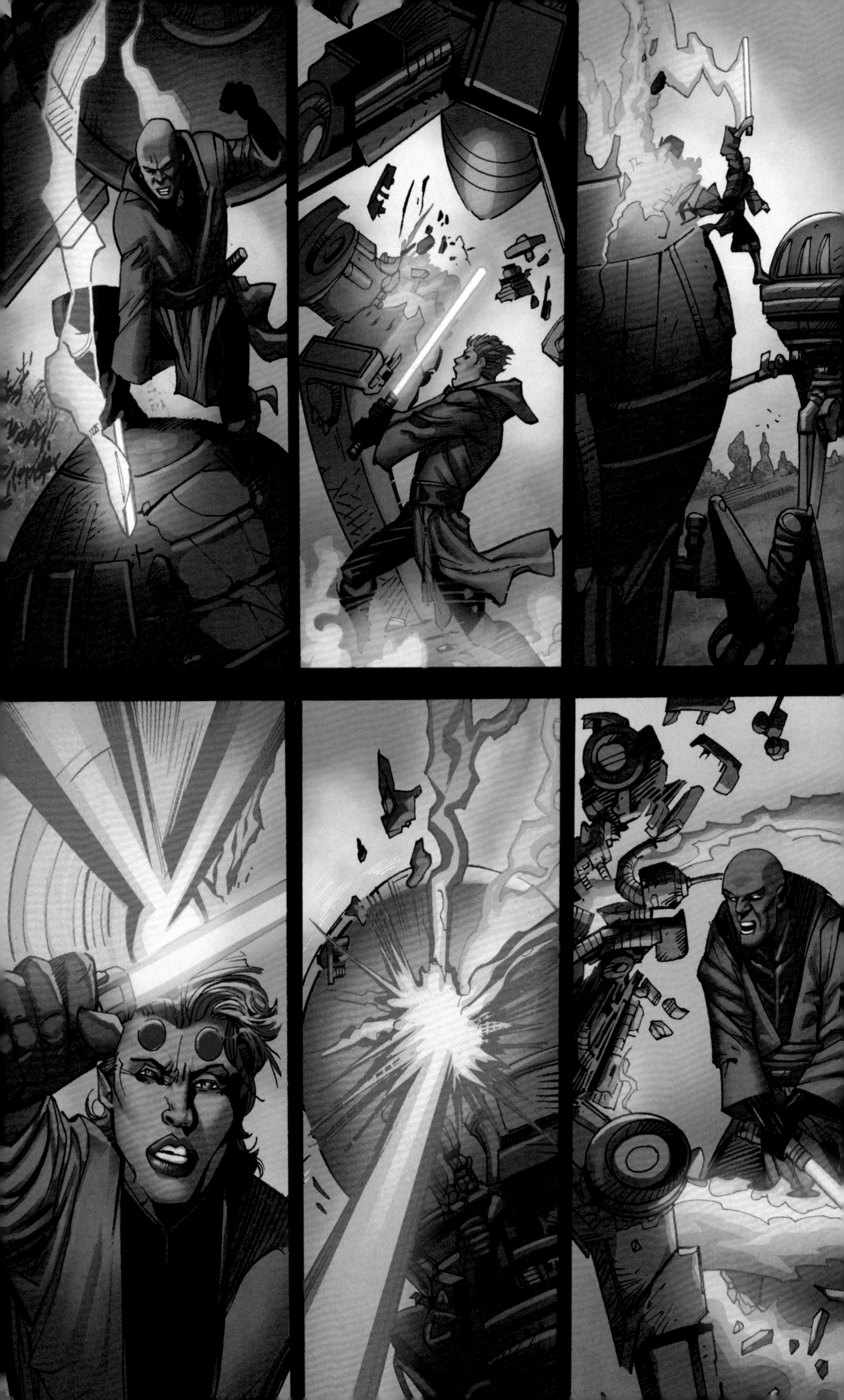

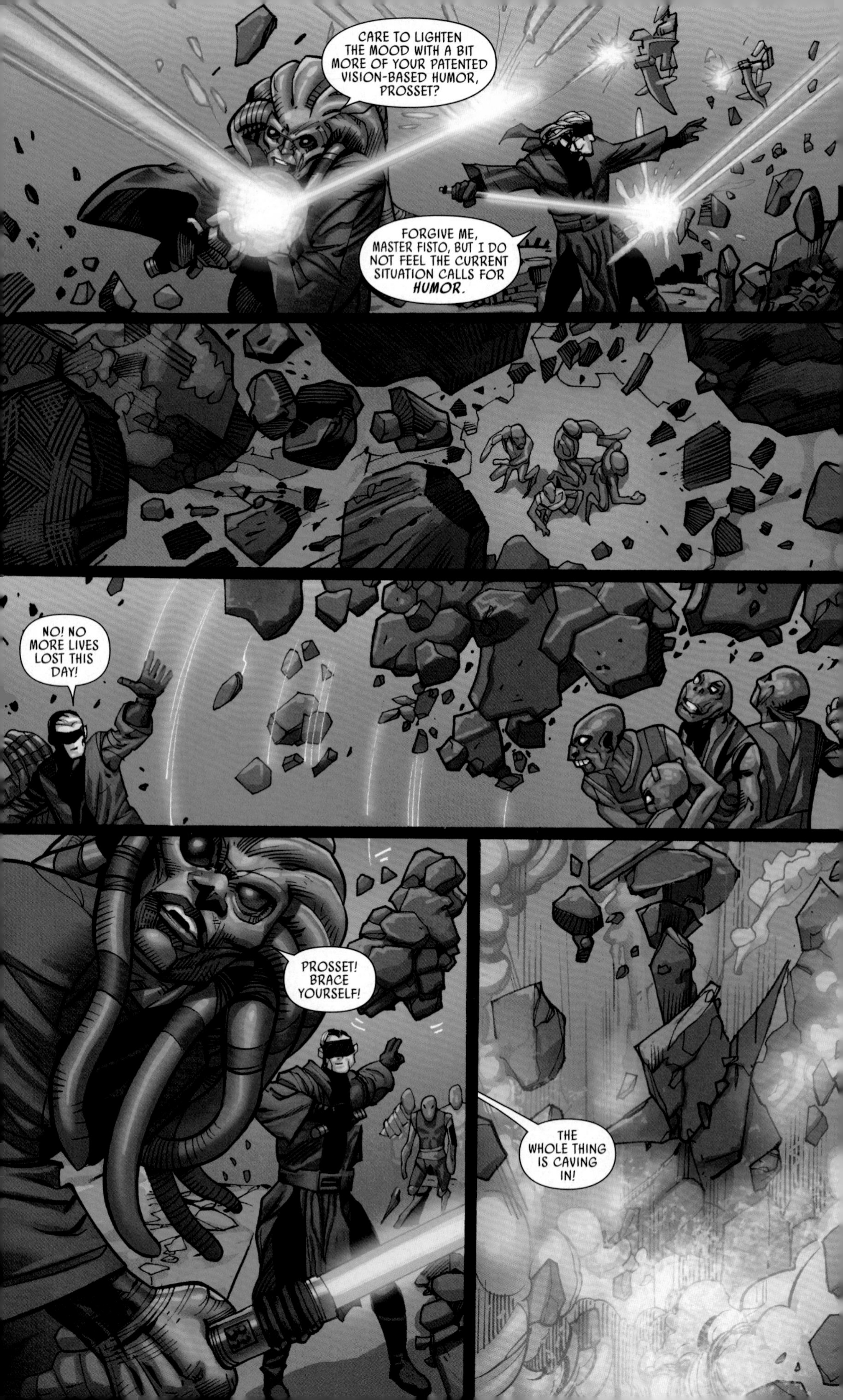
CARE TO LIGHTEN THE MOOD WITH A BIT MORE OF YOUR PATENTED VISION-BASED HUMOR, PROSSET?
FORGIVE ME, MASTER FISTO, BUT I DO NOT FEEL THE CURRENT SITUATION CALLS FOR HUMOR.
NO! NO MORE LIVES LOST THIS DAY!
PROSSET! BRACE YOURSELF!
THE WHOLE THING IS CAVING IN!

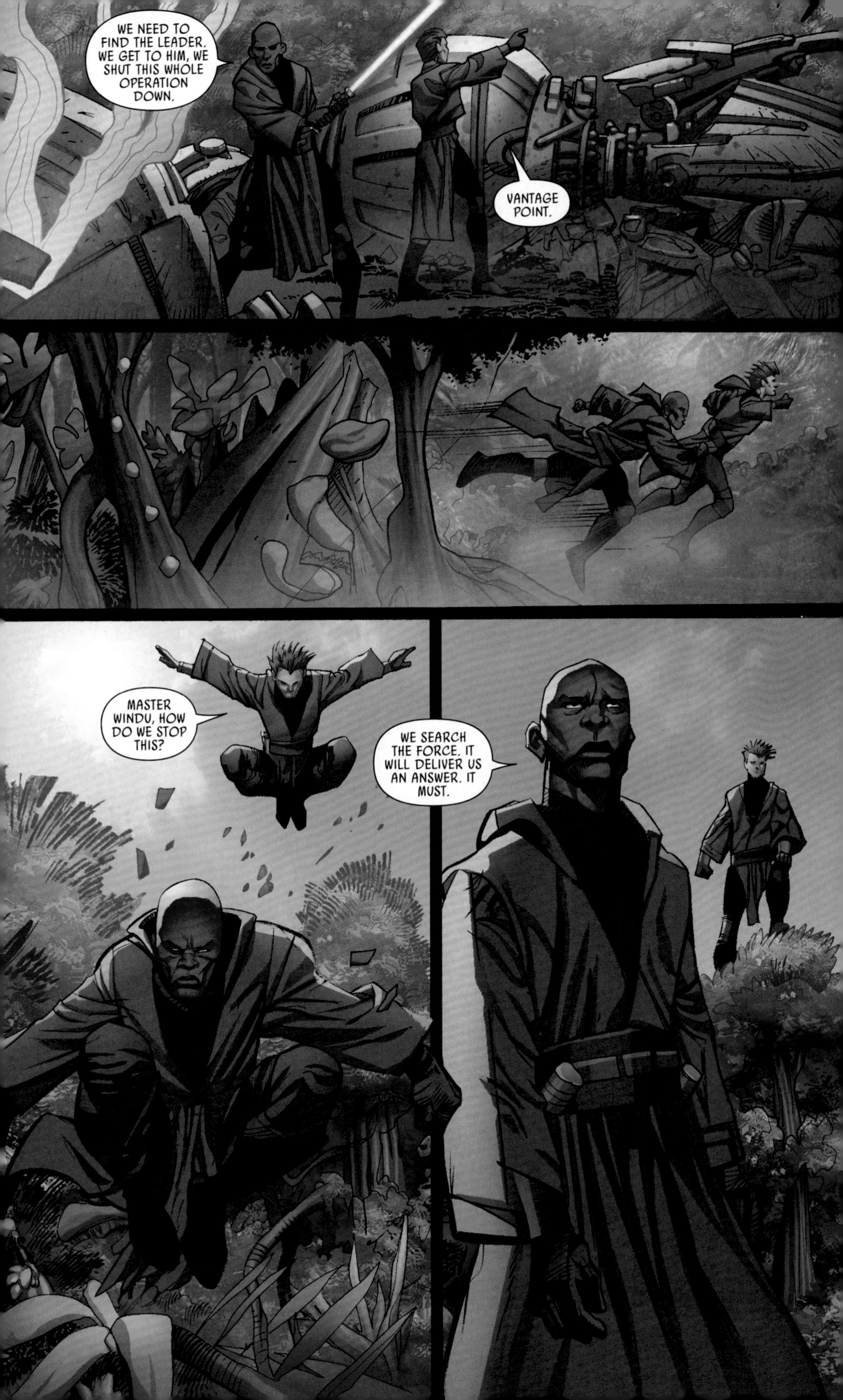
WE NEED TO FIND THE LEADER. WE GET TO HIM, WE SHUT THIS WHOLE OPERATION DOWN.
VANTAGE POINT.
MASTER WINDU, HOW DO WE STOP THIS?
WE SEARCH THE FORCE. IT WILL DELIVER US AN ANSWER. IT MUST.

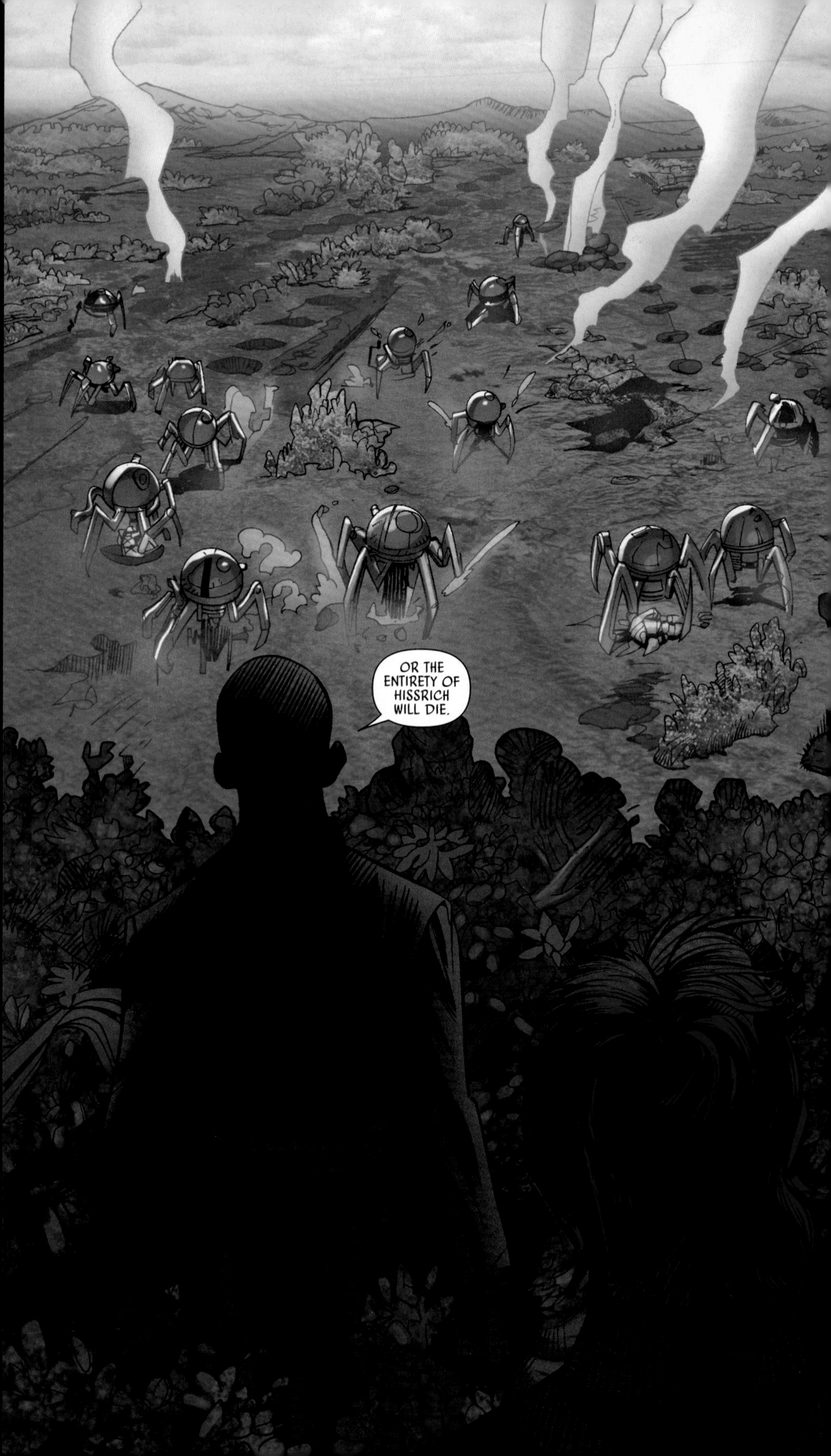
OR THE ENTIRETY OF HISSRICH WILL DIE.

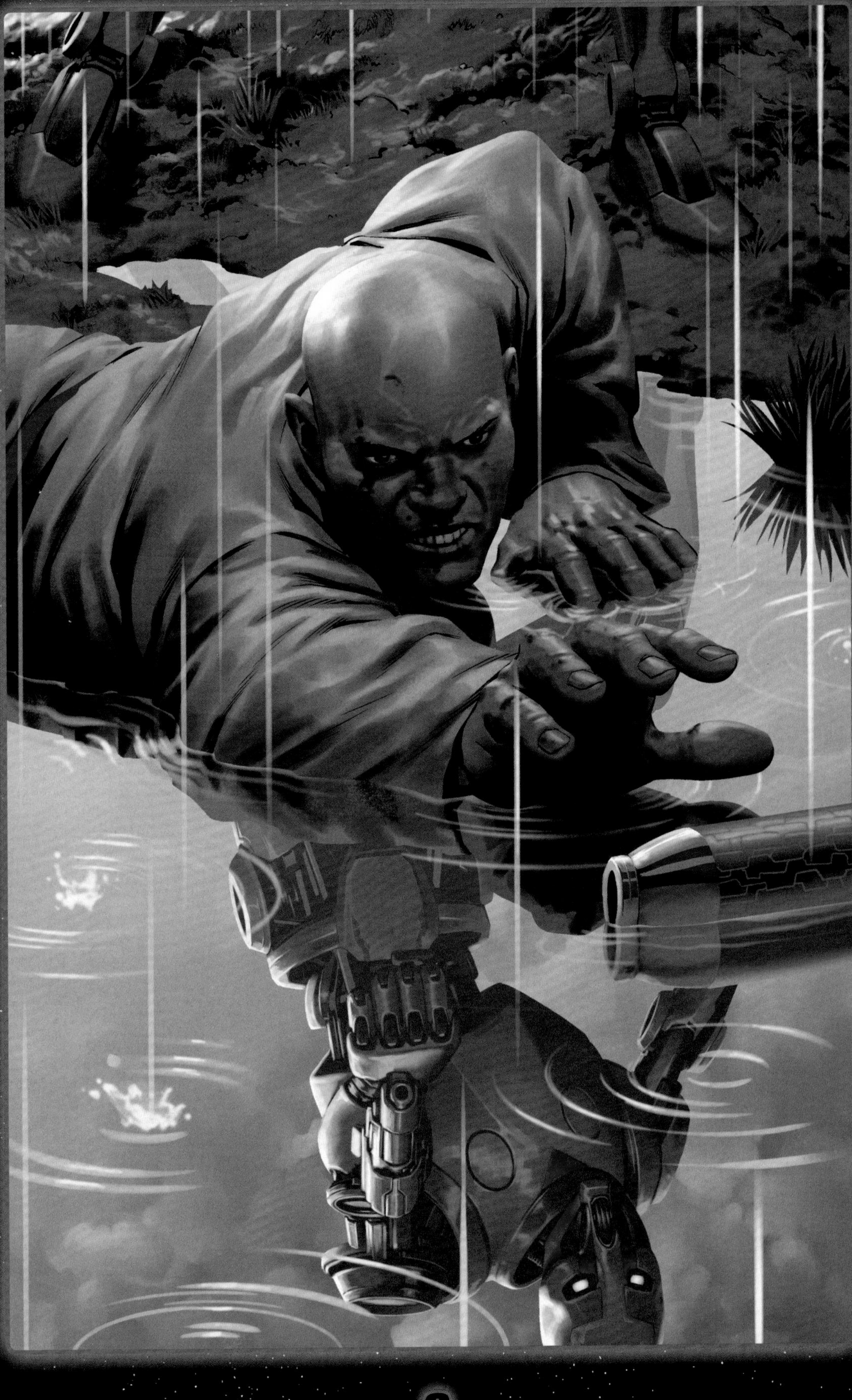

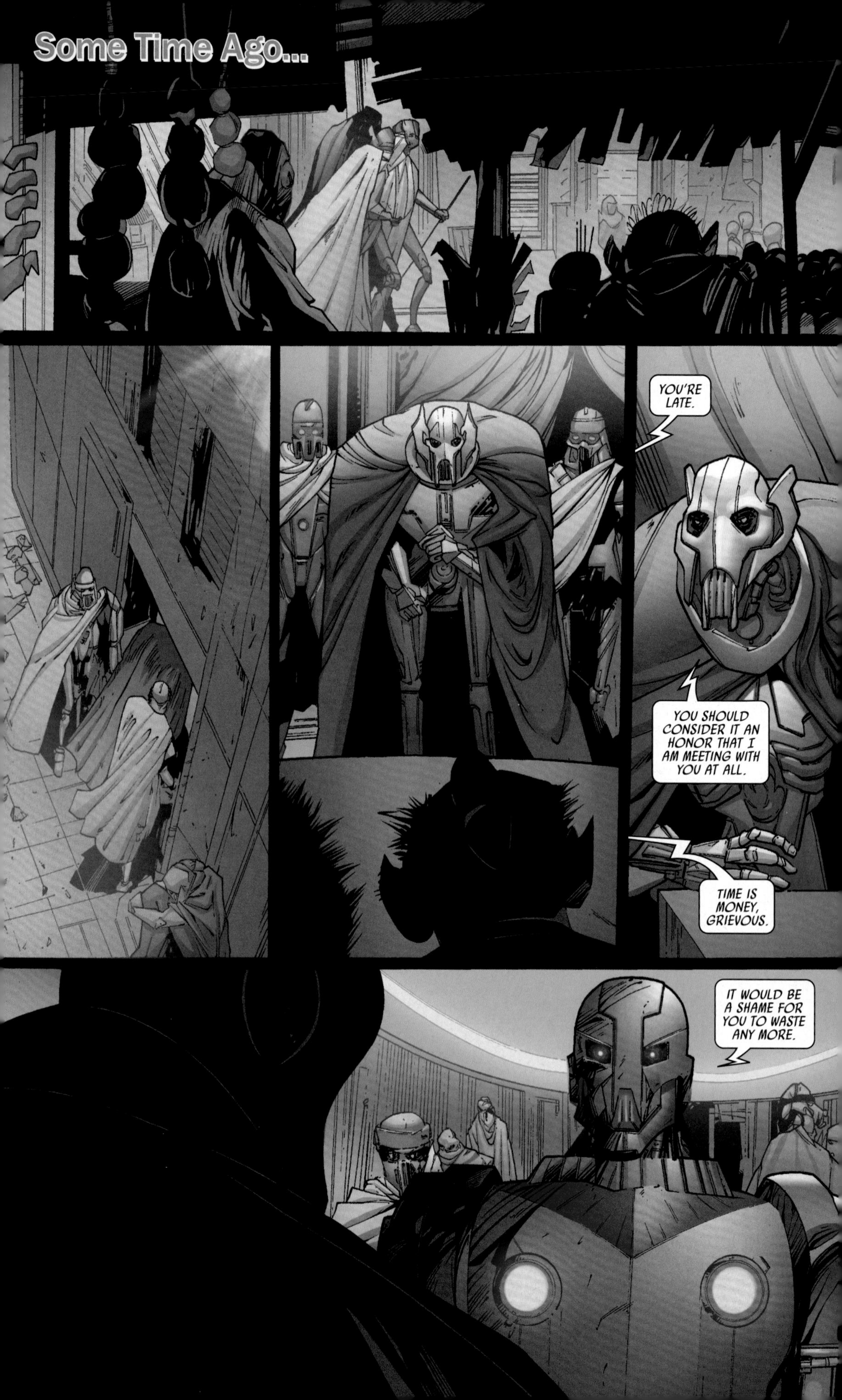
Some Time Ago...
YOU'RE LATE.
YOU SHOULD CONSIDER IT AN HONOR THAT I AM MEETING WITH YOU AT ALL.
TIME IS MONEY, GRIEVOUS.
IT WOULD BE A SHAME FOR YOU TO WASTE ANY MORE.

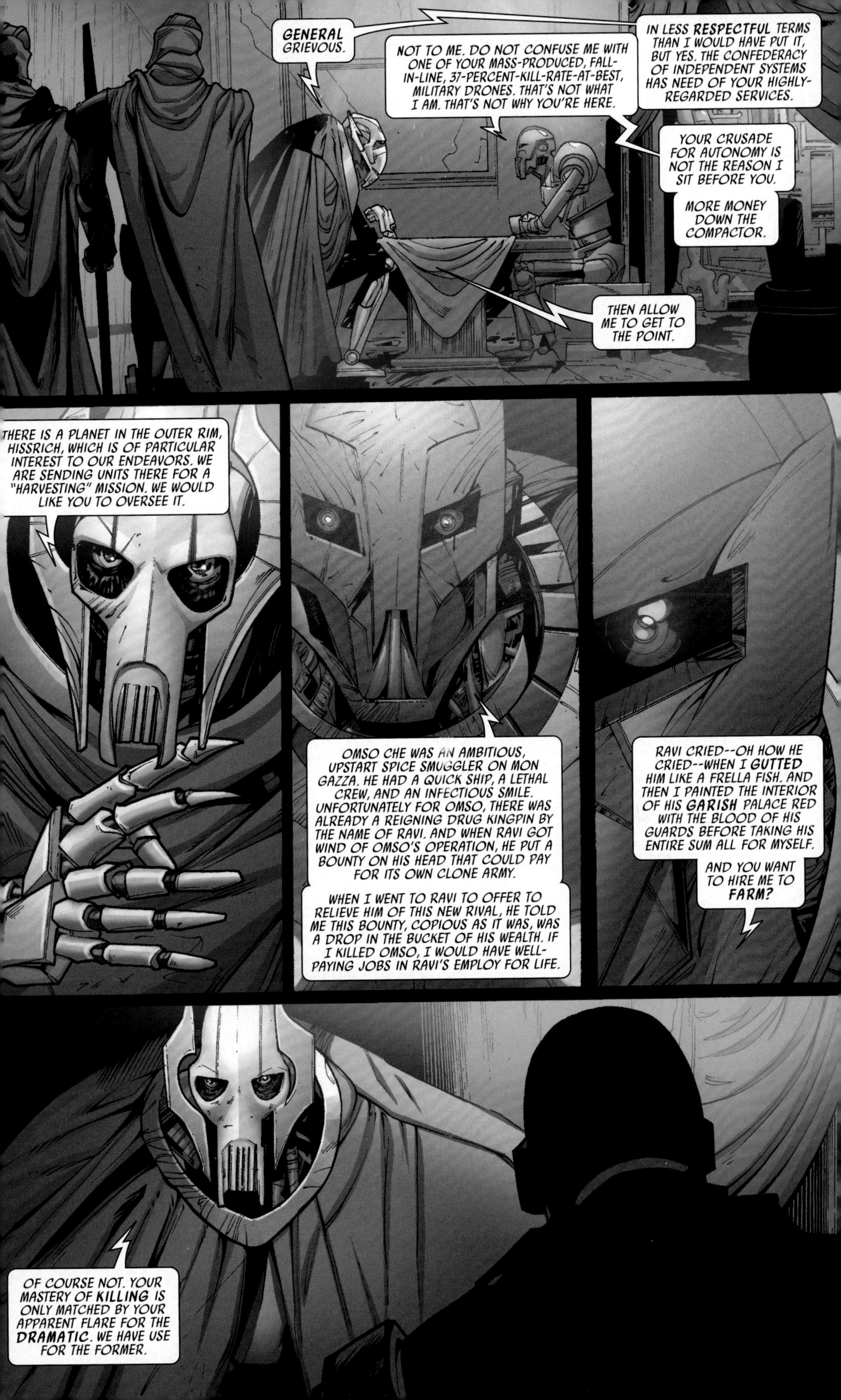
GENERAL GRIEVOUS.
NOT TO ME. DO NOT CONFUSE ME WITH ONE OF YOUR MASS-PRODUCED, FALL-IN-LINE, 37-PERCENT-KILL-RATE-AT-BEST, MILITARY DRONES. THAT'S NOT WHAT I AM. THAT'S NOT WHY YOU'RE HERE.
IN LESS RESPECTFUL TERMS THAN I WOULD HAVE PUT IT, BUT YES. THE CONFEDERACY OF INDEPENDENT SYSTEMS HAS NEED OF YOUR HIGHLY-REGARDED SERVICES.
YOUR CRUSADE FOR AUTONOMY IS NOT THE REASON I SIT BEFORE YOU.
MORE MONEY DOWN THE COMPACTOR.
THEN ALLOW ME TO GET TO THE POINT.
THERE IS A PLANET IN THE OUTER RIM, HISSRICH, WHICH IS OF PARTICULAR INTEREST TO OUR ENDEAVORS. WE ARE SENDING UNITS THERE FOR A "HARVESTING" MISSION. WE WOULD LIKE YOU TO OVERSEE IT.
OMSO CHE WAS AN AMBITIOUS, UPSTART SPICE SMUGGLER ON MON GAZZA. HE HAD A QUICK SHIP, A LETHAL CREW, AND AN INFECTIOUS SMILE. UNFORTUNATELY FOR OMSO, THERE WAS ALREADY A REIGNING DRUG KINGPIN BY THE NAME OF RAVI. AND WHEN RAVI GOT WIND OF OMSO'S OPERATION, HE PUT A BOUNTY ON HIS HEAD THAT COULD PAY FOR ITS OWN CLONE ARMY.
WHEN I WENT TO RAVI TO OFFER TO RELIEVE HIM OF THIS NEW RIVAL, HE TOLD ME THIS BOUNTY, COPIOUS AS IT WAS, WAS A DROP IN THE BUCKET OF HIS WEALTH. IF I KILLED OMSO, I WOULD HAVE WELL-PAYING JOBS IN RAVI'S EMPLOY FOR LIFE.
RAVI CRIED--OH HOW HE CRIED--WHEN I GUTTED HIM LIKE A FRELLA FISH. AND THEN I PAINTED THE INTERIOR OF HIS GARISH PALACE RED WITH THE BLOOD OF HIS GUARDS BEFORE TAKING HIS ENTIRE SUM ALL FOR MYSELF.
AND YOU WANT TO HIRE ME TO FARM?
OF COURSE NOT. YOUR MASTERY OF KILLING IS ONLY MATCHED BY YOUR APPARENT FLARE FOR THE DRAMATIC. WE HAVE USE FOR THE FORMER.

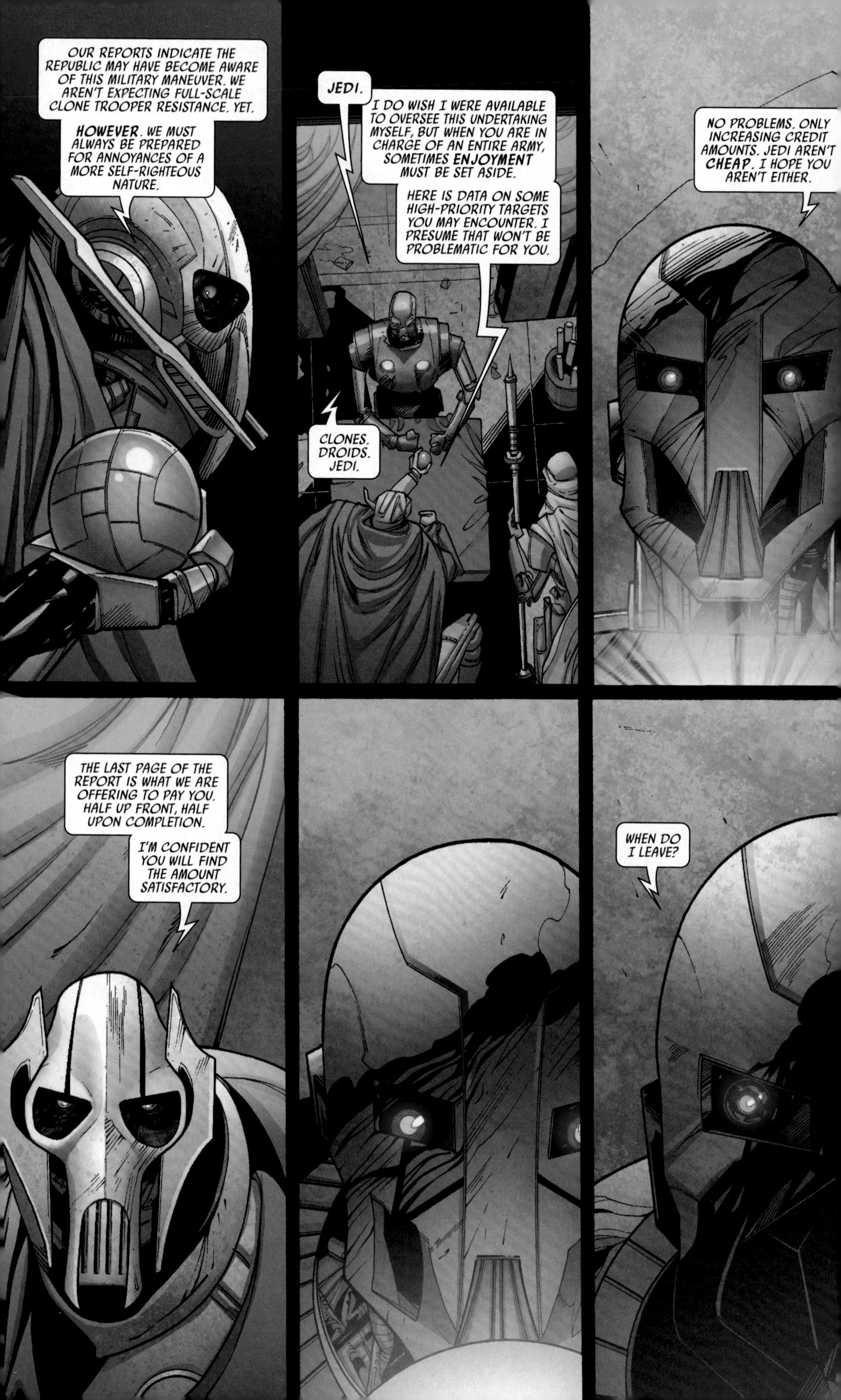

OUR REPORTS INDICATE THE REPUBLIC MAY HAVE BECOME AWARE OF THIS MILITARY MANEUVER. WE AREN'T EXPECTING FULL-SCALE CLONE TROOPER RESISTANCE. YET.
HOWEVER. WE MUST ALWAYS BE PREPARED FOR ANNOYANCES OF A MORE SELF-RIGHTEOUS NATURE.
JEDI.
I DO WISH I WERE AVAILABLE TO OVERSEE THIS UNDERTAKING MYSELF, BUT WHEN YOU ARE IN CHARGE OF AN ENTIRE ARMY, SOMETIMES ENJOYMENT MUST BE SET ASIDE.
HERE IS DATA ON SOME HIGH-PRIORITY TARGETS YOU MAY ENCOUNTER. I PRESUME THAT WON'T BE PROBLEMATIC FOR YOU.
CLONES. DROIDS. JEDI.
NO PROBLEMS. ONLY INCREASING CREDIT AMOUNTS. JEDI AREN'T CHEAP. I HOPE YOU AREN'T EITHER.
THE LAST PAGE OF THE REPORT IS WHAT WE ARE OFFERING TO PAY YOU. HALF UP FRONT, HALF UPON COMPLETION.
I'M CONFIDENT YOU WILL FIND THE AMOUNT SATISFACTORY.
WHEN DO I LEAVE?

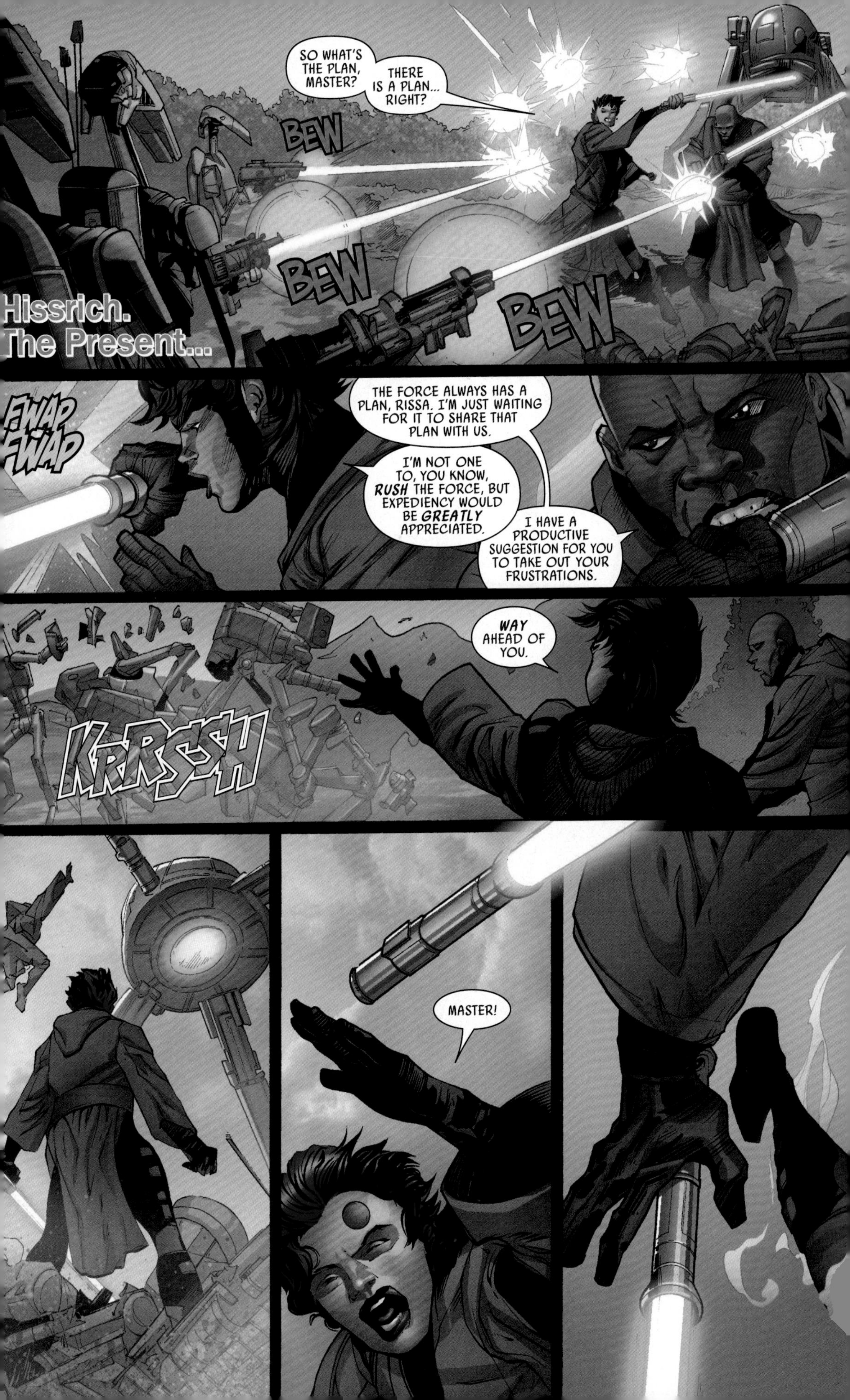

Hissrich.
The Present...
SO WHAT'S THE PLAN, MASTER?
THERE IS A PLAN... RIGHT?
BEW
BEW
BEW
FWAP FWAP
THE FORCE ALWAYS HAS A PLAN, RISSA. I'M JUST WAITING FOR IT TO SHARE THAT PLAN WITH US.
I'M NOT ONE TO, YOU KNOW, RUSH THE FORCE, BUT EXPEDIENCY WOULD BE GREATLY APPRECIATED.
I HAVE A PRODUCTIVE SUGGESTION FOR YOU TO TAKE OUT YOUR FRUSTRATIONS.
WAY AHEAD OF YOU.
KRRRSSH
MASTER!

FFFFFSSSSSSHHHHH

DHHOOOOOOOOOOOOOOOOOHH

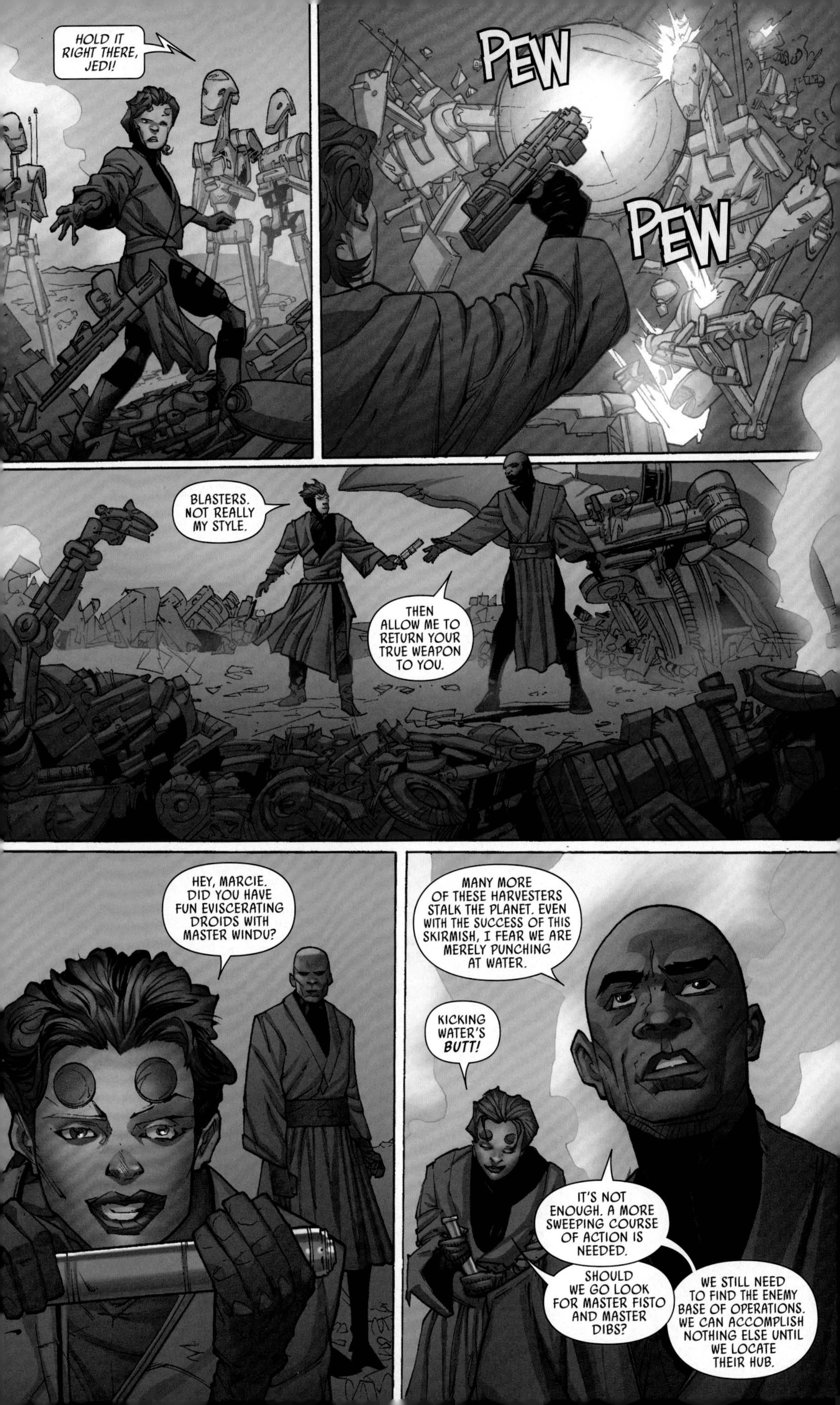
HOLD IT RIGHT THERE, JEDI!
PEW
PEW
BLASTERS. NOT REALLY MY STYLE.
THEN ALLOW ME TO RETURN YOUR TRUE WEAPON TO YOU.
HEY, MARCIE. DID YOU HAVE FUN EVISCERATING DROIDS WITH MASTER WINDU?
MANY MORE OF THESE HARVESTERS STALK THE PLANET. EVEN WITH THE SUCCESS OF THIS SKIRMISH, I FEAR WE ARE MERELY PUNCHING AT WATER.
KICKING WATER'S *BUTT!*
IT'S NOT ENOUGH. A MORE SWEEPING COURSE OF ACTION IS NEEDED.
SHOULD WE GO LOOK FOR MASTER FISTO AND MASTER DIBS?
WE STILL NEED TO FIND THE ENEMY BASE OF OPERATIONS. WE CAN ACCOMPLISH NOTHING ELSE UNTIL WE LOCATE THEIR HUB.

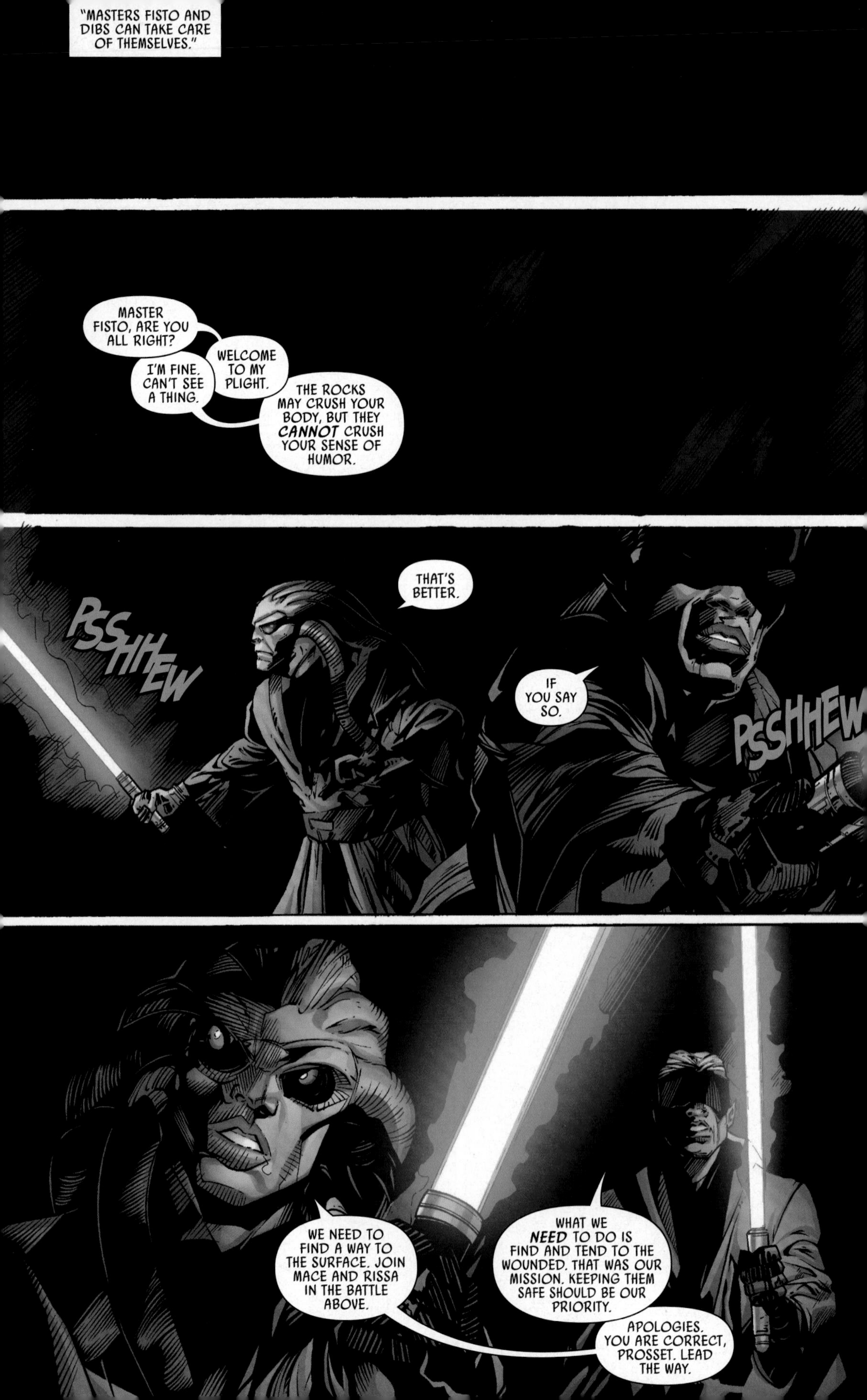
"MASTERS FISTO AND DIBS CAN TAKE CARE OF THEMSELVES."
MASTER FISTO, ARE YOU ALL RIGHT?
I'M FINE. CAN'T SEE A THING.
WELCOME TO MY PLIGHT.
THE ROCKS MAY CRUSH YOUR BODY, BUT THEY *CANNOT* CRUSH YOUR SENSE OF HUMOR.
PSSHHEW
THAT'S BETTER.
IF YOU SAY SO.
PSSHHEW
WE NEED TO FIND A WAY TO THE SURFACE. JOIN MACE AND RISSA IN THE BATTLE ABOVE.
WHAT WE *NEED* TO DO IS FIND AND TEND TO THE WOUNDED. THAT WAS OUR MISSION. KEEPING THEM SAFE SHOULD BE OUR PRIORITY.
APOLOGIES. YOU ARE CORRECT, PROSSET. LEAD THE WAY.

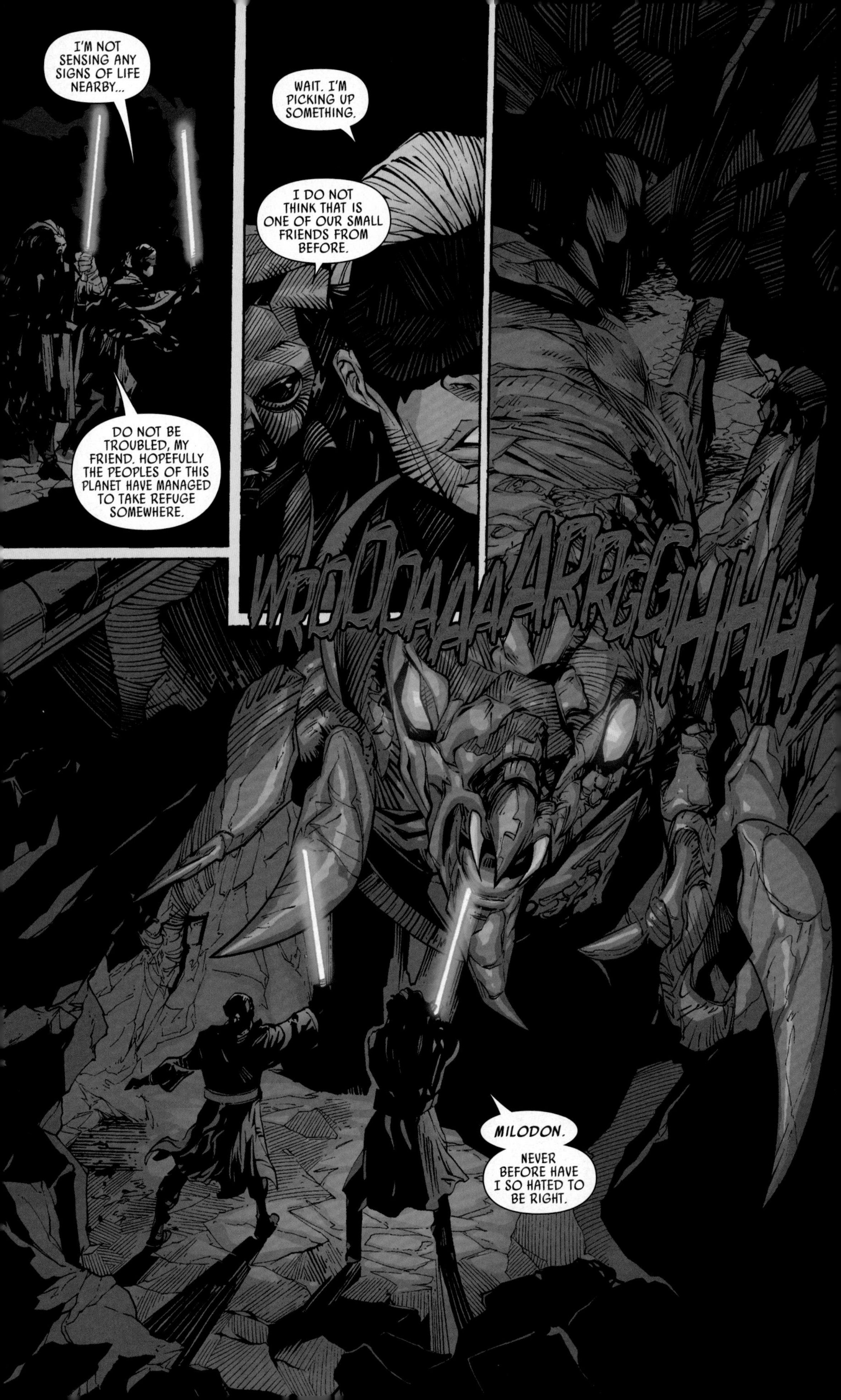

I'M NOT SENSING ANY SIGNS OF LIFE NEARBY...
DO NOT BE TROUBLED, MY FRIEND. HOPEFULLY THE PEOPLES OF THIS PLANET HAVE MANAGED TO TAKE REFUGE SOMEWHERE.
WAIT. I'M PICKING UP SOMETHING.
I DO NOT THINK THAT IS ONE OF OUR SMALL FRIENDS FROM BEFORE.
WROOOAAAAARRGHHH
MILODON.
NEVER BEFORE HAVE I SO HATED TO BE RIGHT.

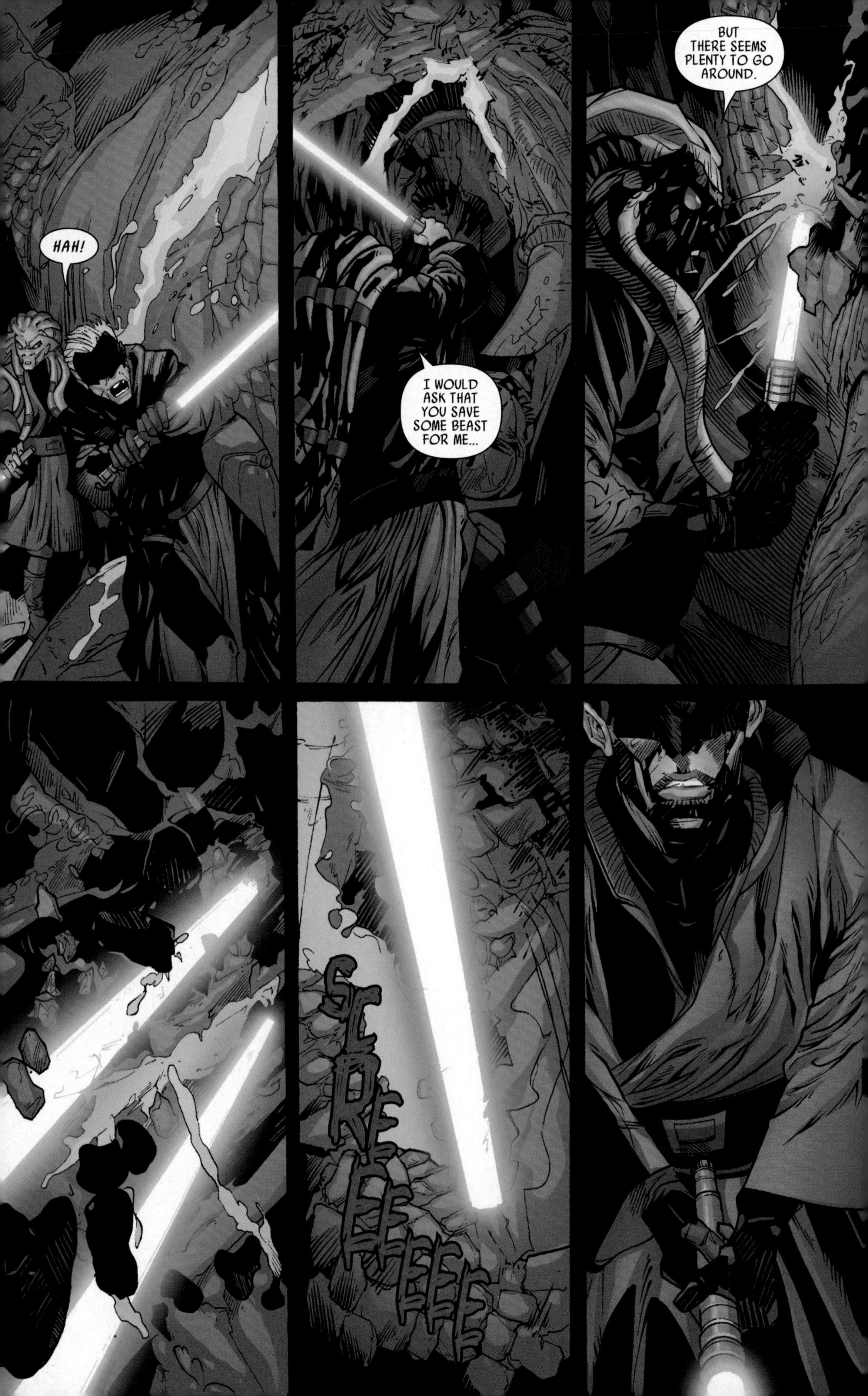
HAH!
I WOULD ASK THAT YOU SAVE SOME BEAST FOR ME...
BUT THERE SEEMS PLENTY TO GO AROUND.
SCREEEEEE

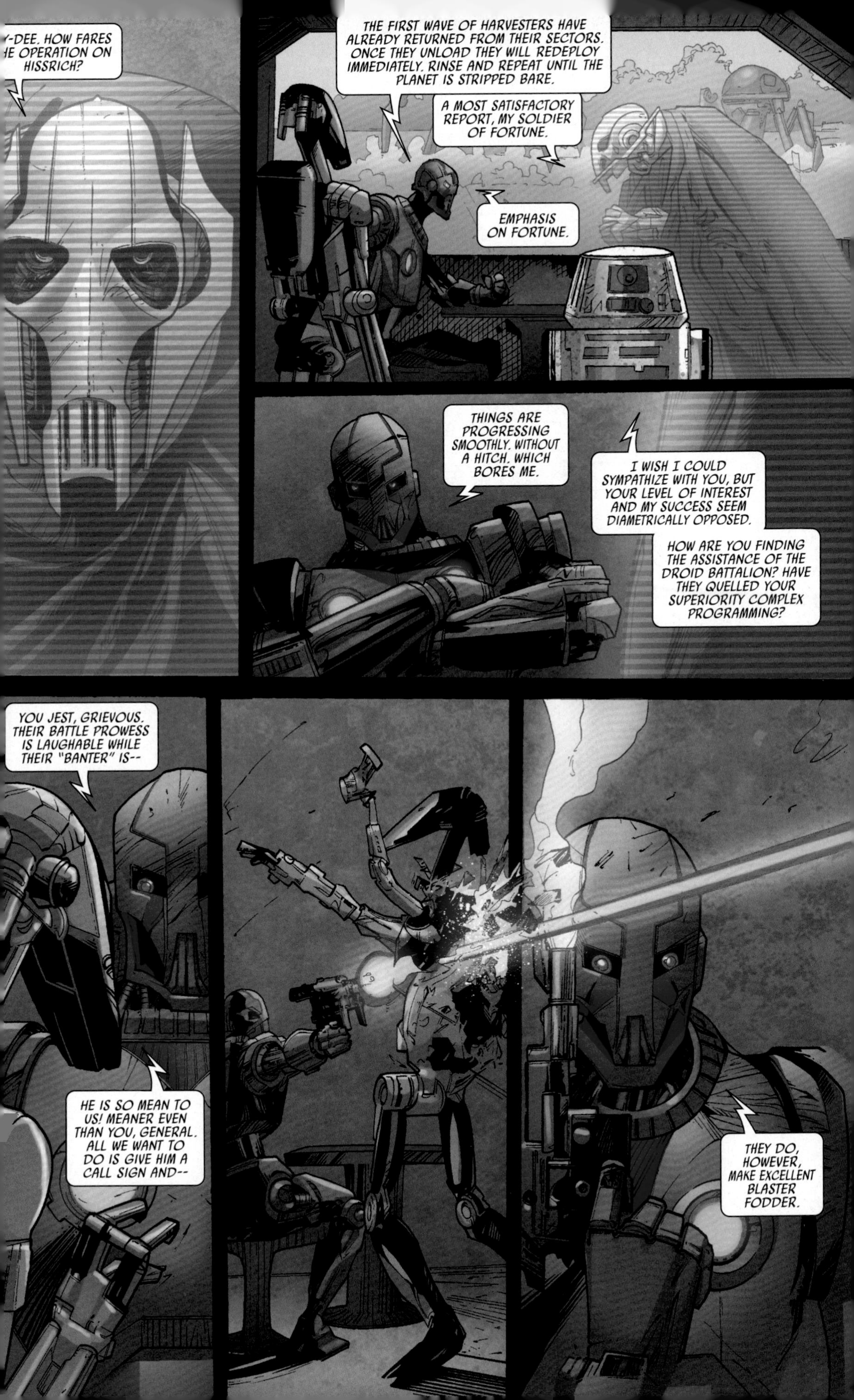
-DEE. HOW FARES HE OPERATION ON HISSRICH?
THE FIRST WAVE OF HARVESTERS HAVE ALREADY RETURNED FROM THEIR SECTORS. ONCE THEY UNLOAD THEY WILL REDEPLOY IMMEDIATELY. RINSE AND REPEAT UNTIL THE PLANET IS STRIPPED BARE.
A MOST SATISFACTORY REPORT, MY SOLDIER OF FORTUNE.
EMPHASIS ON FORTUNE.
THINGS ARE PROGRESSING SMOOTHLY. WITHOUT A HITCH. WHICH BORES ME.
I WISH I COULD SYMPATHIZE WITH YOU, BUT YOUR LEVEL OF INTEREST AND MY SUCCESS SEEM DIAMETRICALLY OPPOSED.
HOW ARE YOU FINDING THE ASSISTANCE OF THE DROID BATTALION? HAVE THEY QUELLED YOUR SUPERIORITY COMPLEX PROGRAMMING?
YOU JEST, GRIEVOUS. THEIR BATTLE PROWESS IS LAUGHABLE WHILE THEIR "BANTER" IS--
HE IS SO MEAN TO US! MEANER EVEN THAN YOU, GENERAL. ALL WE WANT TO DO IS GIVE HIM A CALL SIGN AND--
THEY DO, HOWEVER, MAKE EXCELLENT BLASTER FODDER.

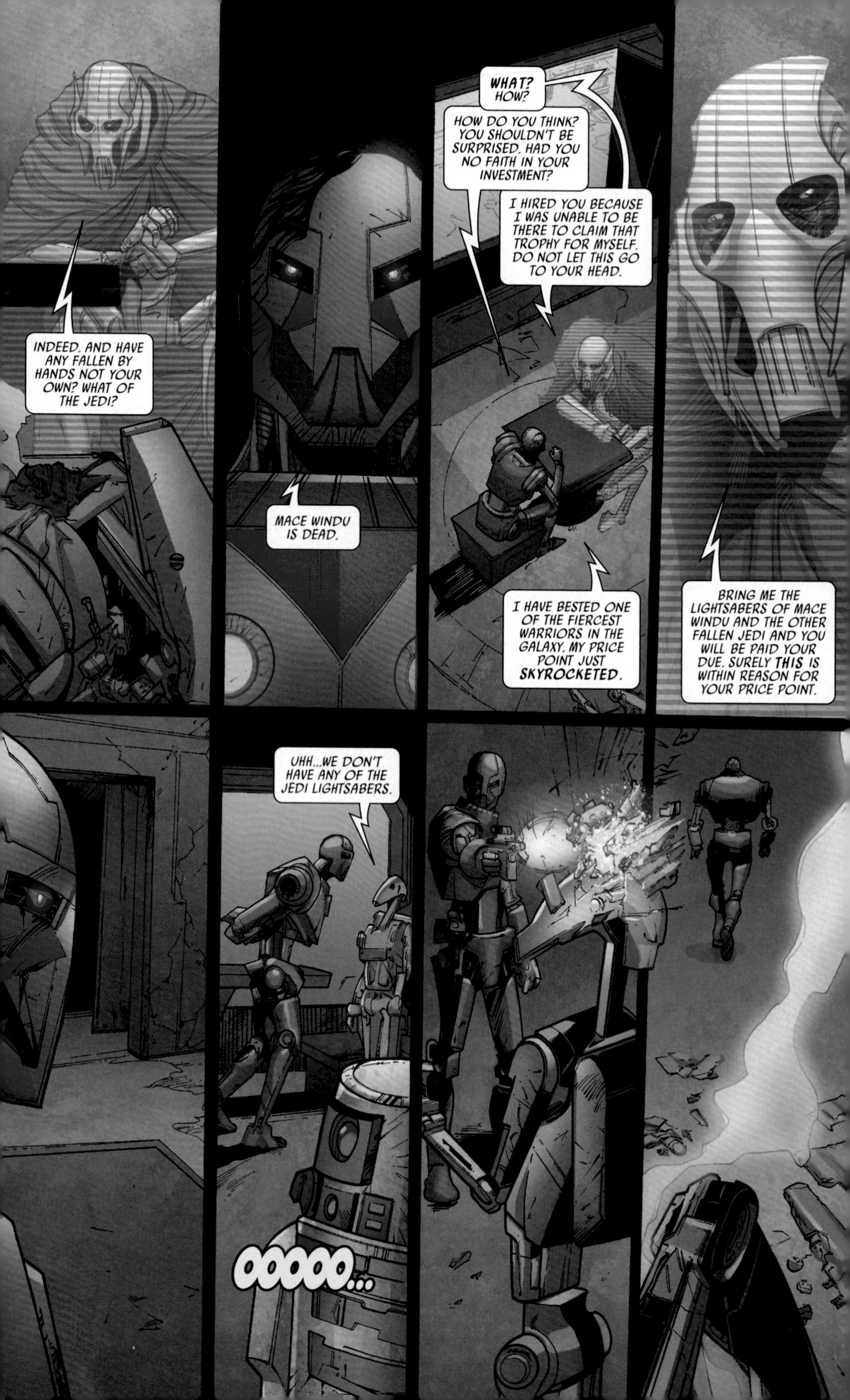
INDEED. AND HAVE ANY FALLEN BY HANDS NOT YOUR OWN? WHAT OF THE JEDI?
MACE WINDU IS DEAD.
WHAT? HOW?
HOW DO YOU THINK? YOU SHOULDN'T BE SURPRISED. HAD YOU NO FAITH IN YOUR INVESTMENT?
I HIRED YOU BECAUSE I WAS UNABLE TO BE THERE TO CLAIM THAT TROPHY FOR MYSELF. DO NOT LET THIS GO TO YOUR HEAD.
I HAVE BESTED ONE OF THE FIERCEST WARRIORS IN THE GALAXY. MY PRICE POINT JUST SKYROCKETED.
BRING ME THE LIGHTSABERS OF MACE WINDU AND THE OTHER FALLEN JEDI AND YOU WILL BE PAID YOUR DUE. SURELY THIS IS WITHIN REASON FOR YOUR PRICE POINT.
UHH...WE DON'T HAVE ANY OF THE JEDI LIGHTSABERS.
OOOOO...

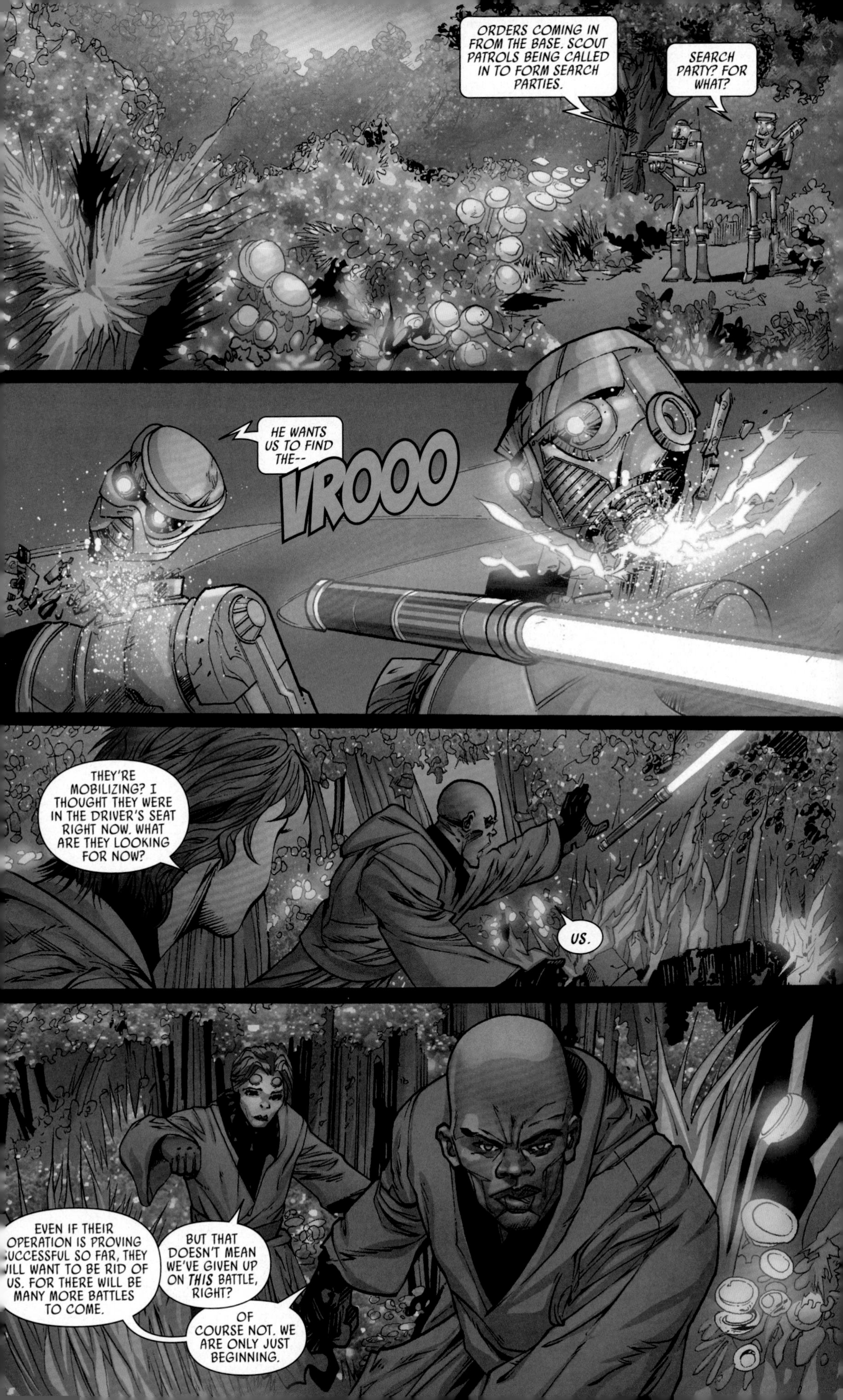
ORDERS COMING IN FROM THE BASE. SCOUT PATROLS BEING CALLED IN TO FORM SEARCH PARTIES.
SEARCH PARTY? FOR WHAT?
HE WANTS US TO FIND THE--
VROOO
THEY'RE MOBILIZING? I THOUGHT THEY WERE IN THE DRIVER'S SEAT RIGHT NOW. WHAT ARE THEY LOOKING FOR NOW?
US.
EVEN IF THEIR OPERATION IS PROVING SUCCESSFUL SO FAR, THEY WILL WANT TO BE RID OF US. FOR THERE WILL BE MANY MORE BATTLES TO COME.
BUT THAT DOESN'T MEAN WE'VE GIVEN UP ON *THIS* BATTLE, RIGHT?
OF COURSE NOT. WE ARE ONLY JUST BEGINNING.

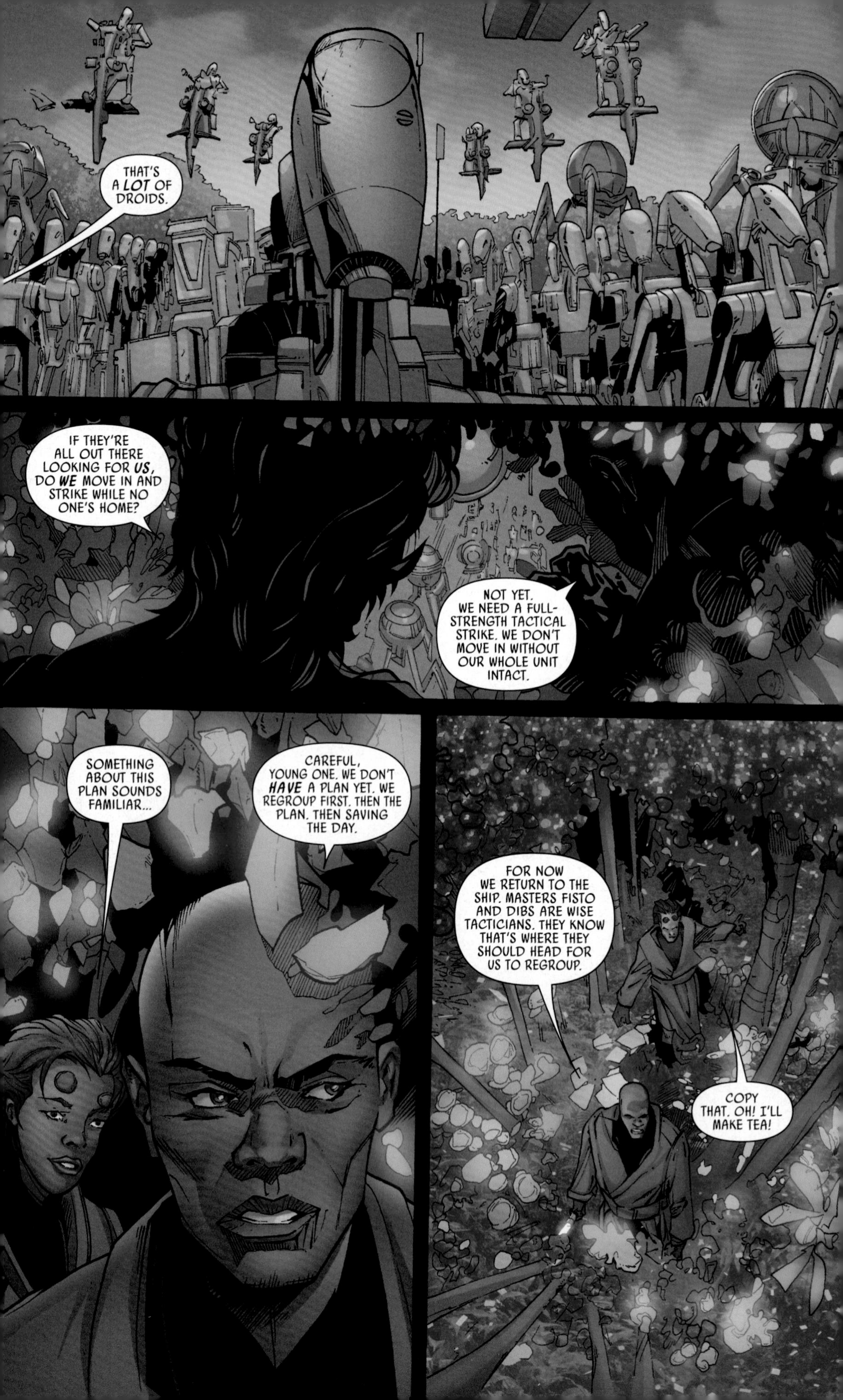
THAT'S A LOT OF DROIDS.
IF THEY'RE ALL OUT THERE LOOKING FOR US, DO WE MOVE IN AND STRIKE WHILE NO ONE'S HOME?
NOT YET. WE NEED A FULL-STRENGTH TACTICAL STRIKE. WE DON'T MOVE IN WITHOUT OUR WHOLE UNIT INTACT.
SOMETHING ABOUT THIS PLAN SOUNDS FAMILIAR...
CAREFUL, YOUNG ONE. WE DON'T HAVE A PLAN YET. WE REGROUP FIRST. THEN THE PLAN. THEN SAVING THE DAY.
FOR NOW WE RETURN TO THE SHIP. MASTERS FISTO AND DIBS ARE WISE TACTICIANS. THEY KNOW THAT'S WHERE THEY SHOULD HEAD FOR US TO REGROUP.
COPY THAT. OH! I'LL MAKE TEA!

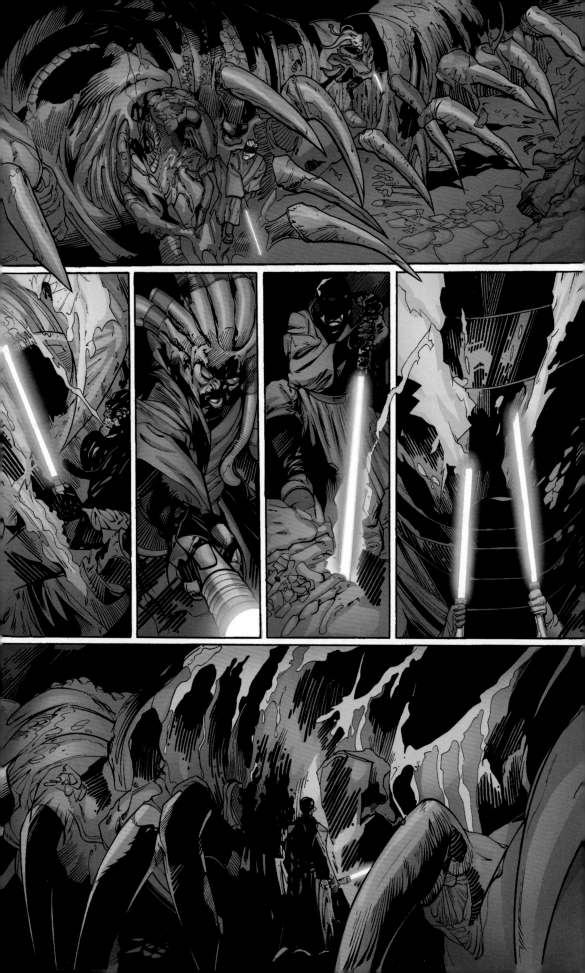

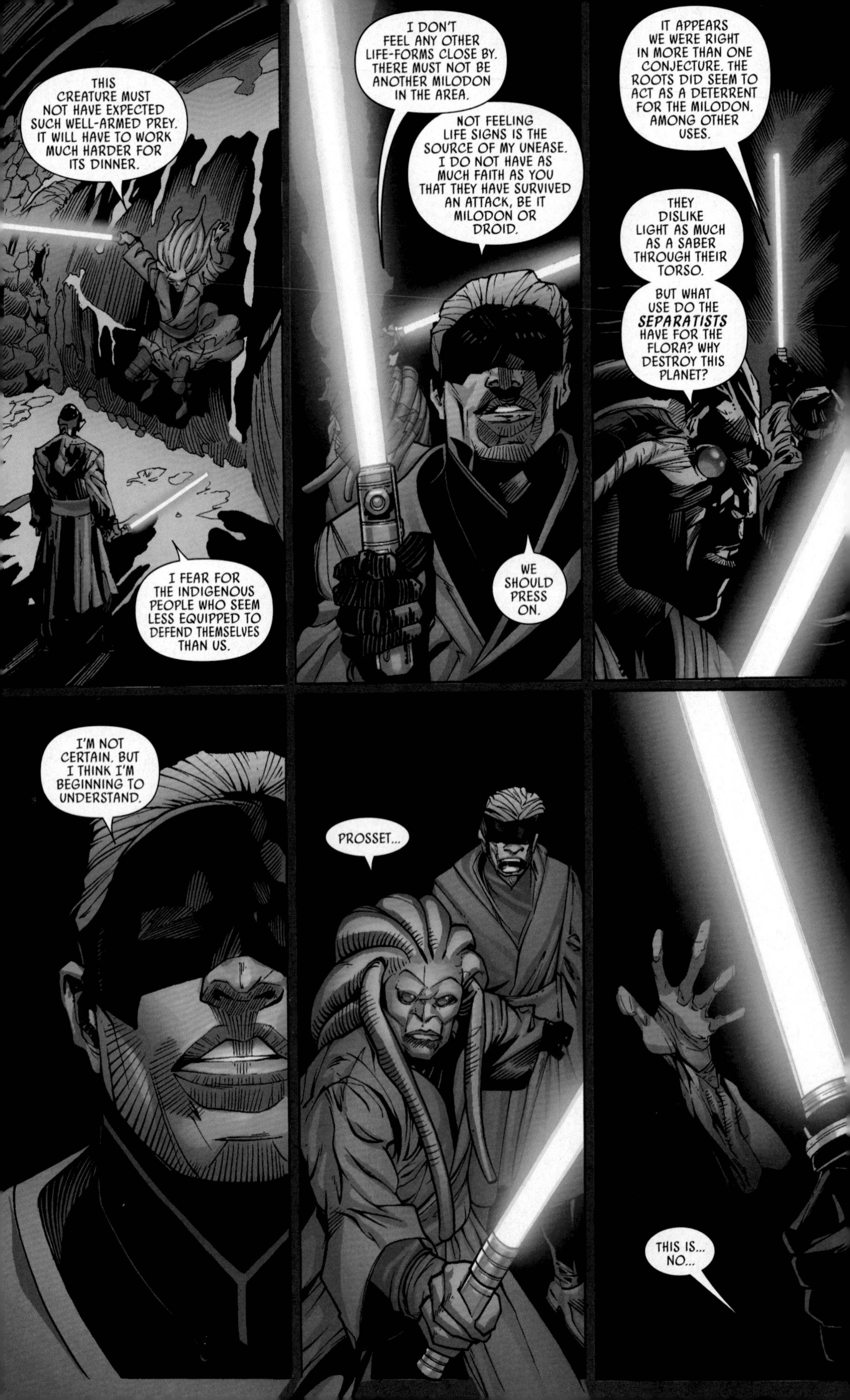
THIS CREATURE MUST NOT HAVE EXPECTED SUCH WELL-ARMED PREY. IT WILL HAVE TO WORK MUCH HARDER FOR ITS DINNER.
I FEAR FOR THE INDIGENOUS PEOPLE WHO SEEM LESS EQUIPPED TO DEFEND THEMSELVES THAN US.
I DON'T FEEL ANY OTHER LIFE-FORMS CLOSE BY. THERE MUST NOT BE ANOTHER MILODON IN THE AREA.
NOT FEELING LIFE SIGNS IS THE SOURCE OF MY UNEASE. I DO NOT HAVE AS MUCH FAITH AS YOU THAT THEY HAVE SURVIVED AN ATTACK, BE IT MILODON OR DROID.
WE SHOULD PRESS ON.
IT APPEARS WE WERE RIGHT IN MORE THAN ONE CONJECTURE. THE ROOTS DID SEEM TO ACT AS A DETERRENT FOR THE MILODON. AMONG OTHER USES.
THEY DISLIKE LIGHT AS MUCH AS A SABER THROUGH THEIR TORSO.
BUT WHAT USE DO THE *SEPARATISTS* HAVE FOR THE FLORA? WHY DESTROY THIS PLANET?
I'M NOT CERTAIN. BUT I THINK I'M BEGINNING TO UNDERSTAND.
PROSSET...
THIS IS... NO...

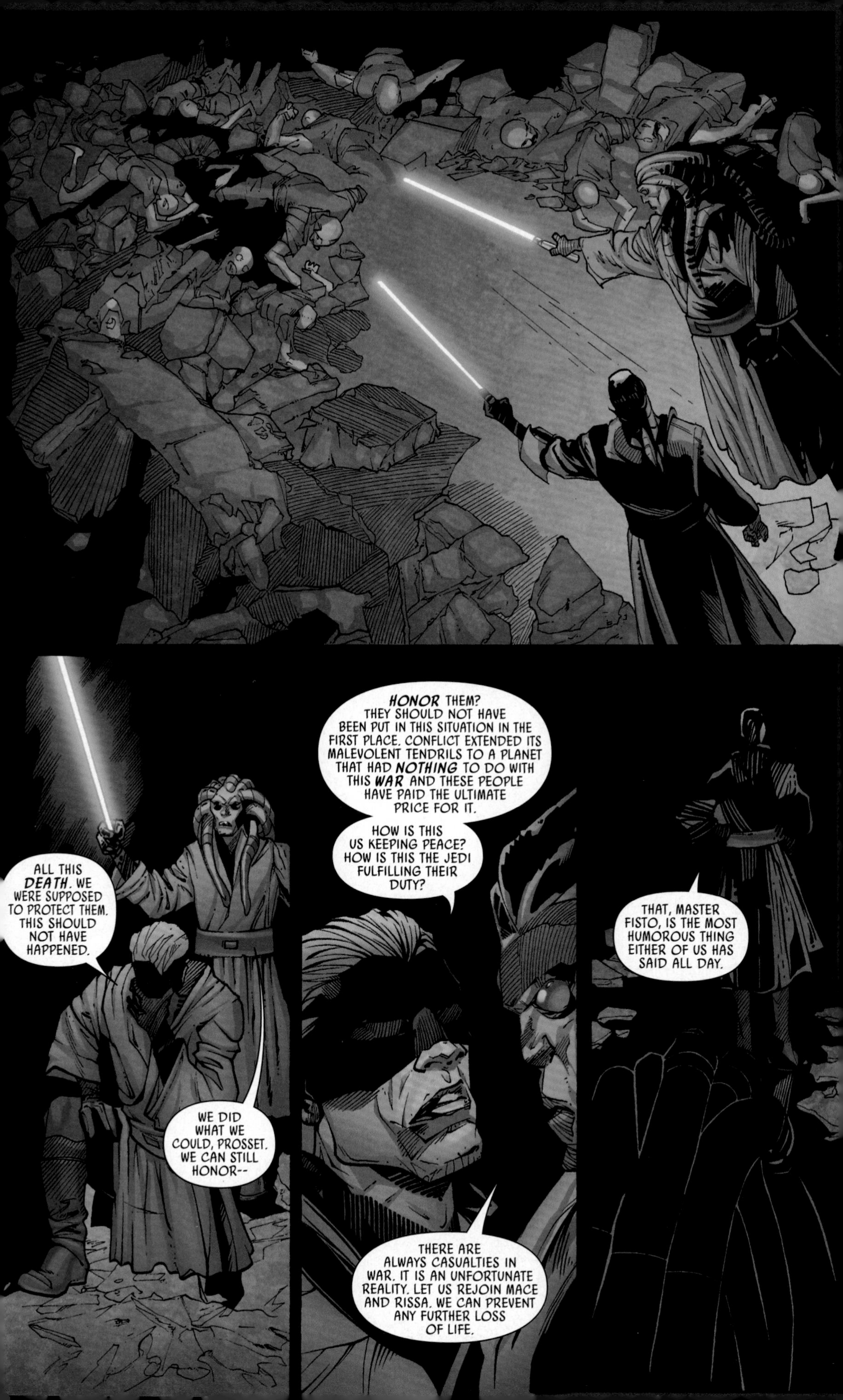
ALL THIS DEATH. WE WERE SUPPOSED TO PROTECT THEM. THIS SHOULD NOT HAVE HAPPENED.
WE DID WHAT WE COULD, PROSSET. WE CAN STILL HONOR--
HONOR THEM? THEY SHOULD NOT HAVE BEEN PUT IN THIS SITUATION IN THE FIRST PLACE. CONFLICT EXTENDED ITS MALEVOLENT TENDRILS TO A PLANET THAT HAD NOTHING TO DO WITH THIS WAR AND THESE PEOPLE HAVE PAID THE ULTIMATE PRICE FOR IT.
HOW IS THIS US KEEPING PEACE? HOW IS THIS THE JEDI FULFILLING THEIR DUTY?
THERE ARE ALWAYS CASUALTIES IN WAR. IT IS AN UNFORTUNATE REALITY. LET US REJOIN MACE AND RISSA. WE CAN PREVENT ANY FURTHER LOSS OF LIFE.
THAT, MASTER FISTO, IS THE MOST HUMOROUS THING EITHER OF US HAS SAID ALL DAY.

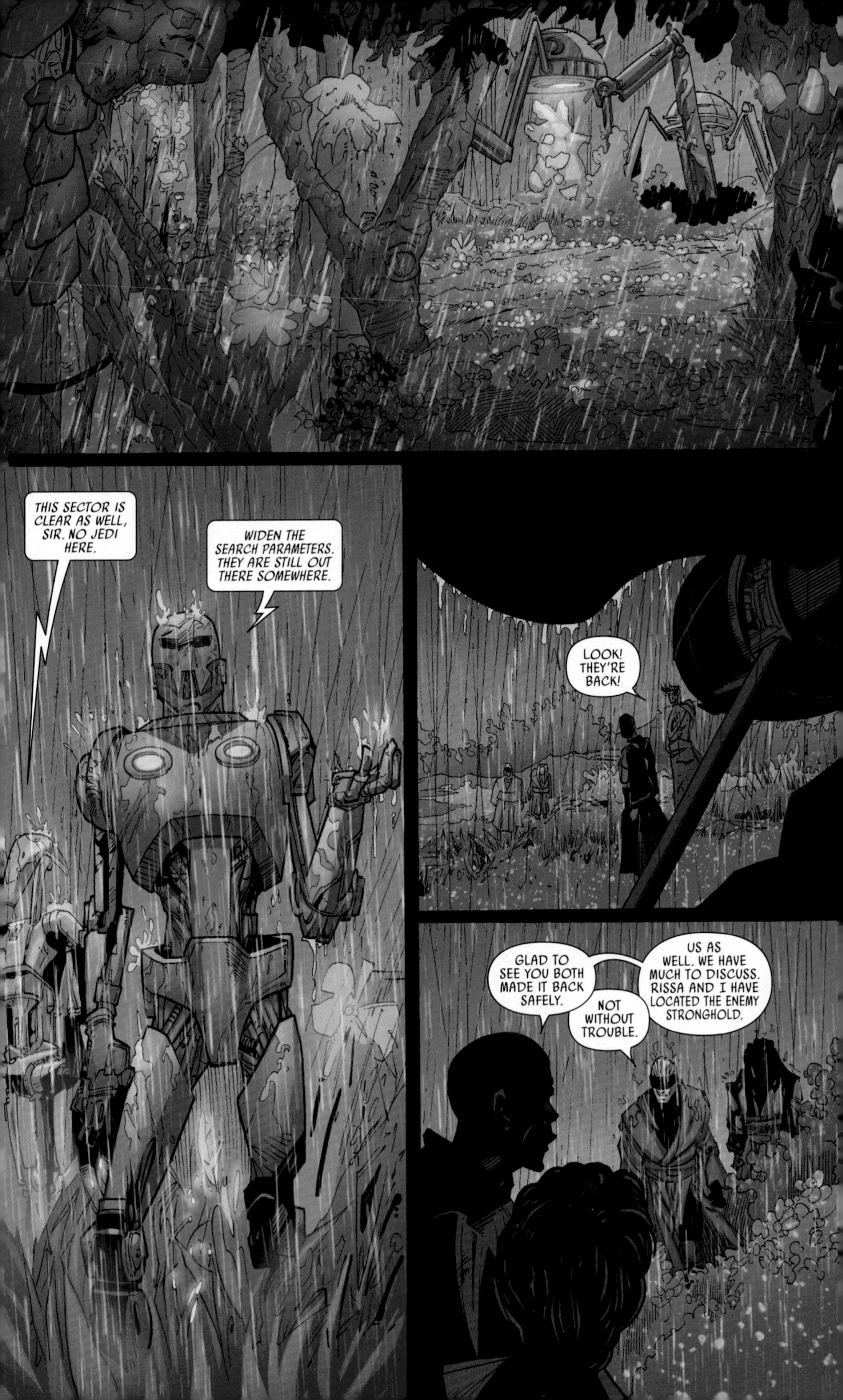
THIS SECTOR IS CLEAR AS WELL, SIR. NO JEDI HERE.
WIDEN THE SEARCH PARAMETERS. THEY ARE STILL OUT THERE SOMEWHERE.
LOOK! THEY'RE BACK!
GLAD TO SEE YOU BOTH MADE IT BACK SAFELY.
US AS WELL. WE HAVE MUCH TO DISCUSS. RISSA AND I HAVE LOCATED THE ENEMY STRONGHOLD.
NOT WITHOUT TROUBLE.

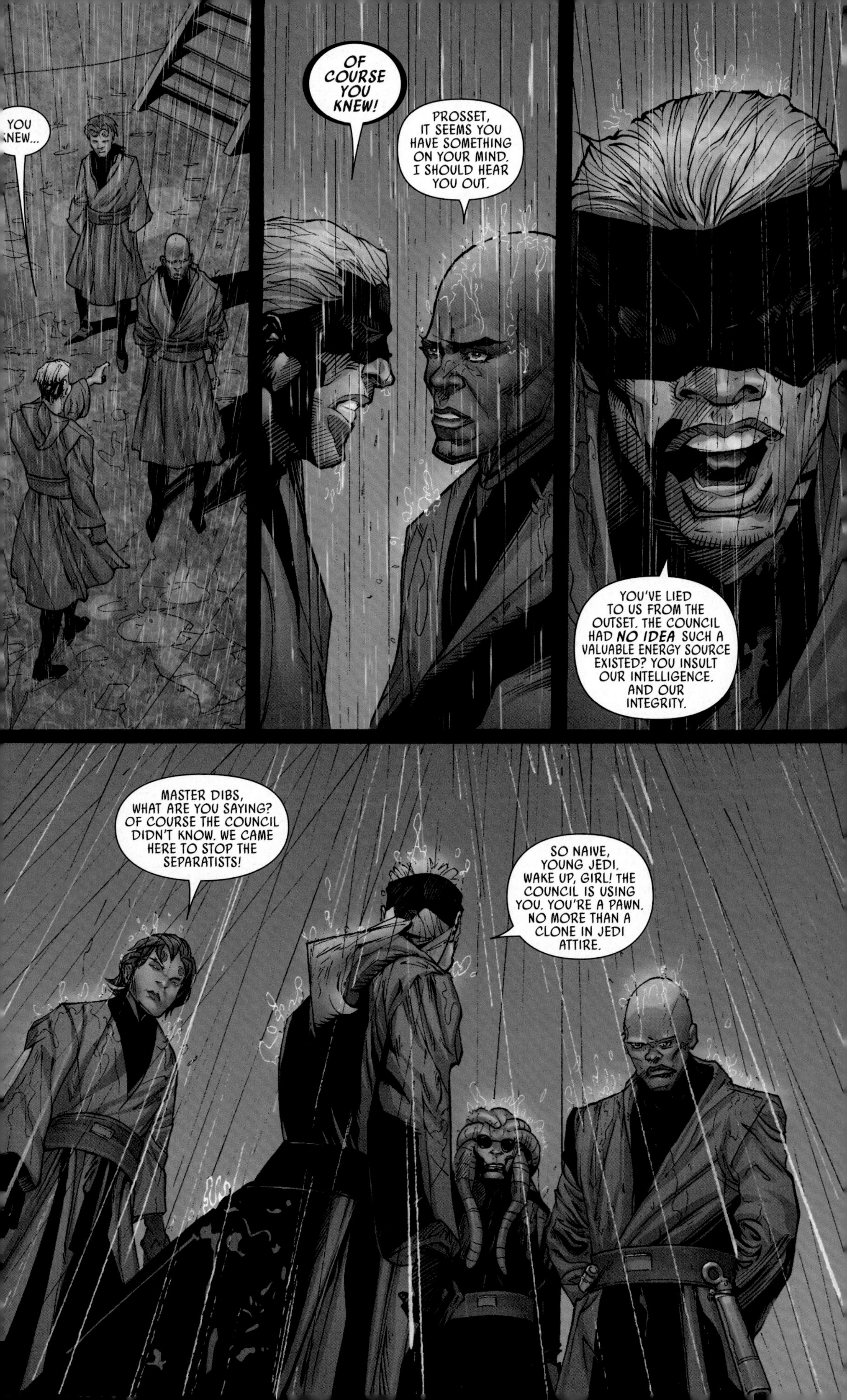
YOU KNEW...
OF COURSE YOU KNEW!
PROSSET, IT SEEMS YOU HAVE SOMETHING ON YOUR MIND. I SHOULD HEAR YOU OUT.
YOU'VE LIED TO US FROM THE OUTSET. THE COUNCIL HAD NO IDEA SUCH A VALUABLE ENERGY SOURCE EXISTED? YOU INSULT OUR INTELLIGENCE. AND OUR INTEGRITY.
MASTER DIBS, WHAT ARE YOU SAYING? OF COURSE THE COUNCIL DIDN'T KNOW. WE CAME HERE TO STOP THE SEPARATISTS!
SO NAIVE, YOUNG JEDI. WAKE UP, GIRL! THE COUNCIL IS USING YOU. YOU'RE A PAWN. NO MORE THAN A CLONE IN JEDI ATTIRE.

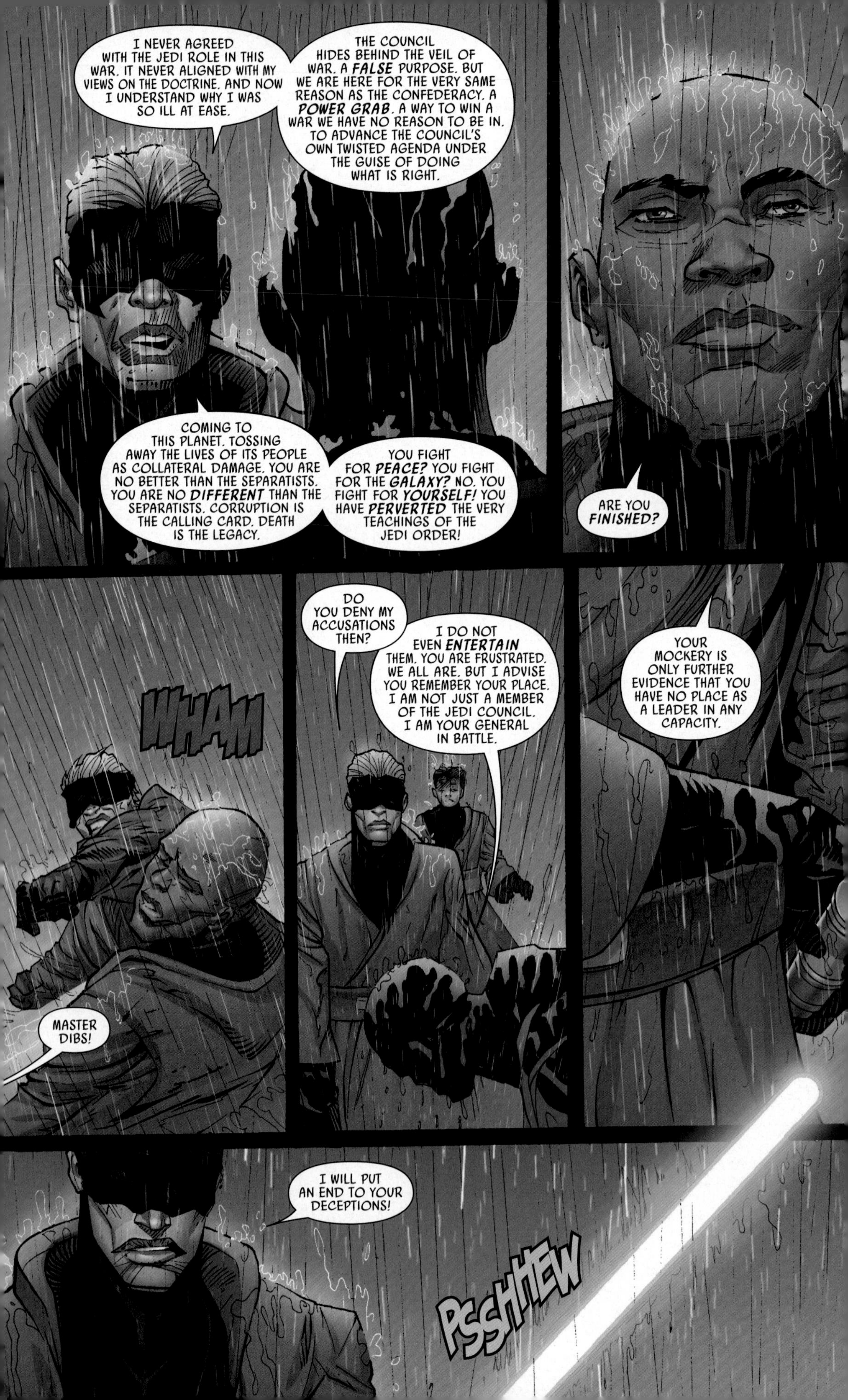
I NEVER AGREED WITH THE JEDI ROLE IN THIS WAR. IT NEVER ALIGNED WITH MY VIEWS ON THE DOCTRINE, AND NOW I UNDERSTAND WHY I WAS SO ILL AT EASE.
THE COUNCIL HIDES BEHIND THE VEIL OF WAR. A FALSE PURPOSE. BUT WE ARE HERE FOR THE VERY SAME REASON AS THE CONFEDERACY. A POWER GRAB. A WAY TO WIN A WAR WE HAVE NO REASON TO BE IN. TO ADVANCE THE COUNCIL'S OWN TWISTED AGENDA UNDER THE GUISE OF DOING WHAT IS RIGHT.
COMING TO THIS PLANET. TOSSING AWAY THE LIVES OF ITS PEOPLE AS COLLATERAL DAMAGE. YOU ARE NO BETTER THAN THE SEPARATISTS. YOU ARE NO DIFFERENT THAN THE SEPARATISTS. CORRUPTION IS THE CALLING CARD. DEATH IS THE LEGACY.
YOU FIGHT FOR PEACE? YOU FIGHT FOR THE GALAXY? NO. YOU FIGHT FOR YOURSELF! YOU HAVE PERVERTED THE VERY TEACHINGS OF THE JEDI ORDER!
ARE YOU FINISHED?
DO YOU DENY MY ACCUSATIONS THEN?
I DO NOT EVEN ENTERTAIN THEM. YOU ARE FRUSTRATED. WE ALL ARE. BUT I ADVISE YOU REMEMBER YOUR PLACE. I AM NOT JUST A MEMBER OF THE JEDI COUNCIL. I AM YOUR GENERAL IN BATTLE.
YOUR MOCKERY IS ONLY FURTHER EVIDENCE THAT YOU HAVE NO PLACE AS A LEADER IN ANY CAPACITY.
WHAM
MASTER DIBS!
I WILL PUT AN END TO YOUR DECEPTIONS!
PSSHHEW

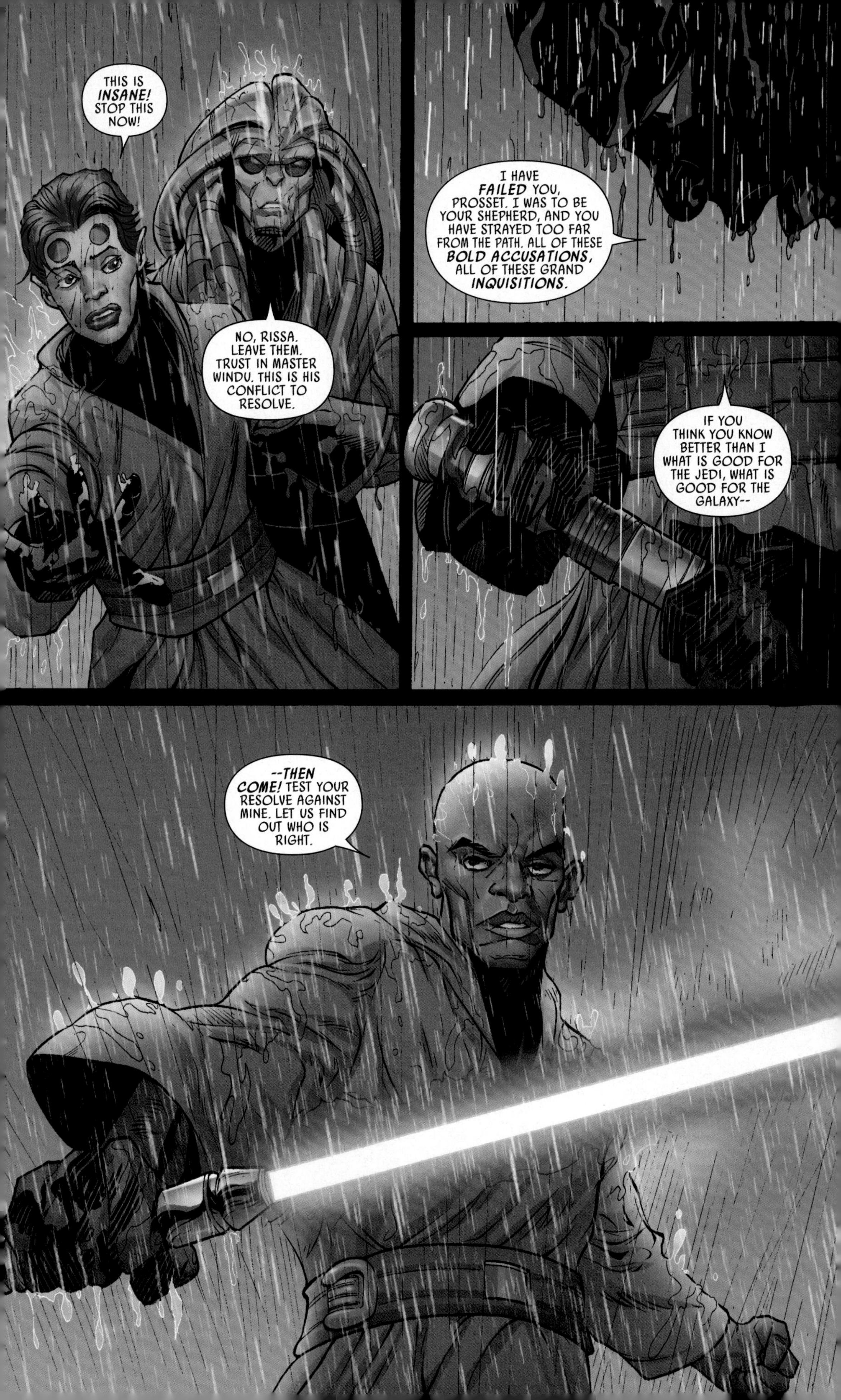
THIS IS INSANE! STOP THIS NOW!
NO, RISSA. LEAVE THEM. TRUST IN MASTER WINDU. THIS IS HIS CONFLICT TO RESOLVE.
I HAVE FAILED YOU, PROSSET. I WAS TO BE YOUR SHEPHERD, AND YOU HAVE STRAYED TOO FAR FROM THE PATH. ALL OF THESE BOLD ACCUSATIONS, ALL OF THESE GRAND INQUISITIONS.
IF YOU THINK YOU KNOW BETTER THAN I WHAT IS GOOD FOR THE JEDI, WHAT IS GOOD FOR THE GALAXY--
--THEN COME! TEST YOUR RESOLVE AGAINST MINE. LET US FIND OUT WHO IS RIGHT.

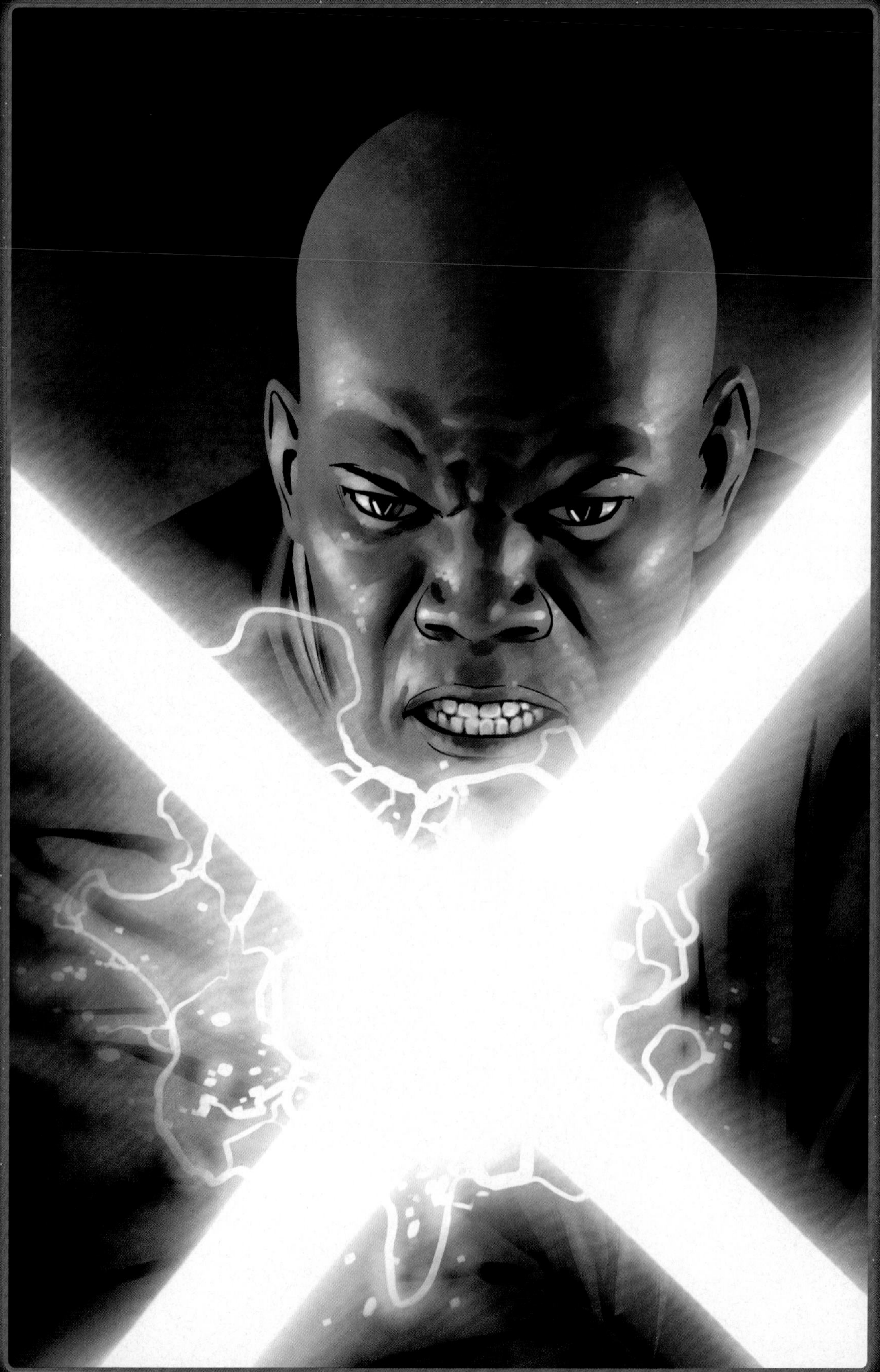

4

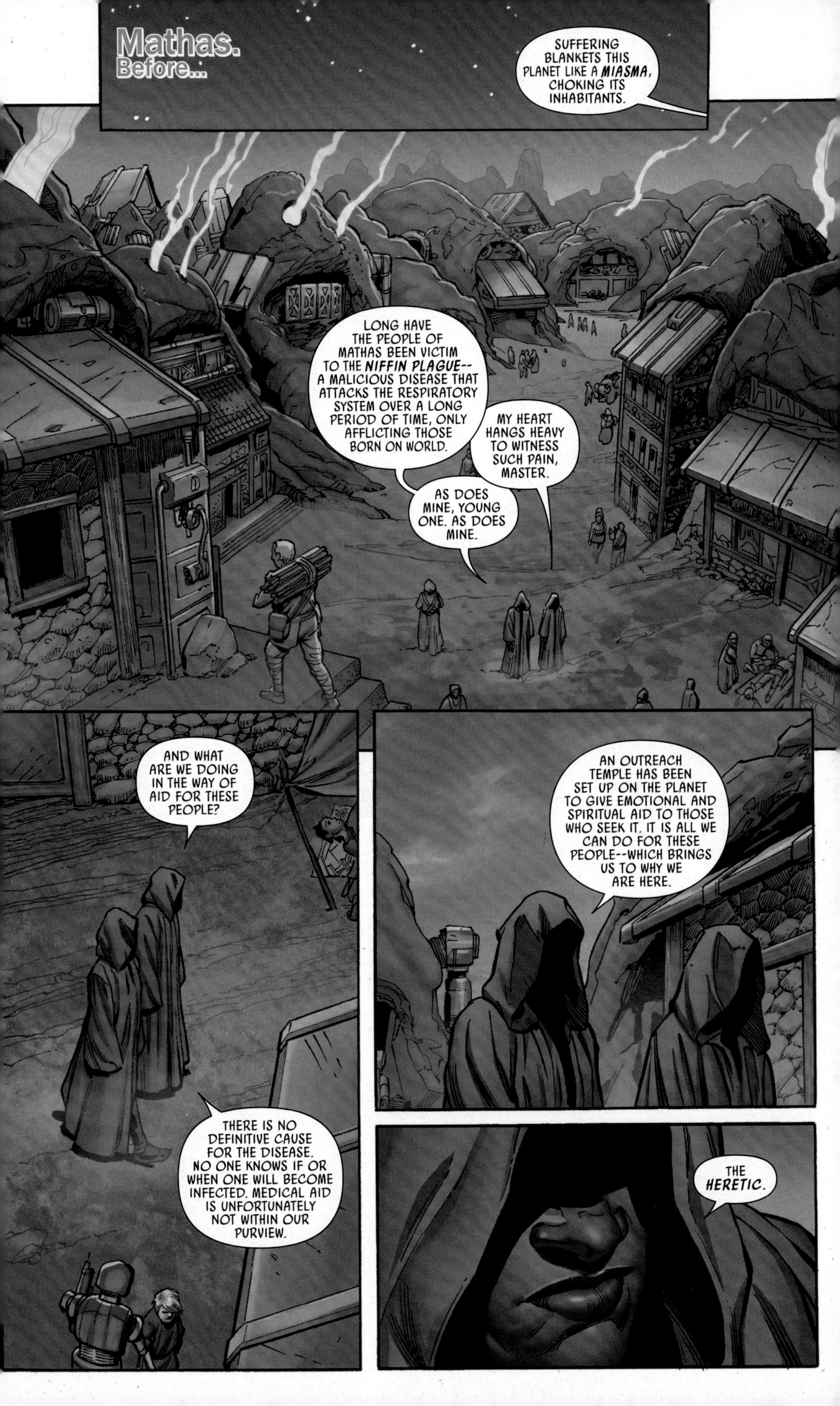
Mathas.
Before...
SUFFERING BLANKETS THIS PLANET LIKE A MIASMA, CHOKING ITS INHABITANTS.
LONG HAVE THE PEOPLE OF MATHAS BEEN VICTIM TO THE NIFFIN PLAGUE-- A MALICIOUS DISEASE THAT ATTACKS THE RESPIRATORY SYSTEM OVER A LONG PERIOD OF TIME, ONLY AFFLICTING THOSE BORN ON WORLD.
MY HEART HANGS HEAVY TO WITNESS SUCH PAIN, MASTER.
AS DOES MINE, YOUNG ONE. AS DOES MINE.
AND WHAT ARE WE DOING IN THE WAY OF AID FOR THESE PEOPLE?
THERE IS NO DEFINITIVE CAUSE FOR THE DISEASE. NO ONE KNOWS IF OR WHEN ONE WILL BECOME INFECTED. MEDICAL AID IS UNFORTUNATELY NOT WITHIN OUR PURVIEW.
AN OUTREACH TEMPLE HAS BEEN SET UP ON THE PLANET TO GIVE EMOTIONAL AND SPIRITUAL AID TO THOSE WHO SEEK IT. IT IS ALL WE CAN DO FOR THESE PEOPLE--WHICH BRINGS US TO WHY WE ARE HERE.
THE HERETIC.

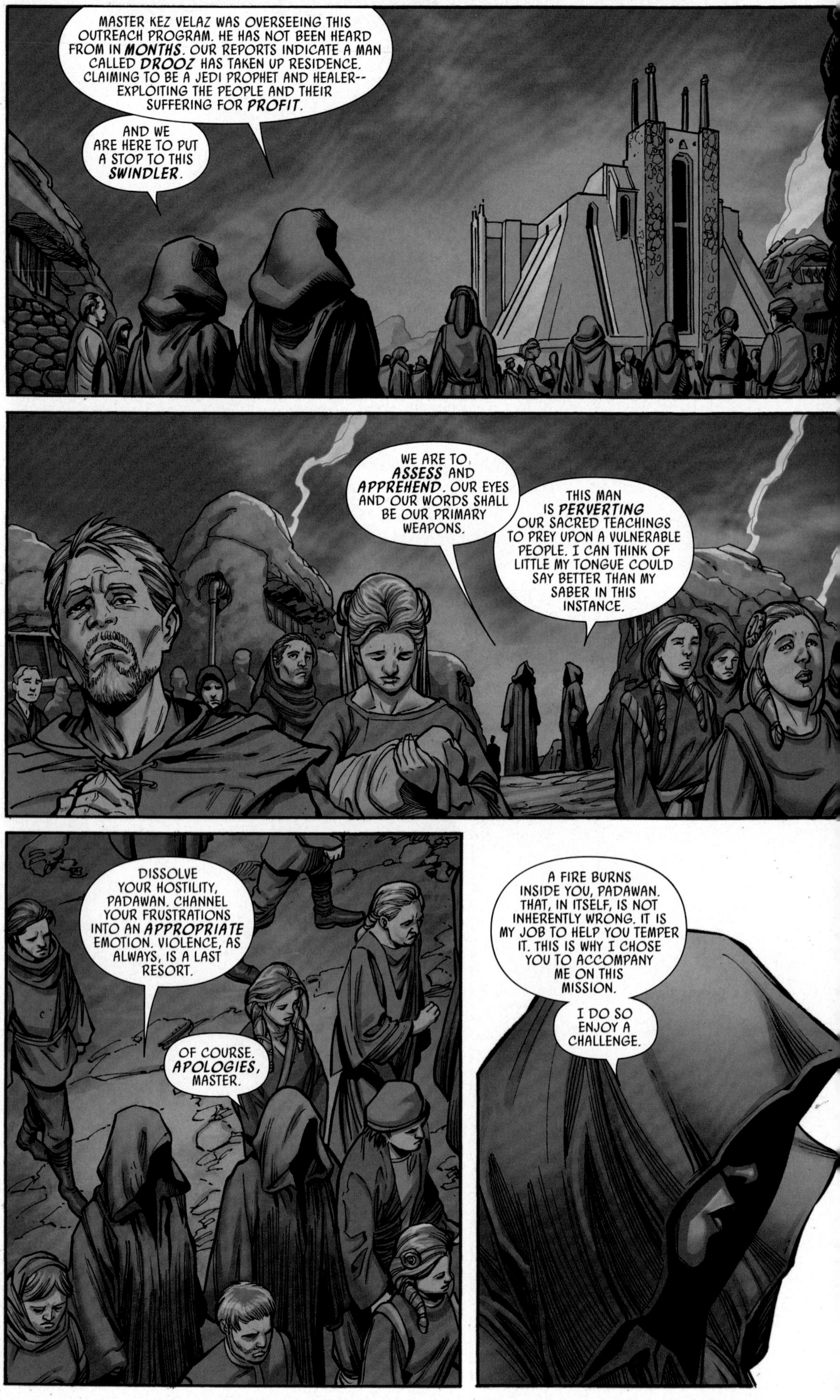
MASTER KEZ VELAZ WAS OVERSEEING THIS OUTREACH PROGRAM. HE HAS NOT BEEN HEARD FROM IN MONTHS. OUR REPORTS INDICATE A MAN CALLED DROOZ HAS TAKEN UP RESIDENCE. CLAIMING TO BE A JEDI PROPHET AND HEALER-- EXPLOITING THE PEOPLE AND THEIR SUFFERING FOR PROFIT.
AND WE ARE HERE TO PUT A STOP TO THIS SWINDLER.
WE ARE TO ASSESS AND APPREHEND. OUR EYES AND OUR WORDS SHALL BE OUR PRIMARY WEAPONS.
THIS MAN IS PERVERTING OUR SACRED TEACHINGS TO PREY UPON A VULNERABLE PEOPLE. I CAN THINK OF LITTLE MY TONGUE COULD SAY BETTER THAN MY SABER IN THIS INSTANCE.
DISSOLVE YOUR HOSTILITY, PADAWAN. CHANNEL YOUR FRUSTRATIONS INTO AN APPROPRIATE EMOTION. VIOLENCE, AS ALWAYS, IS A LAST RESORT.
OF COURSE. APOLOGIES, MASTER.
A FIRE BURNS INSIDE YOU, PADAWAN. THAT, IN ITSELF, IS NOT INHERENTLY WRONG. IT IS MY JOB TO HELP YOU TEMPER IT. THIS IS WHY I CHOSE YOU TO ACCOMPANY ME ON THIS MISSION.
I DO SO ENJOY A CHALLENGE.

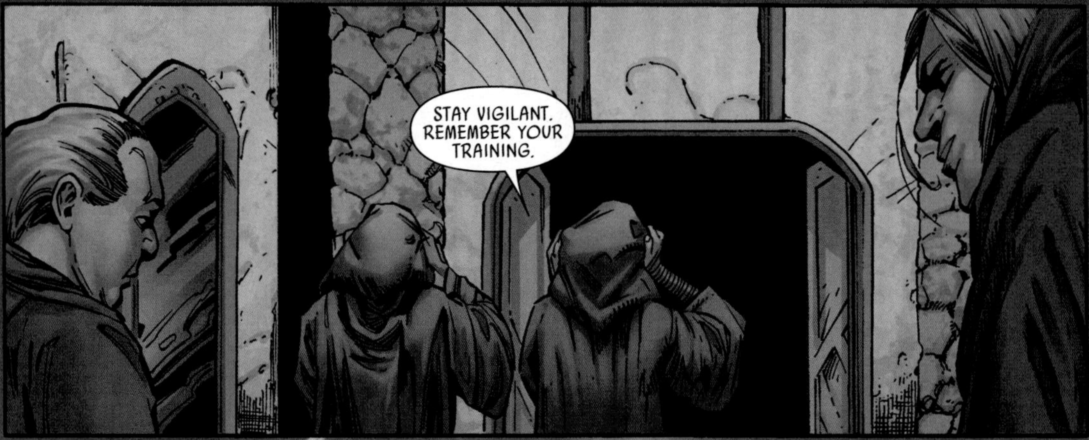
STAY VIGILANT. REMEMBER YOUR TRAINING.

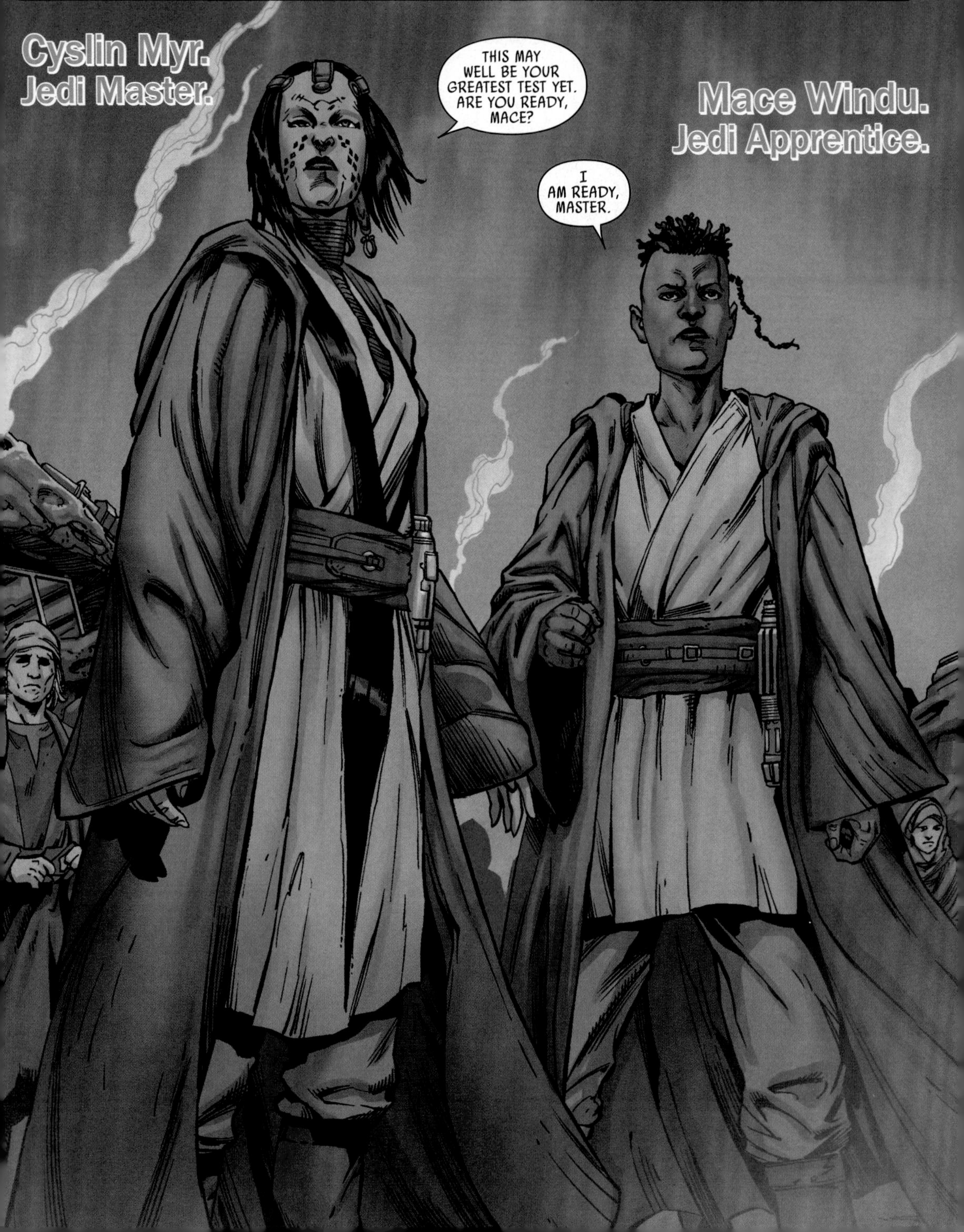
Cyslin Myr. Jedi Master.
THIS MAY WELL BE YOUR GREATEST TEST YET. ARE YOU READY, MACE?
Mace Windu. Jedi Apprentice.
I AM READY, MASTER.

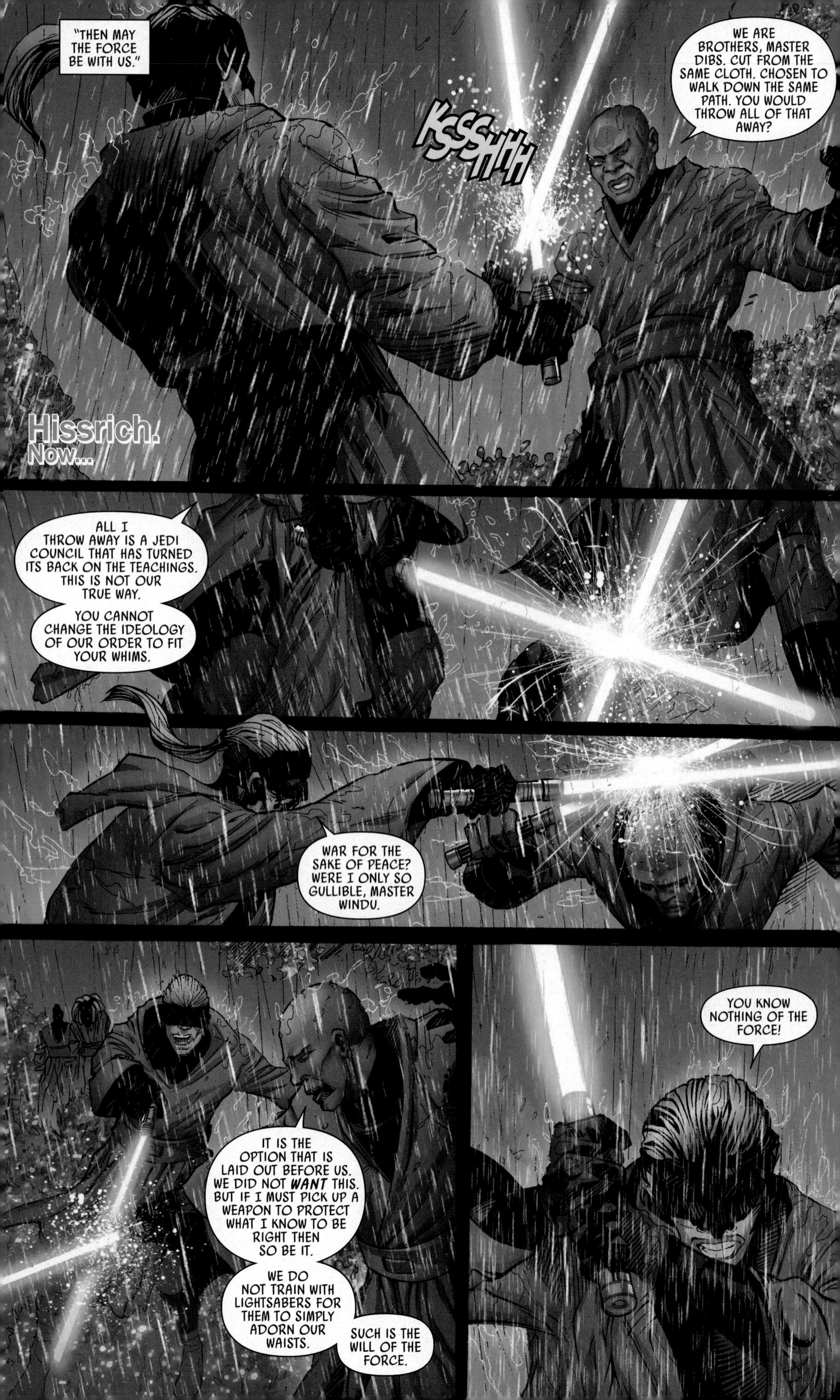
"THEN MAY THE FORCE BE WITH US."
KSSSHHH
WE ARE BROTHERS, MASTER DIBS. CUT FROM THE SAME CLOTH. CHOSEN TO WALK DOWN THE SAME PATH. YOU WOULD THROW ALL OF THAT AWAY?
Hissrich. Now...
ALL I THROW AWAY IS A JEDI COUNCIL THAT HAS TURNED ITS BACK ON THE TEACHINGS. THIS IS NOT OUR TRUE WAY.
YOU CANNOT CHANGE THE IDEOLOGY OF OUR ORDER TO FIT YOUR WHIMS.
WAR FOR THE SAKE OF PEACE? WERE I ONLY SO GULLIBLE, MASTER WINDU.
IT IS THE OPTION THAT IS LAID OUT BEFORE US. WE DID NOT WANT THIS. BUT IF I MUST PICK UP A WEAPON TO PROTECT WHAT I KNOW TO BE RIGHT THEN SO BE IT.
WE DO NOT TRAIN WITH LIGHTSABERS FOR THEM TO SIMPLY ADORN OUR WAISTS.
SUCH IS THE WILL OF THE FORCE.
YOU KNOW NOTHING OF THE FORCE!

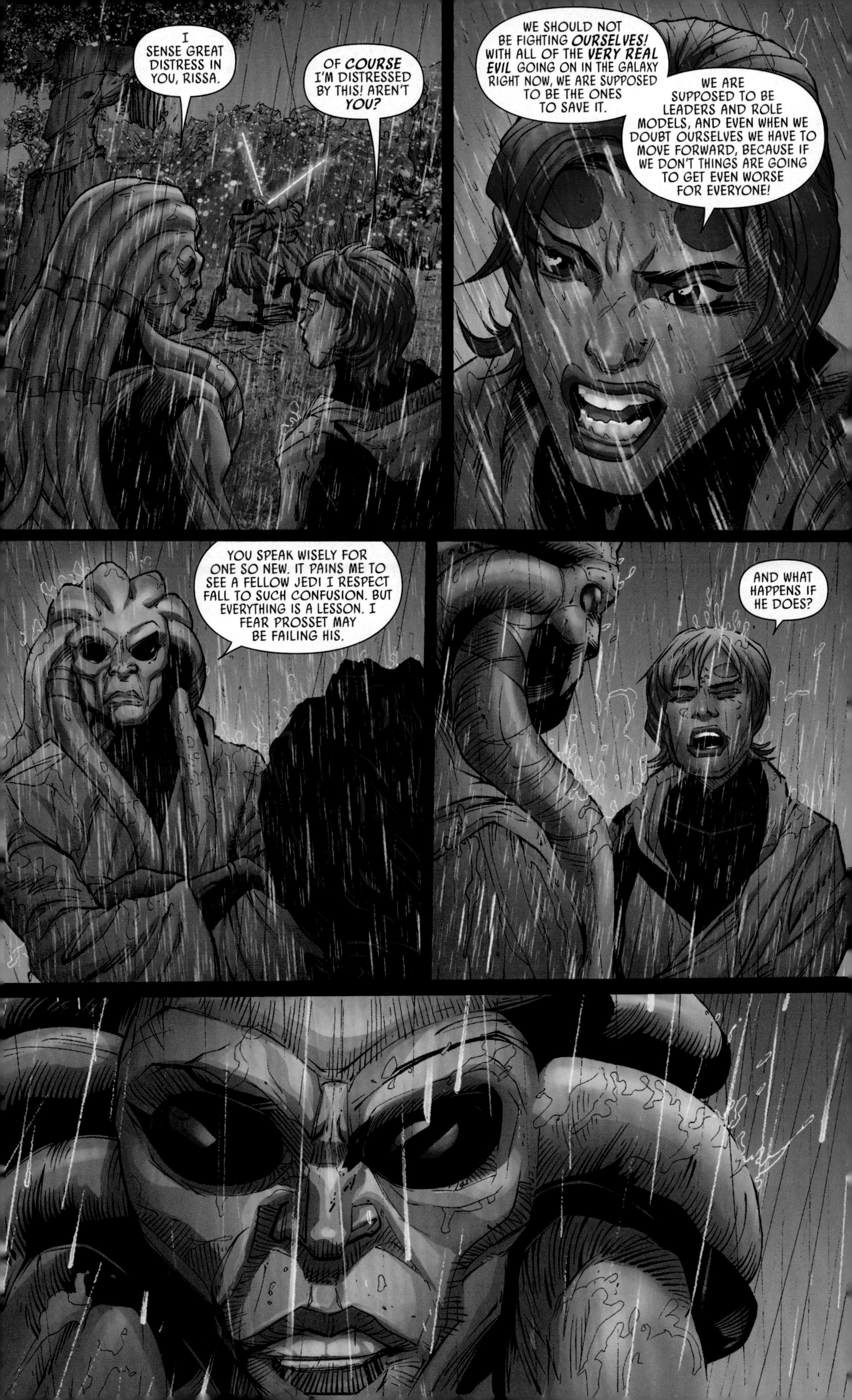
I SENSE GREAT DISTRESS IN YOU, RISSA.
OF *COURSE* I'M DISTRESSED BY THIS! AREN'T *YOU?*
WE SHOULD NOT BE FIGHTING *OURSELVES!* WITH ALL OF THE *VERY REAL EVIL* GOING ON IN THE GALAXY RIGHT NOW, WE ARE SUPPOSED TO BE THE ONES TO SAVE IT.
WE ARE SUPPOSED TO BE LEADERS AND ROLE MODELS, AND EVEN WHEN WE DOUBT OURSELVES WE HAVE TO MOVE FORWARD, BECAUSE IF WE DON'T THINGS ARE GOING TO GET EVEN WORSE FOR EVERYONE!
YOU SPEAK WISELY FOR ONE SO NEW. IT PAINS ME TO SEE A FELLOW JEDI I RESPECT FALL TO SUCH CONFUSION. BUT EVERYTHING IS A LESSON. I FEAR PROSSET MAY BE FAILING HIS.
AND WHAT HAPPENS IF HE DOES?

I HAVE **PRAYED** AND **PRAYED** IN YOUR GOOD NAME. BUT THE FORCE DOES NOT HEED MY PLEAS. I **CANNOT** LOSE ANOTHER CHILD SO EARLY.

**PLEASE**, MASTER DROOZ! SAVE MY CHILD'S LIFE!

THE FORCE IS A COMPLEX, STAR-SHATTERING POWER OF NATURE. IT IS MY DUTY AS A JEDI MASTER TO ACT AS A CONDUIT FOR ITS WISDOM AND POTENTIAL. I SEARCH THE ETHER, BRINGING HOPE AND ANSWERS TO THOSE LESS IN TUNE WITH ITS AWESOME MIGHT.

SO I MUST ASK YOU...

...HAVE YOU GIVEN YOURSELF **FULLY** TO THE FORCE?

I PRAY **EVERY DAY**. I HAVE GIVEN MONEY AS YOU HAVE INSTRUCTED. AND YET THE FORCE STILL DOES NOT ANSWER. I DO NOT KNOW WHAT ELSE I CAN DO.

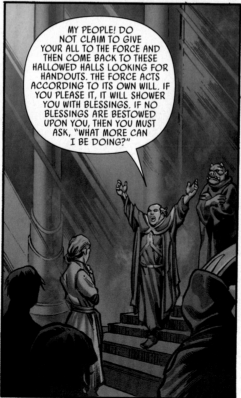

MY PEOPLE! DO NOT CLAIM TO GIVE YOUR ALL TO THE FORCE AND THEN COME BACK TO THESE HALLOWED HALLS LOOKING FOR HANDOUTS. THE FORCE ACTS ACCORDING TO ITS OWN WILL. IF YOU PLEASE IT, IT WILL SHOWER YOU WITH BLESSINGS. IF NO BLESSINGS ARE BESTOWED UPON YOU, THEN YOU MUST ASK, "WHAT MORE CAN I BE DOING?"

WHAT MORE COULD YOU BE **DOING**, MY CHILD?

EXCUSE ME. **MASTER DROOZ**, WAS IT?

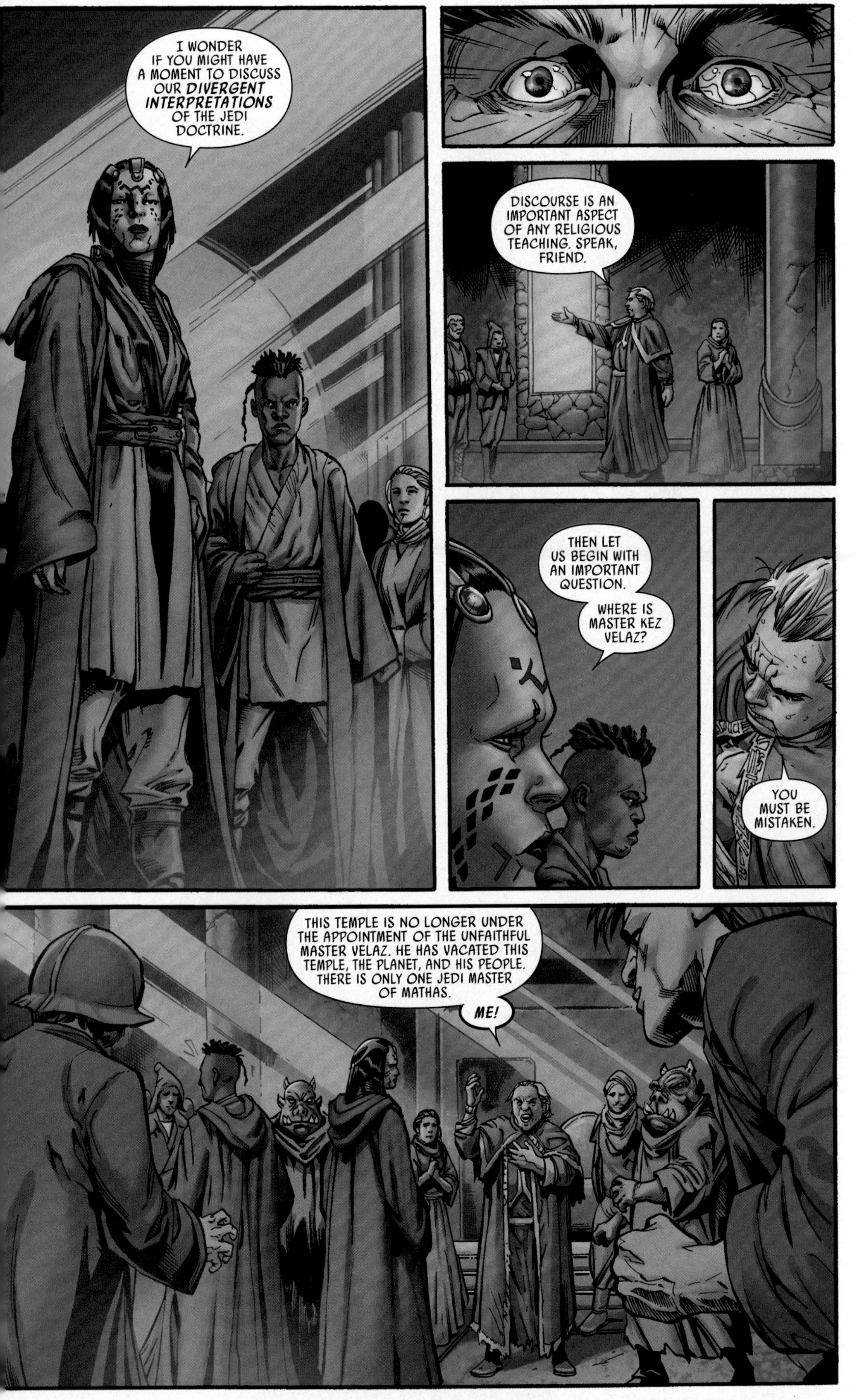
I WONDER IF YOU MIGHT HAVE A MOMENT TO DISCUSS OUR DIVERGENT INTERPRETATIONS OF THE JEDI DOCTRINE.
DISCOURSE IS AN IMPORTANT ASPECT OF ANY RELIGIOUS TEACHING. SPEAK, FRIEND.
THEN LET US BEGIN WITH AN IMPORTANT QUESTION.
WHERE IS MASTER KEZ VELAZ?
YOU MUST BE MISTAKEN.
THIS TEMPLE IS NO LONGER UNDER THE APPOINTMENT OF THE UNFAITHFUL MASTER VELAZ. HE HAS VACATED THIS TEMPLE, THE PLANET, AND HIS PEOPLE. THERE IS ONLY ONE JEDI MASTER OF MATHAS.
ME!

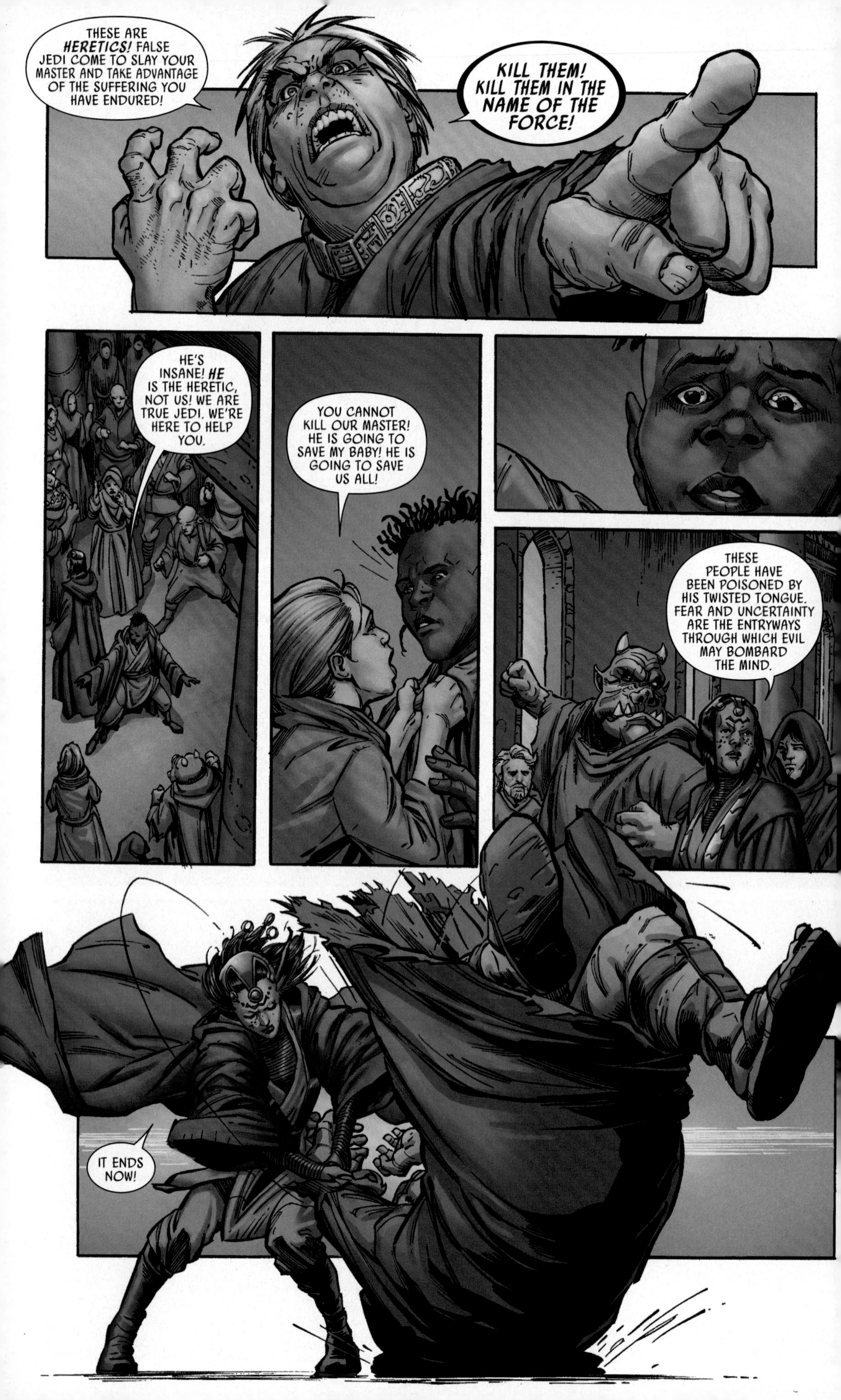
THESE ARE HERETICS! FALSE JEDI COME TO SLAY YOUR MASTER AND TAKE ADVANTAGE OF THE SUFFERING YOU HAVE ENDURED!
KILL THEM! KILL THEM IN THE NAME OF THE FORCE!
HE'S INSANE! HE IS THE HERETIC, NOT US! WE ARE TRUE JEDI. WE'RE HERE TO HELP YOU.
YOU CANNOT KILL OUR MASTER! HE IS GOING TO SAVE MY BABY! HE IS GOING TO SAVE US ALL!
THESE PEOPLE HAVE BEEN POISONED BY HIS TWISTED TONGUE. FEAR AND UNCERTAINTY ARE THE ENTRYWAYS THROUGH WHICH EVIL MAY BOMBARD THE MIND.
IT ENDS NOW!

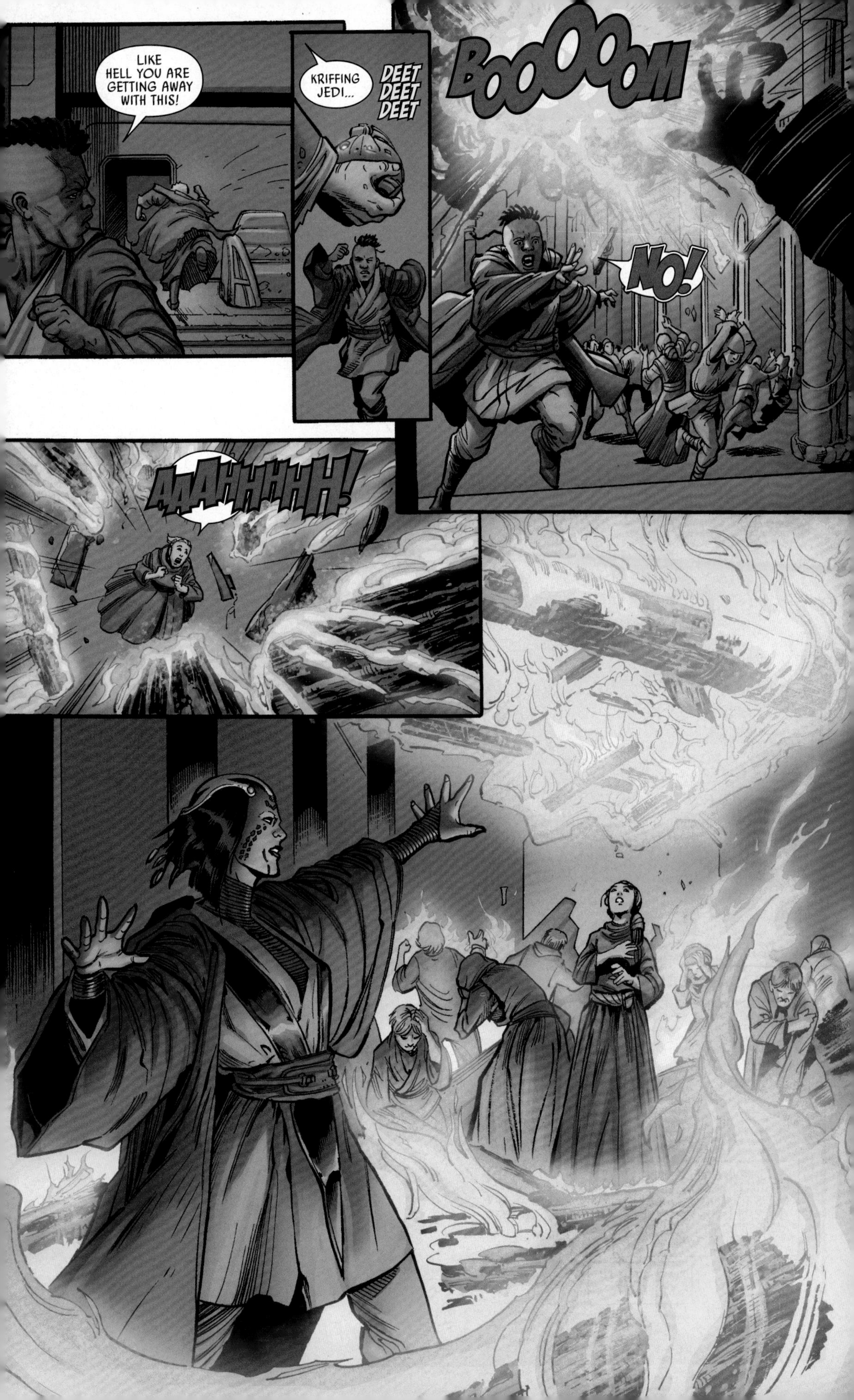
LIKE HELL YOU ARE GETTING AWAY WITH THIS!
KRIFFING JEDI...
DEET DEET DEET
BOOOOOOM
NO!
AAAHHHHH!

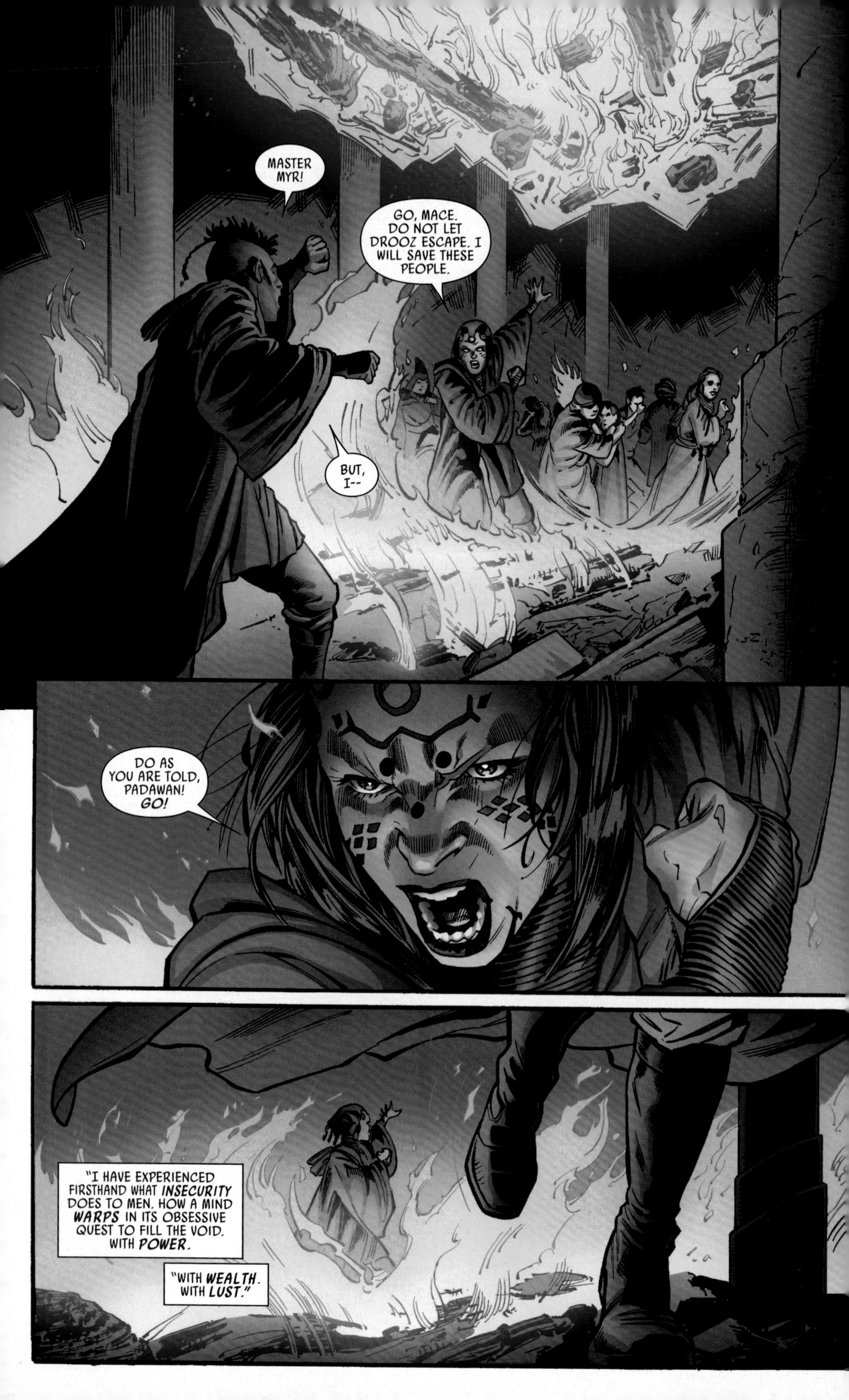
MASTER MYR!
GO, MACE. DO NOT LET DROOZ ESCAPE. I WILL SAVE THESE PEOPLE.
BUT, I--
DO AS YOU ARE TOLD, PADAWAN! GO!
"I HAVE EXPERIENCED FIRSTHAND WHAT INSECURITY DOES TO MEN. HOW A MIND WARPS IN ITS OBSESSIVE QUEST TO FILL THE VOID. WITH POWER.
"WITH WEALTH. WITH LUST."

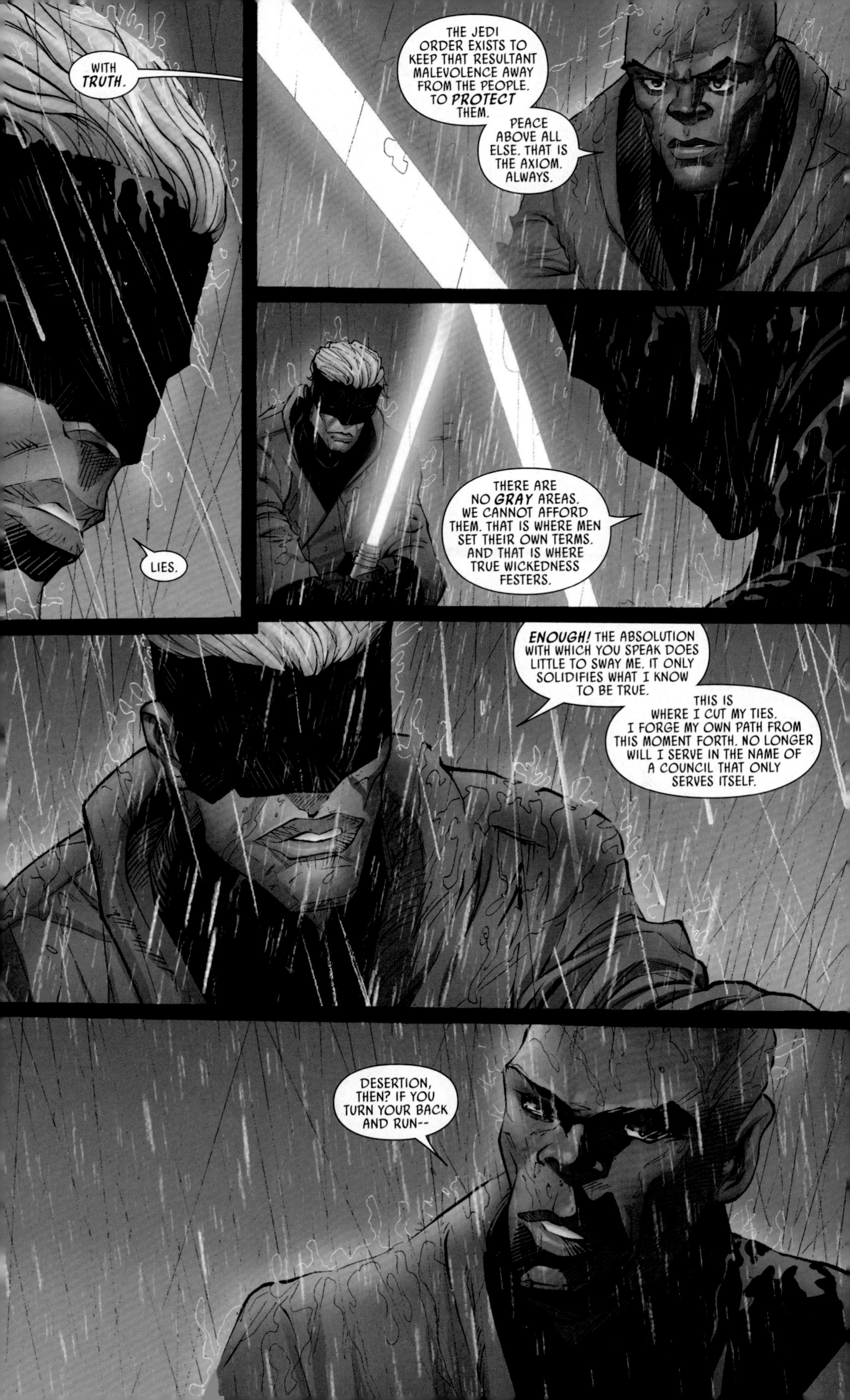
WITH TRUTH.
THE JEDI ORDER EXISTS TO KEEP THAT RESULTANT MALEVOLENCE AWAY FROM THE PEOPLE. TO PROTECT THEM.
PEACE ABOVE ALL ELSE. THAT IS THE AXIOM. ALWAYS.
LIES.
THERE ARE NO GRAY AREAS. WE CANNOT AFFORD THEM. THAT IS WHERE MEN SET THEIR OWN TERMS. AND THAT IS WHERE TRUE WICKEDNESS FESTERS.
ENOUGH! THE ABSOLUTION WITH WHICH YOU SPEAK DOES LITTLE TO SWAY ME. IT ONLY SOLIDIFIES WHAT I KNOW TO BE TRUE.
THIS IS WHERE I CUT MY TIES. I FORGE MY OWN PATH FROM THIS MOMENT FORTH. NO LONGER WILL I SERVE IN THE NAME OF A COUNCIL THAT ONLY SERVES ITSELF.
DESERTION, THEN? IF YOU TURN YOUR BACK AND RUN--

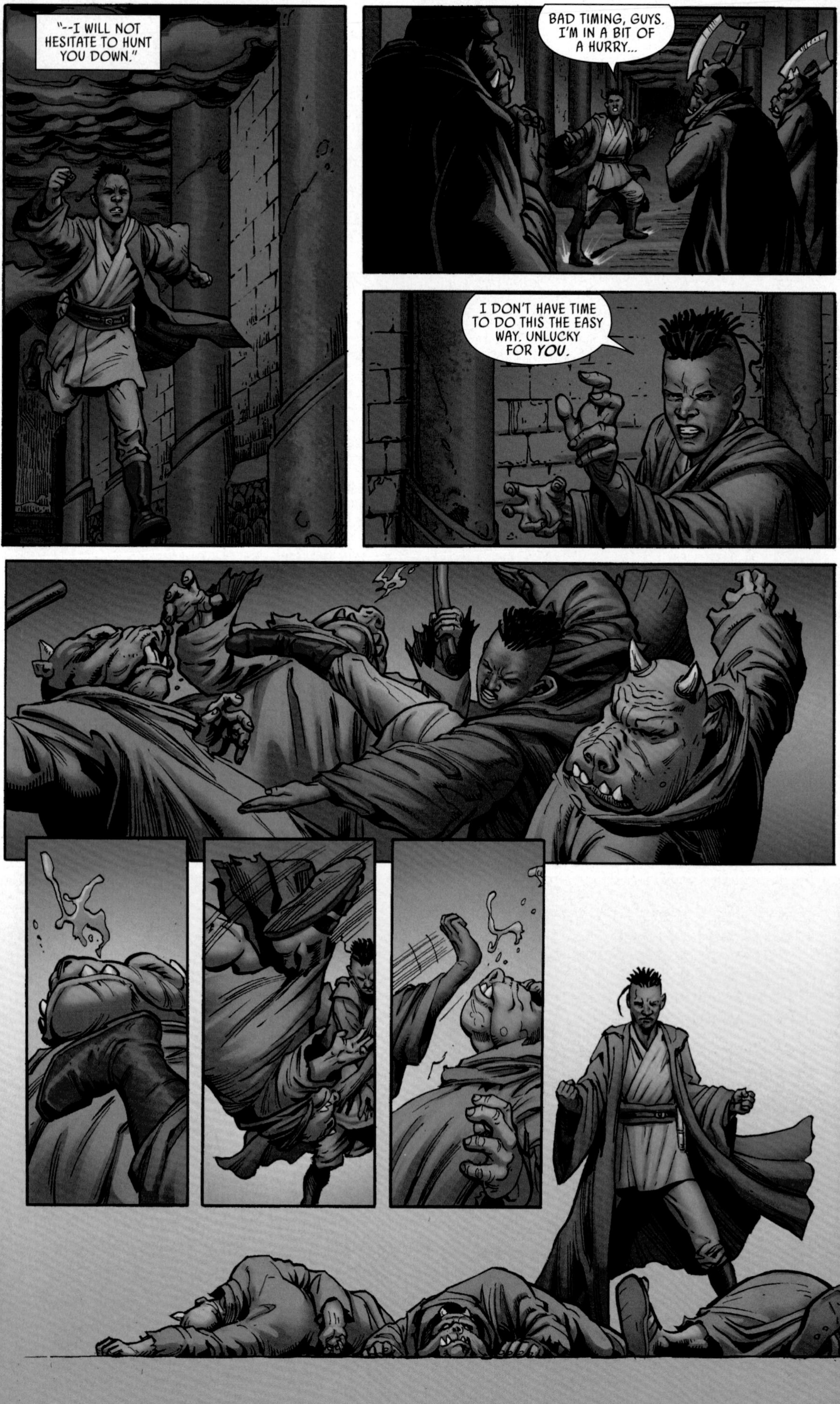
"--I WILL NOT HESITATE TO HUNT YOU DOWN."
BAD TIMING, GUYS. I'M IN A BIT OF A HURRY...
I DON'T HAVE TIME TO DO THIS THE EASY WAY. UNLUCKY FOR *YOU*.

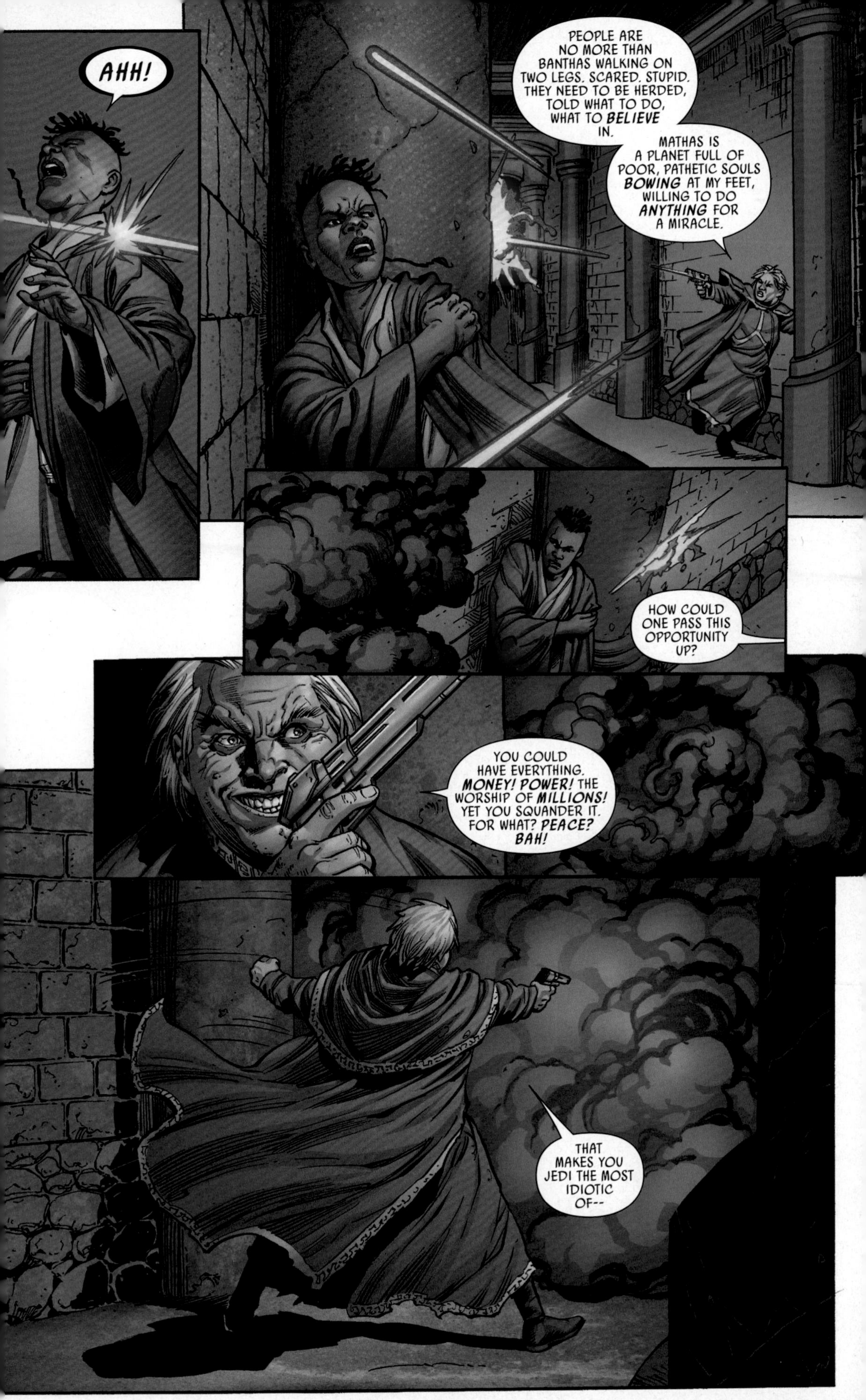
AHH!
PEOPLE ARE NO MORE THAN BANTHAS WALKING ON TWO LEGS. SCARED. STUPID. THEY NEED TO BE HERDED, TOLD WHAT TO DO, WHAT TO BELIEVE IN.
MATHAS IS A PLANET FULL OF POOR, PATHETIC SOULS BOWING AT MY FEET, WILLING TO DO ANYTHING FOR A MIRACLE.
HOW COULD ONE PASS THIS OPPORTUNITY UP?
YOU COULD HAVE EVERYTHING. MONEY! POWER! THE WORSHIP OF MILLIONS! YET YOU SQUANDER IT. FOR WHAT? PEACE? BAH!
THAT MAKES YOU JEDI THE MOST IDIOTIC OF--

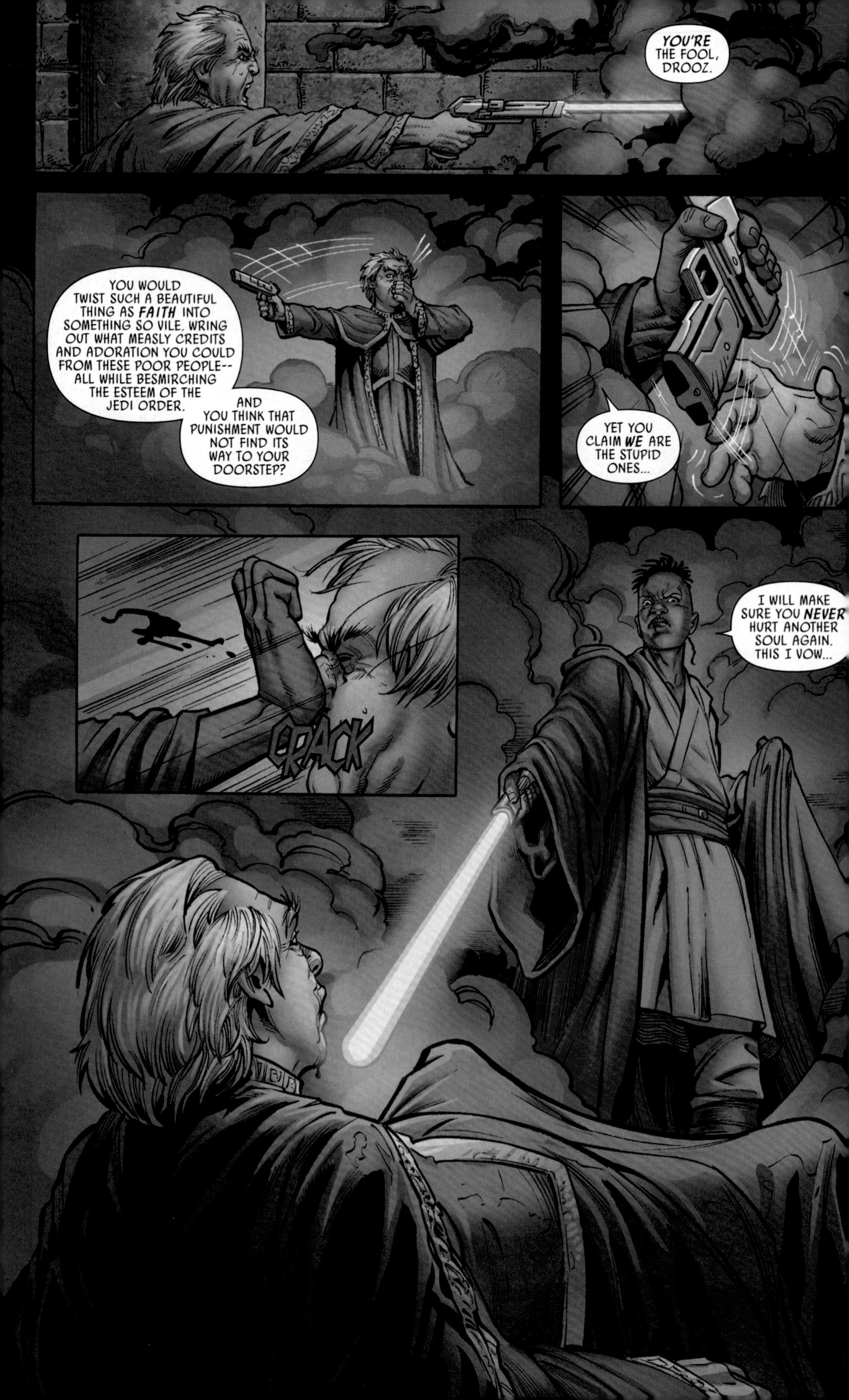
YOU'RE THE FOOL, DROOZ.
YOU WOULD TWIST SUCH A BEAUTIFUL THING AS FAITH INTO SOMETHING SO VILE. WRING OUT WHAT MEASLY CREDITS AND ADORATION YOU COULD FROM THESE POOR PEOPLE-- ALL WHILE BESMIRCHING THE ESTEEM OF THE JEDI ORDER.
AND YOU THINK THAT PUNISHMENT WOULD NOT FIND ITS WAY TO YOUR DOORSTEP?
YET YOU CLAIM WE ARE THE STUPID ONES...
CRACK
I WILL MAKE SURE YOU NEVER HURT ANOTHER SOUL AGAIN. THIS I VOW...

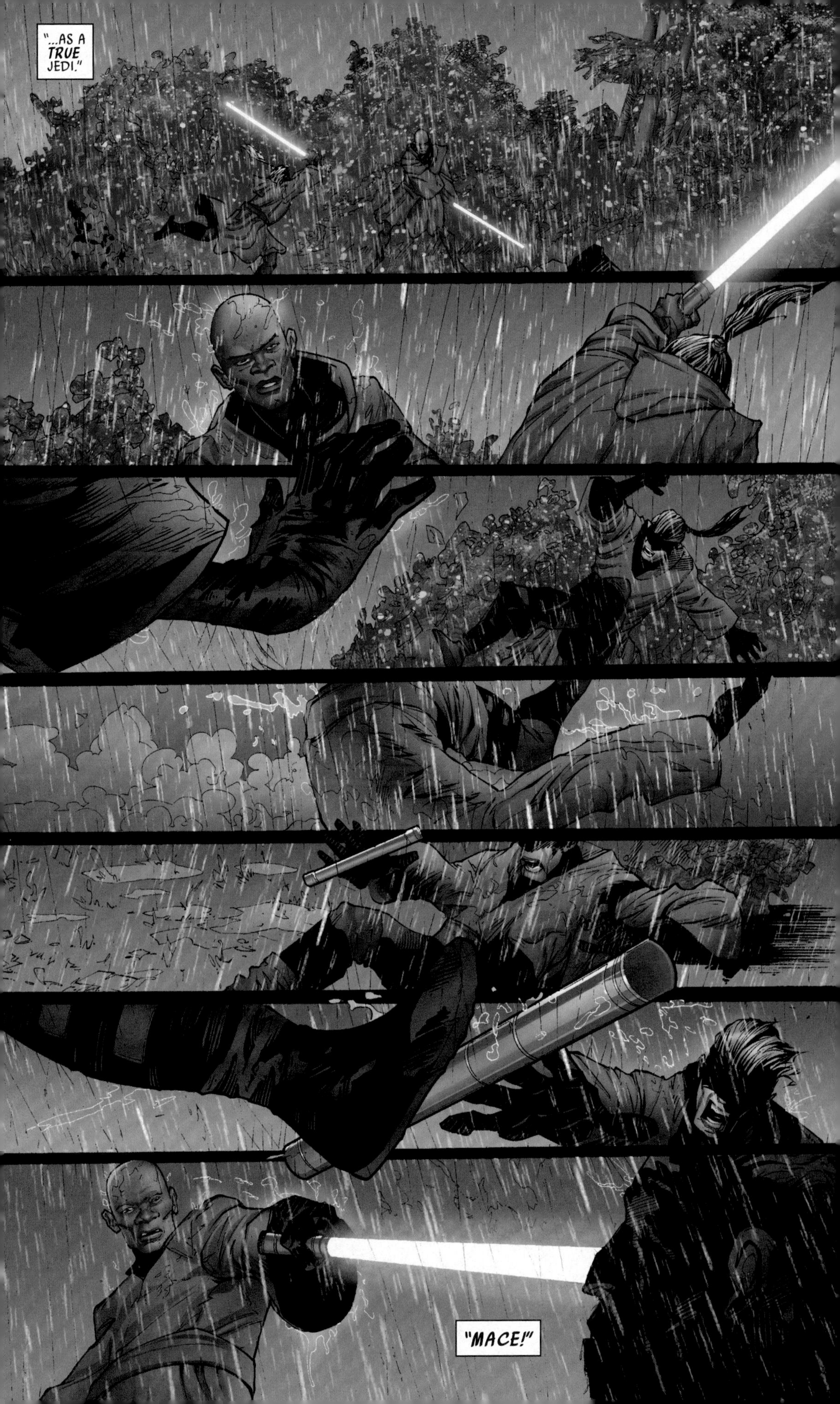
"...AS A TRUE JEDI."
"MACE!"

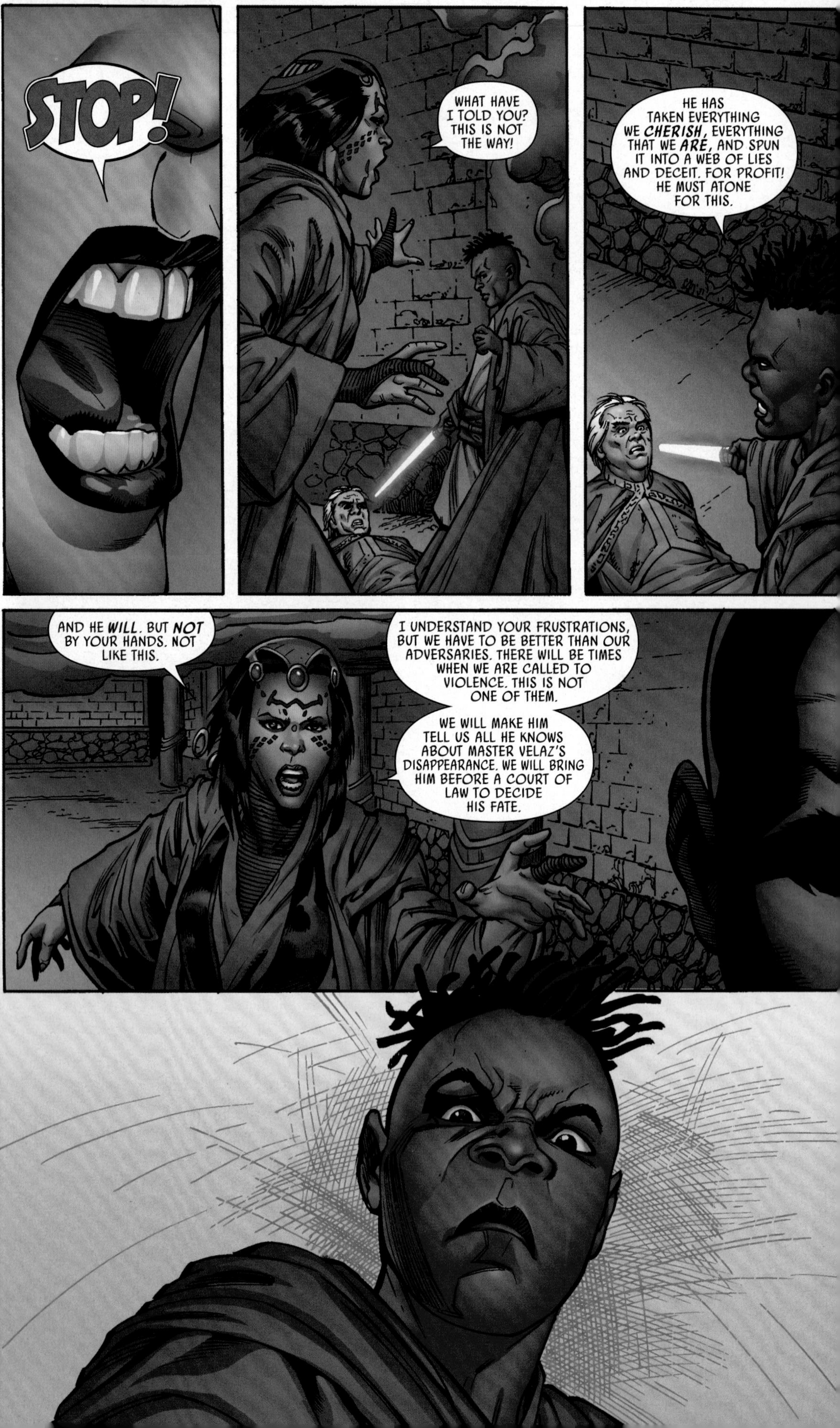

STOP!
WHAT HAVE I TOLD YOU? THIS IS NOT THE WAY!
HE HAS TAKEN EVERYTHING WE CHERISH, EVERYTHING THAT WE ARE, AND SPUN IT INTO A WEB OF LIES AND DECEIT. FOR PROFIT! HE MUST ATONE FOR THIS.
AND HE WILL. BUT NOT BY YOUR HANDS. NOT LIKE THIS.
I UNDERSTAND YOUR FRUSTRATIONS, BUT WE HAVE TO BE BETTER THAN OUR ADVERSARIES. THERE WILL BE TIMES WHEN WE ARE CALLED TO VIOLENCE. THIS IS NOT ONE OF THEM.
WE WILL MAKE HIM TELL US ALL HE KNOWS ABOUT MASTER VELAZ'S DISAPPEARANCE. WE WILL BRING HIM BEFORE A COURT OF LAW TO DECIDE HIS FATE.

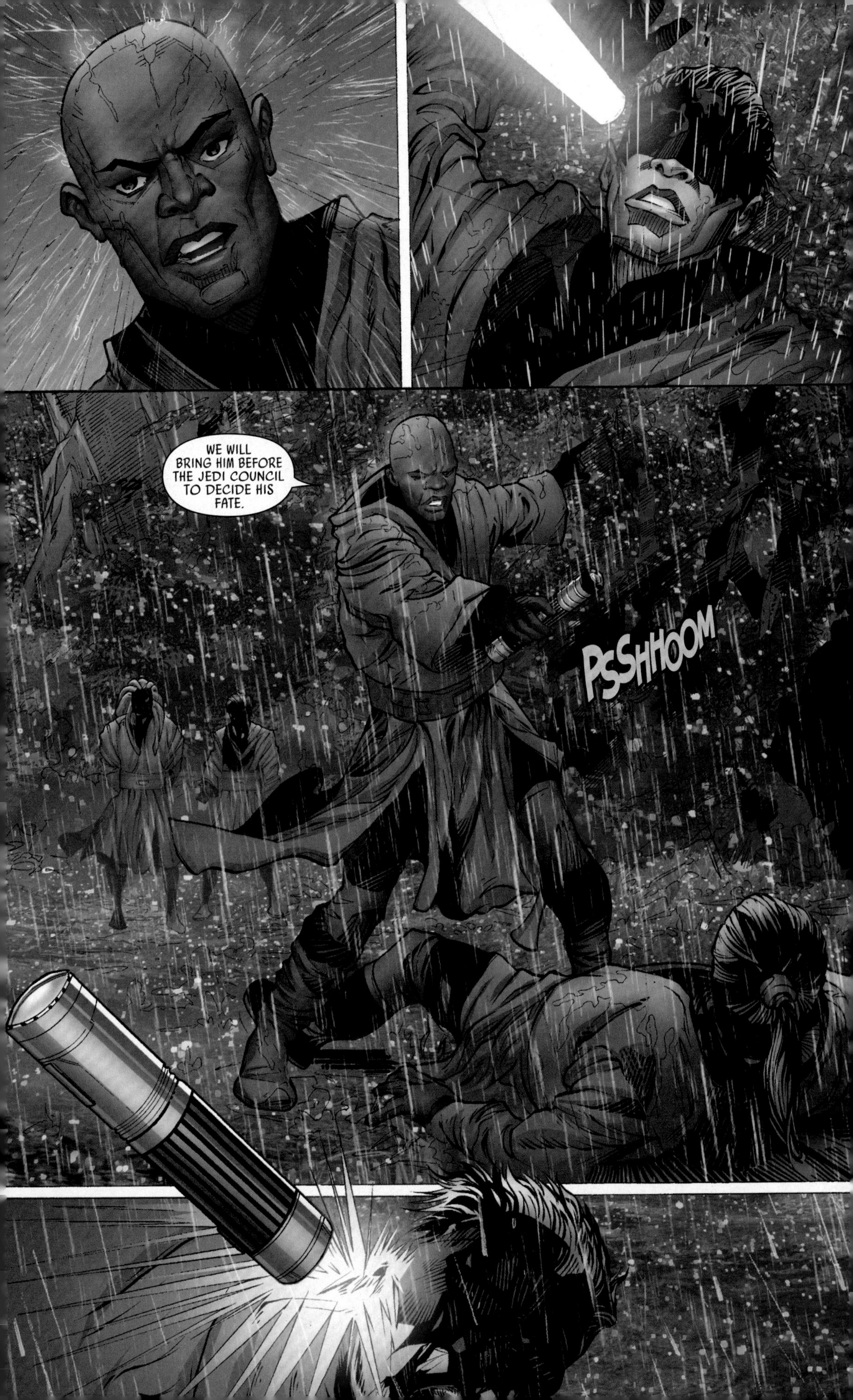
WE WILL BRING HIM BEFORE THE JEDI COUNCIL TO DECIDE HIS FATE.
PSSHHOOM

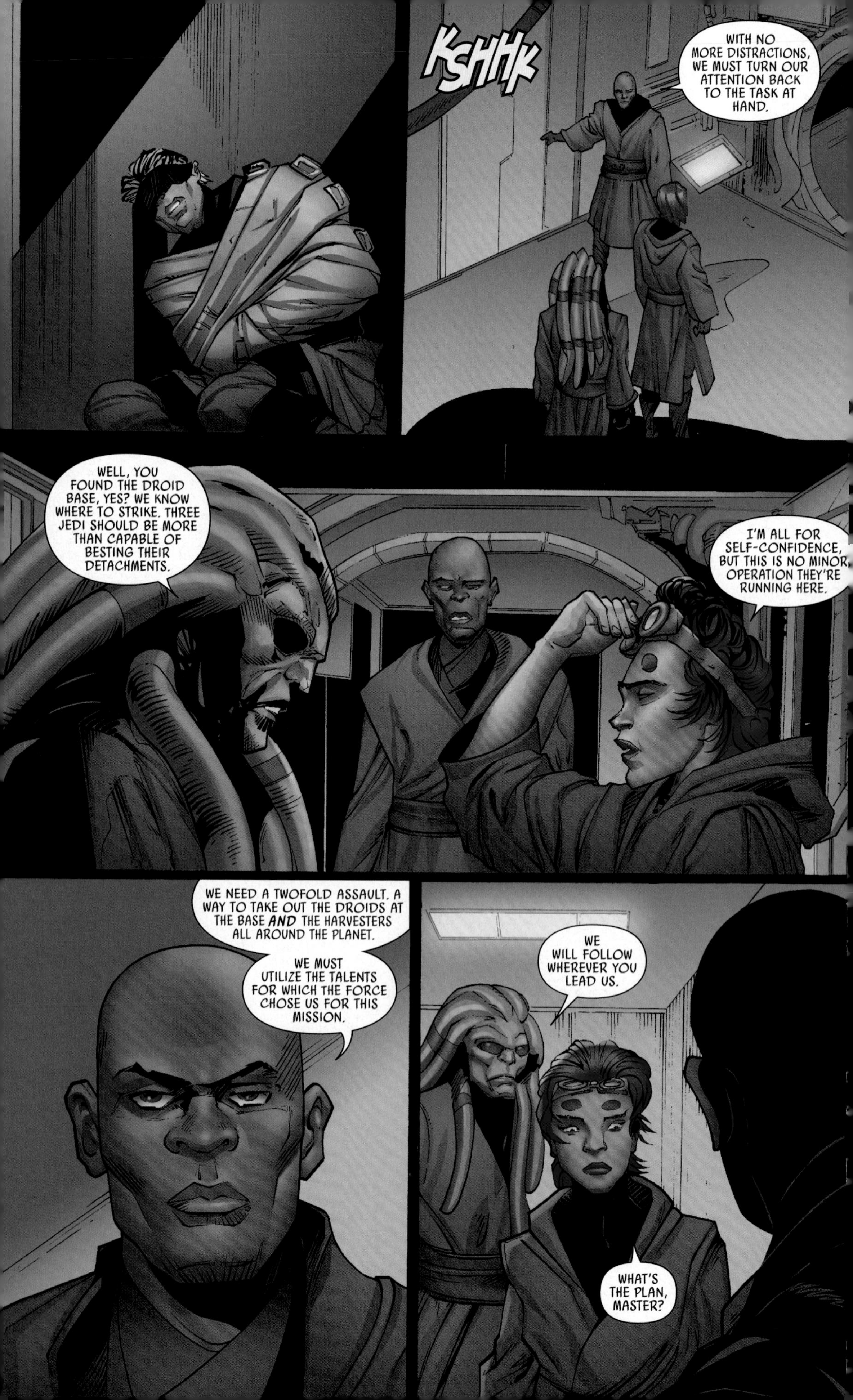
KSHHK
WITH NO MORE DISTRACTIONS, WE MUST TURN OUR ATTENTION BACK TO THE TASK AT HAND.
WELL, YOU FOUND THE DROID BASE, YES? WE KNOW WHERE TO STRIKE. THREE JEDI SHOULD BE MORE THAN CAPABLE OF BESTING THEIR DETACHMENTS.
I'M ALL FOR SELF-CONFIDENCE, BUT THIS IS NO MINOR OPERATION THEY'RE RUNNING HERE.
WE NEED A TWOFOLD ASSAULT. A WAY TO TAKE OUT THE DROIDS AT THE BASE AND THE HARVESTERS ALL AROUND THE PLANET.
WE MUST UTILIZE THE TALENTS FOR WHICH THE FORCE CHOSE US FOR THIS MISSION.
WE WILL FOLLOW WHEREVER YOU LEAD US.
WHAT'S THE PLAN, MASTER?

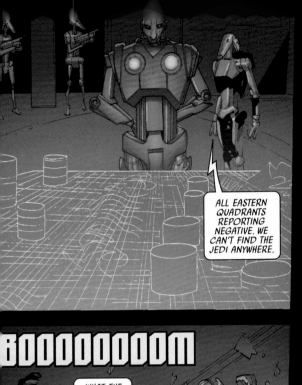

ALL EASTERN QUADRANTS REPORTING NEGATIVE. WE CAN'T FIND THE JEDI ANYWHERE.

TIRESOME AS THIS SEARCH HAS BECOME, ITS END DRAWS NEAR. THE JEDI WON'T HAVE MUCH LEFT TO HIDE BEHIND FOR LONG.

AND THEN THE REAL GAME BEGINS.

BOOOOOOOOM

WHAT THE HELL IS GOING ON?

UHH...IT LOOKS LIKE THE JEDI HAVE FOUND US.

STAND ASIDE!

HOW ANXIOUSLY THEY RUN TO THEIR SLAUGHTER. I'M MORE THAN HAPPY TO GIVE THEM THE END THEY SO DESIRE.

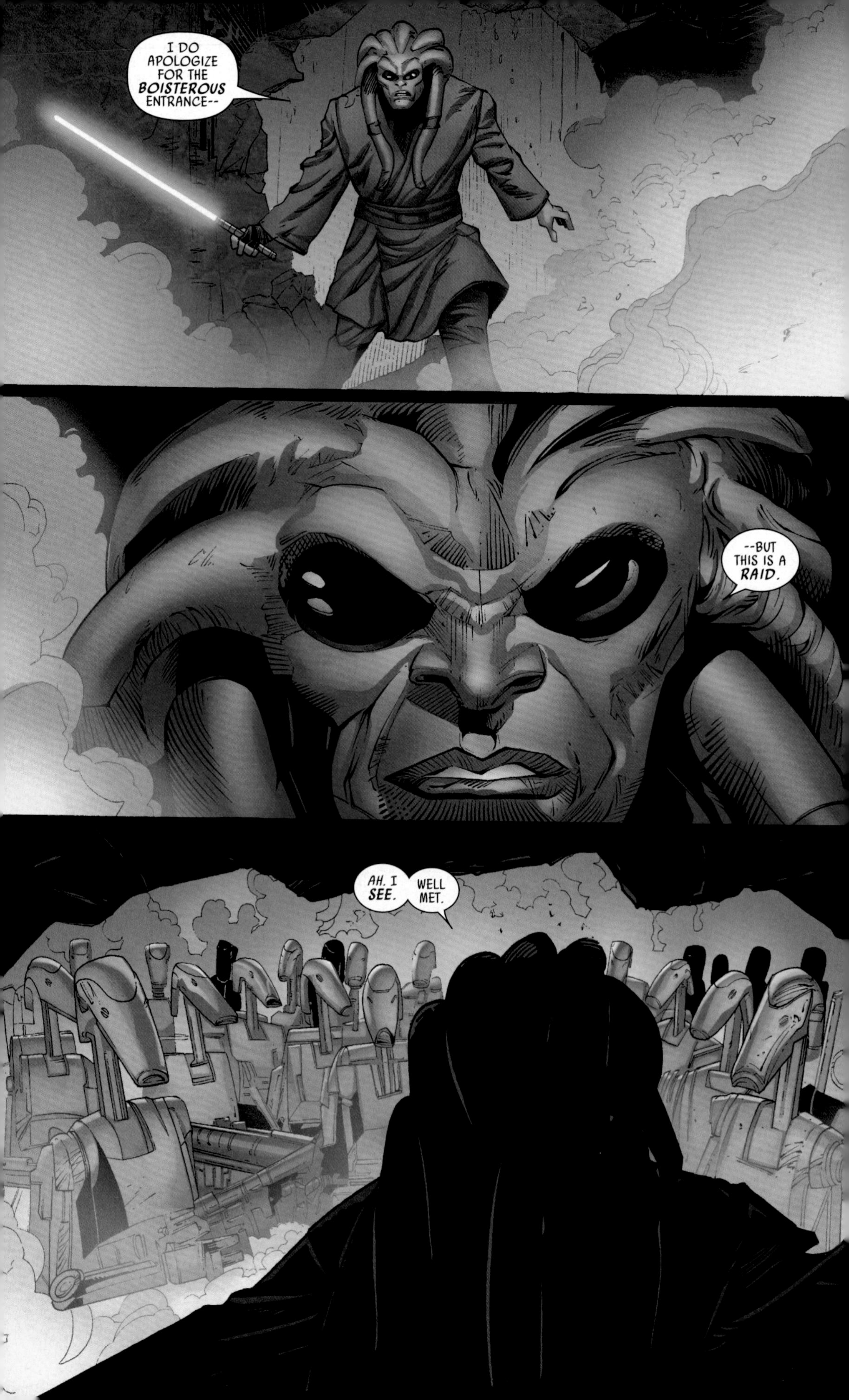

I DO APOLOGIZE FOR THE BOISTEROUS ENTRANCE--
--BUT THIS IS A RAID.
AH. I SEE.
WELL MET.

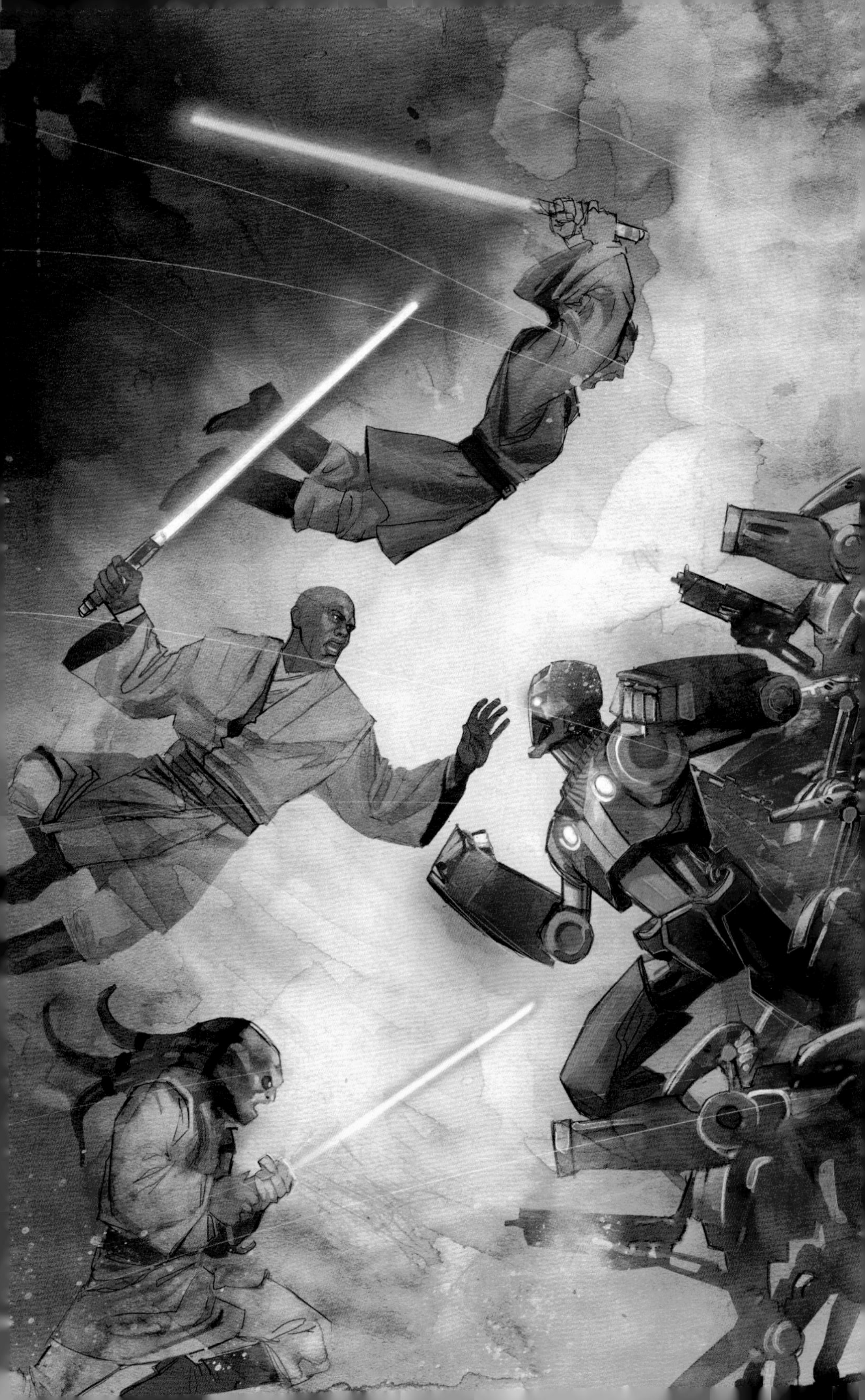

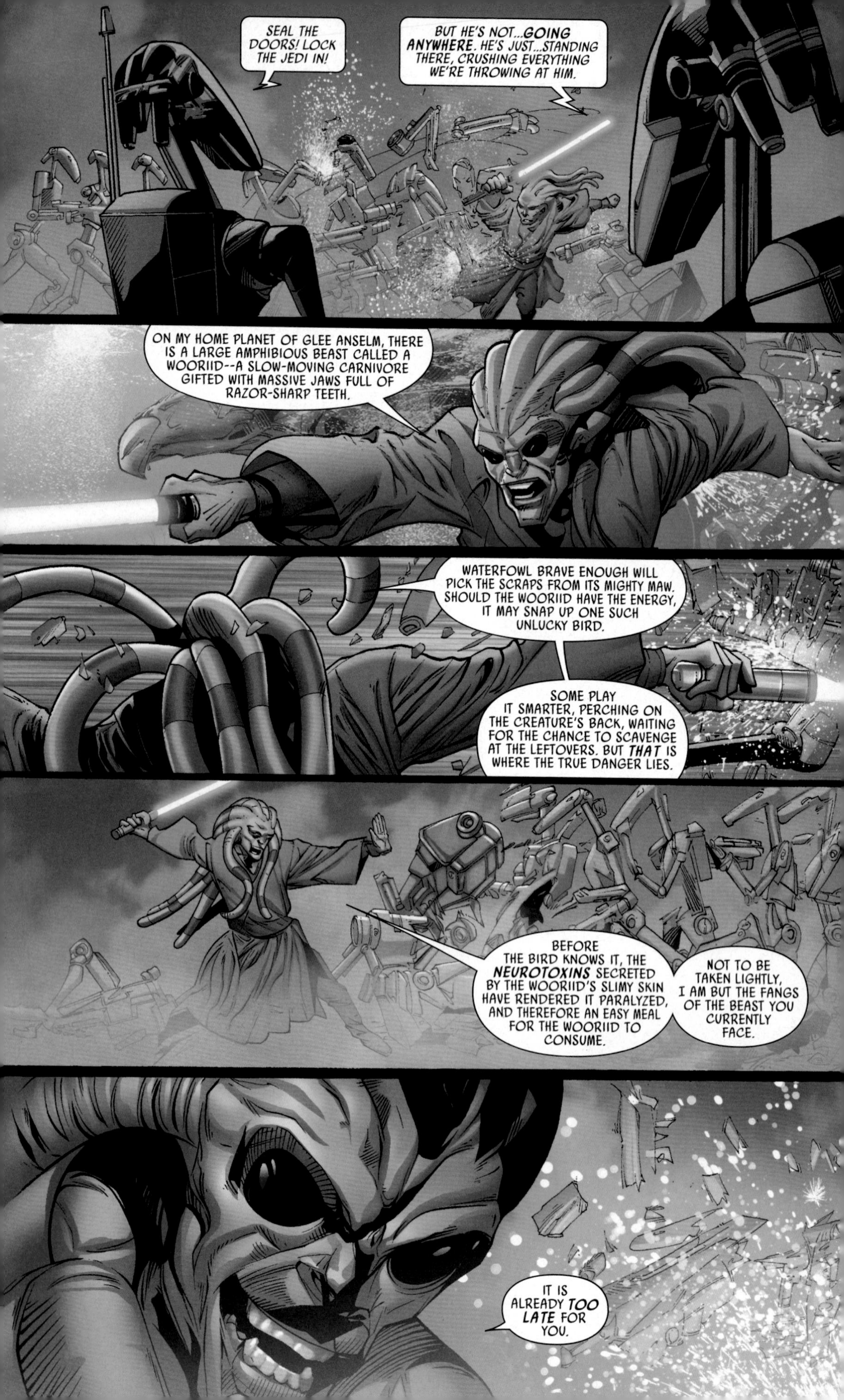
SEAL THE DOORS! LOCK THE JEDI IN!
BUT HE'S NOT...GOING ANYWHERE. HE'S JUST...STANDING THERE, CRUSHING EVERYTHING WE'RE THROWING AT HIM.
ON MY HOME PLANET OF GLEE ANSELM, THERE IS A LARGE AMPHIBIOUS BEAST CALLED A WOORIID--A SLOW-MOVING CARNIVORE GIFTED WITH MASSIVE JAWS FULL OF RAZOR-SHARP TEETH.
WATERFOWL BRAVE ENOUGH WILL PICK THE SCRAPS FROM ITS MIGHTY MAW. SHOULD THE WOORIID HAVE THE ENERGY, IT MAY SNAP UP ONE SUCH UNLUCKY BIRD.
SOME PLAY IT SMARTER, PERCHING ON THE CREATURE'S BACK, WAITING FOR THE CHANCE TO SCAVENGE AT THE LEFTOVERS. BUT THAT IS WHERE THE TRUE DANGER LIES.
BEFORE THE BIRD KNOWS IT, THE NEUROTOXINS SECRETED BY THE WOORIID'S SLIMY SKIN HAVE RENDERED IT PARALYZED, AND THEREFORE AN EASY MEAL FOR THE WOORIID TO CONSUME.
NOT TO BE TAKEN LIGHTLY, I AM BUT THE FANGS OF THE BEAST YOU CURRENTLY FACE.
IT IS ALREADY TOO LATE FOR YOU.

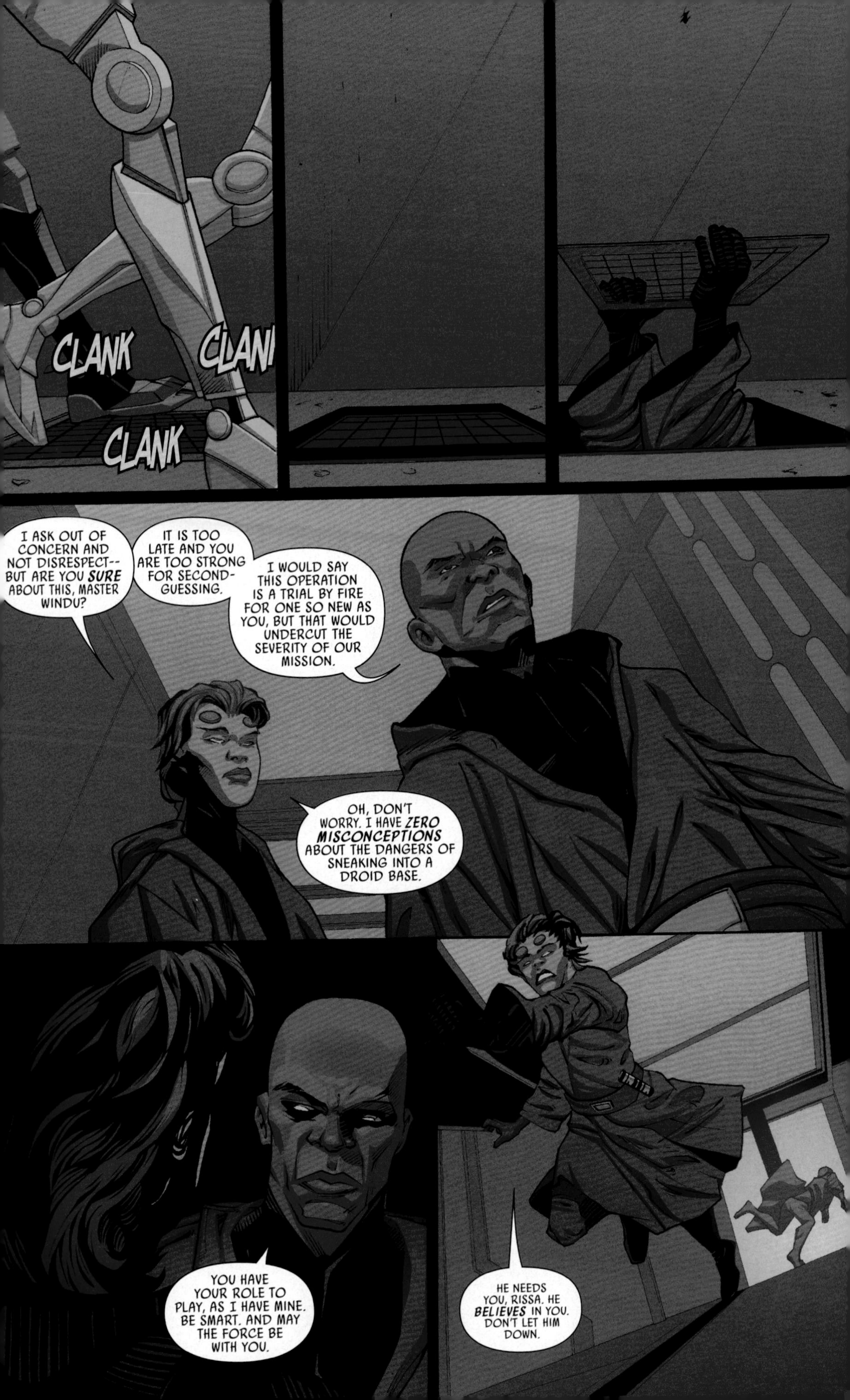
CLANK
CLANK
CLANK
I ASK OUT OF CONCERN AND NOT DISRESPECT-- BUT ARE YOU SURE ABOUT THIS, MASTER WINDU?
IT IS TOO LATE AND YOU ARE TOO STRONG FOR SECOND-GUESSING.
I WOULD SAY THIS OPERATION IS A TRIAL BY FIRE FOR ONE SO NEW AS YOU, BUT THAT WOULD UNDERCUT THE SEVERITY OF OUR MISSION.
OH, DON'T WORRY. I HAVE ZERO MISCONCEPTIONS ABOUT THE DANGERS OF SNEAKING INTO A DROID BASE.
YOU HAVE YOUR ROLE TO PLAY, AS I HAVE MINE. BE SMART. AND MAY THE FORCE BE WITH YOU.
HE NEEDS YOU, RISSA. HE BELIEVES IN YOU. DON'T LET HIM DOWN.

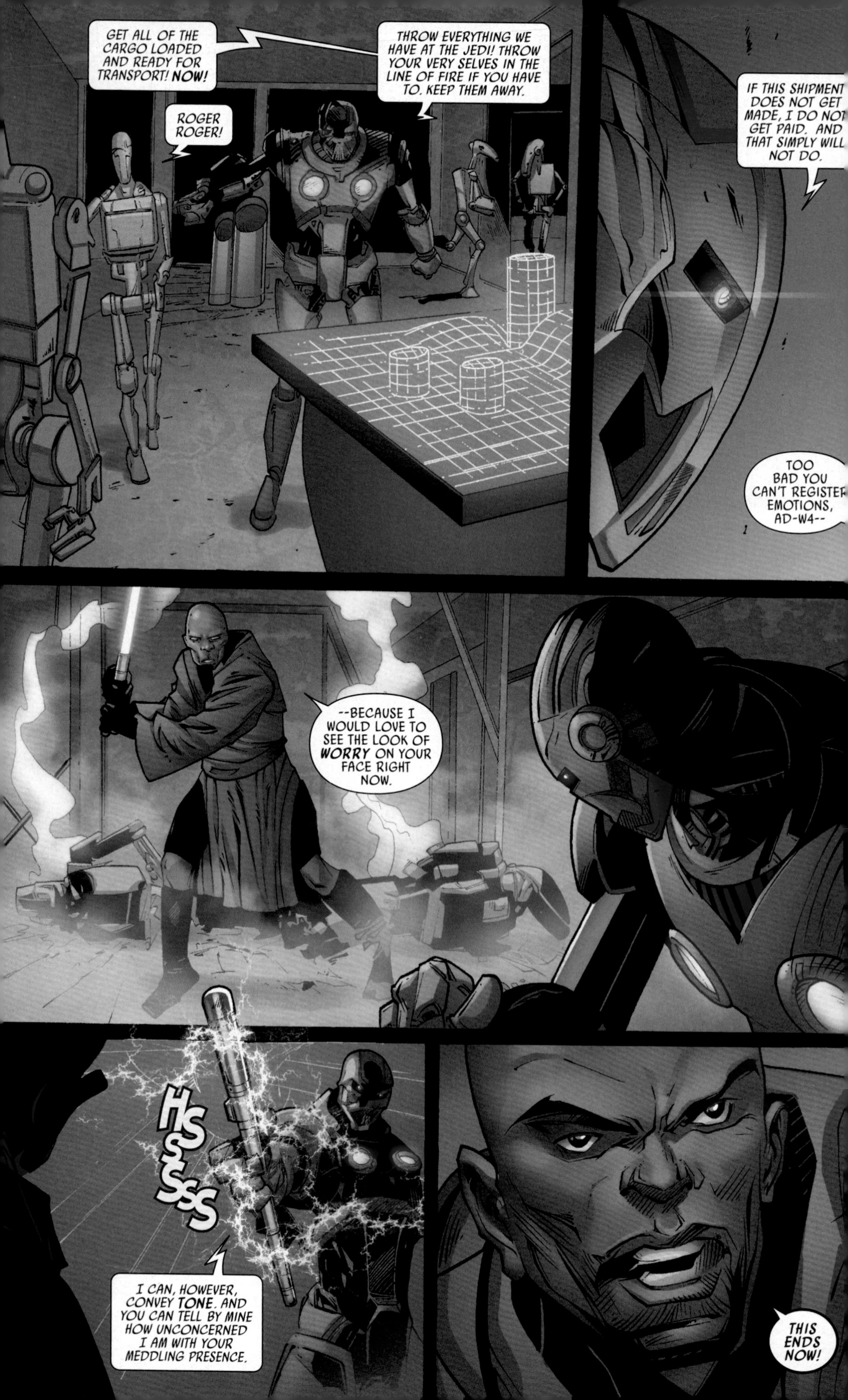
GET ALL OF THE CARGO LOADED AND READY FOR TRANSPORT! NOW!
THROW EVERYTHING WE HAVE AT THE JEDI! THROW YOUR VERY SELVES IN THE LINE OF FIRE IF YOU HAVE TO. KEEP THEM AWAY.
ROGER ROGER!
IF THIS SHIPMENT DOES NOT GET MADE, I DO NOT GET PAID. AND THAT SIMPLY WILL NOT DO.
TOO BAD YOU CAN'T REGISTER EMOTIONS, AD-W4--
--BECAUSE I WOULD LOVE TO SEE THE LOOK OF WORRY ON YOUR FACE RIGHT NOW.
HSSSSS
I CAN, HOWEVER, CONVEY TONE. AND YOU CAN TELL BY MINE HOW UNCONCERNED I AM WITH YOUR MEDDLING PRESENCE.
THIS ENDS NOW!

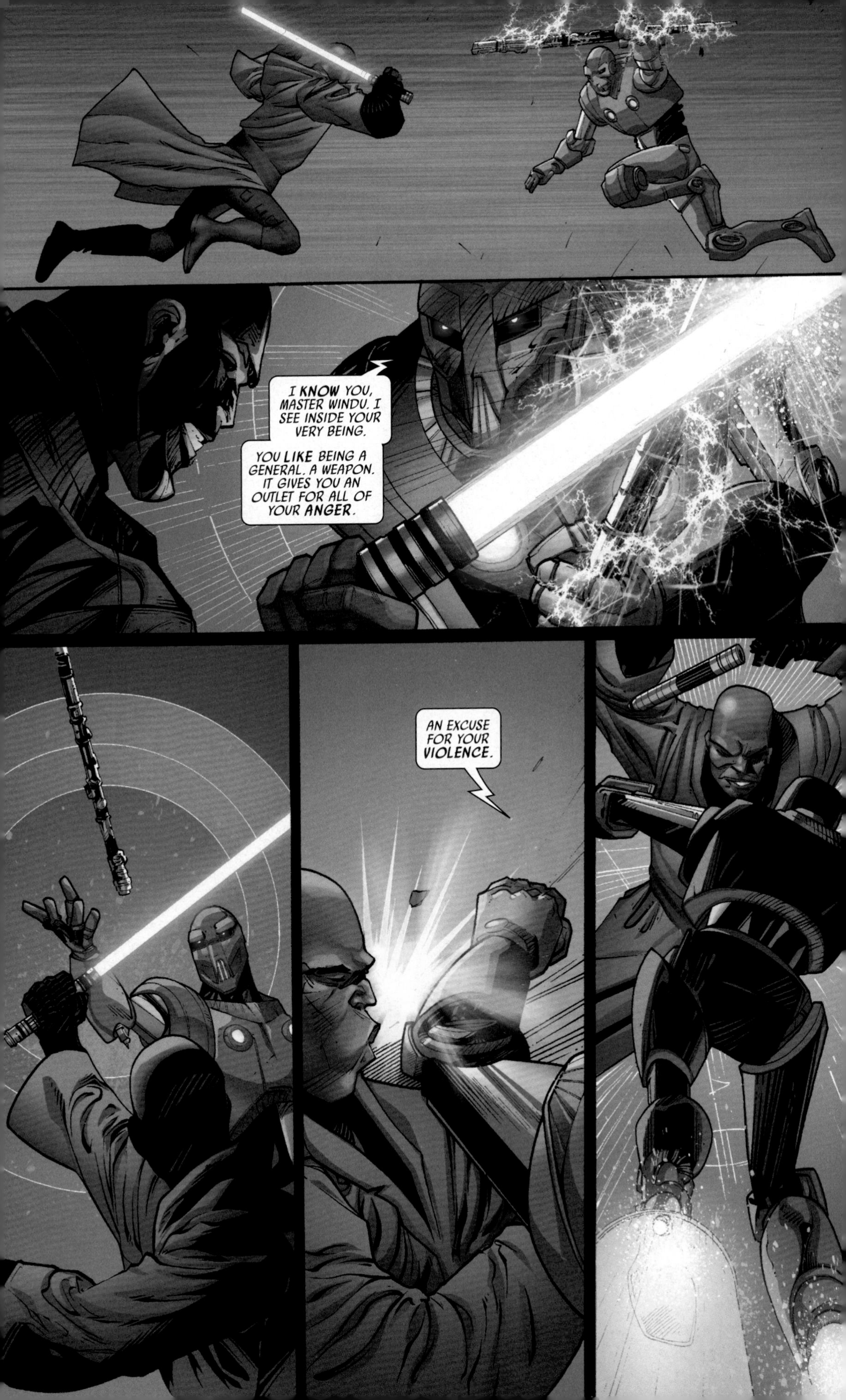
I **KNOW** YOU, MASTER WINDU. I SEE INSIDE YOUR VERY BEING.
YOU **LIKE** BEING A GENERAL. A WEAPON. IT GIVES YOU AN OUTLET FOR ALL OF YOUR **ANGER**.
AN EXCUSE FOR YOUR **VIOLENCE**.

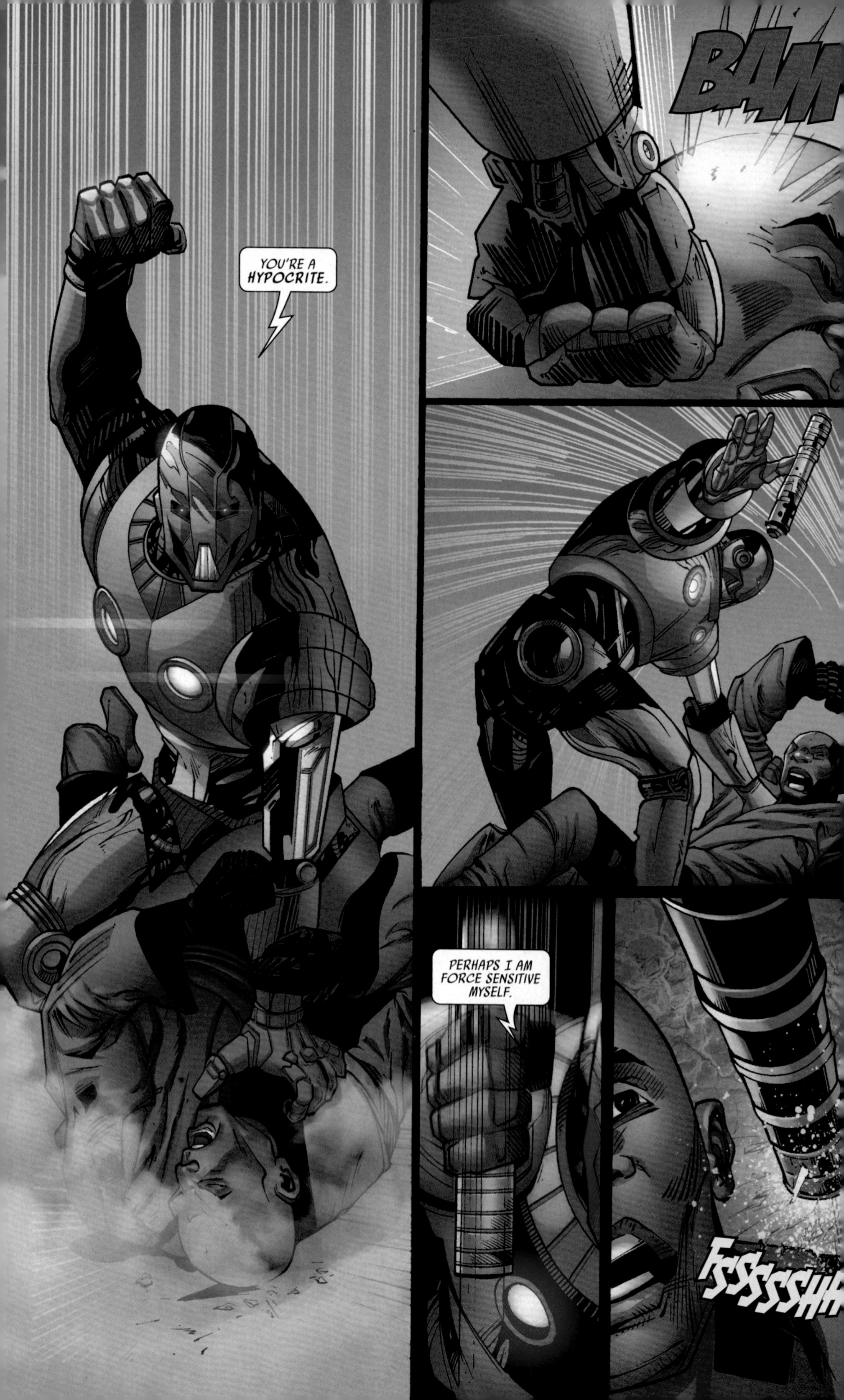
YOU'RE A HYPOCRITE.
BAM
PERHAPS I AM FORCE SENSITIVE MYSELF.
FSSSSHH

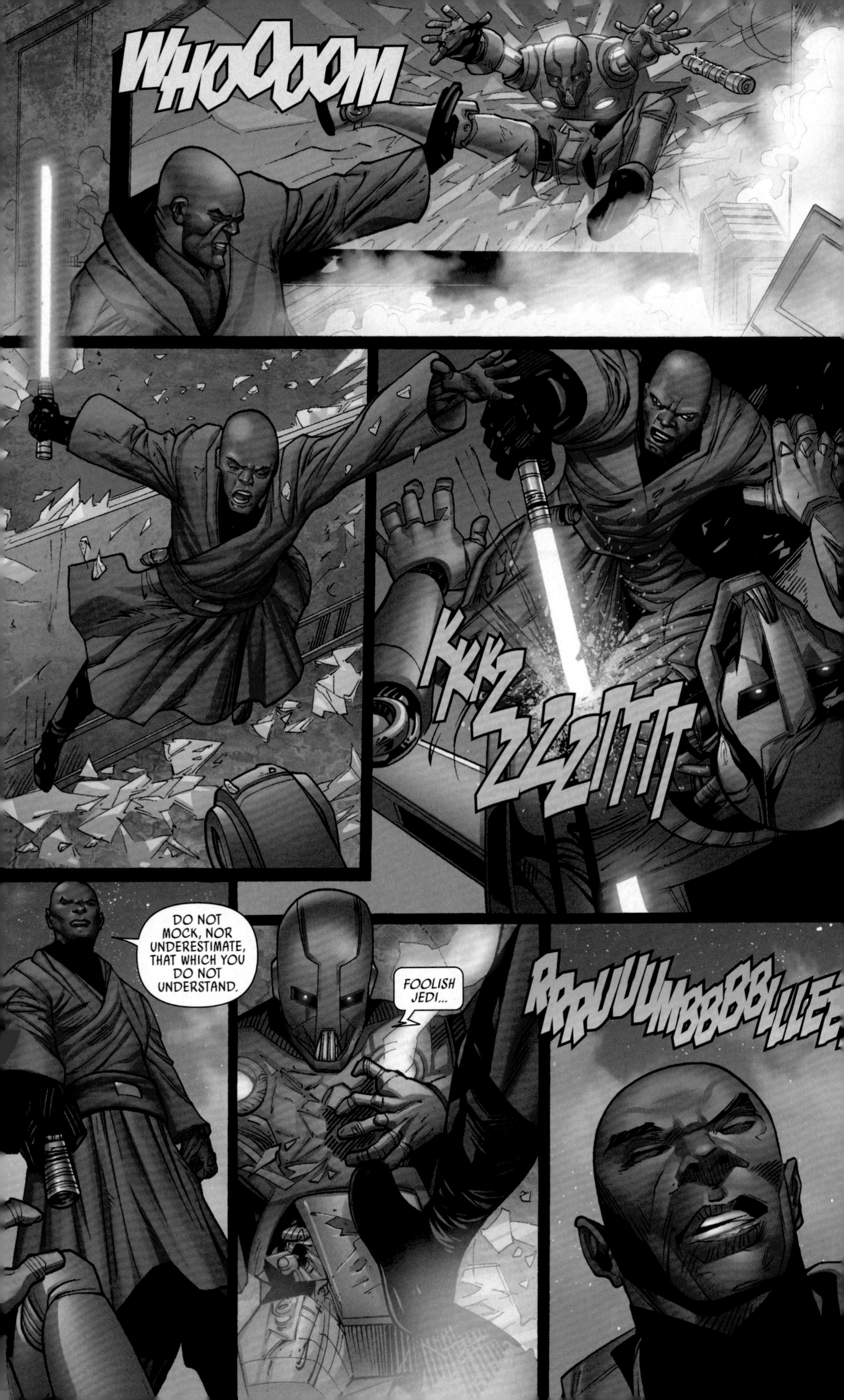
WHOOOOM
KKKZZZZTTTT
DO NOT MOCK, NOR UNDERESTIMATE, THAT WHICH YOU DO NOT UNDERSTAND.
FOOLISH JEDI...
RRRUUUMBBBBLLLEE

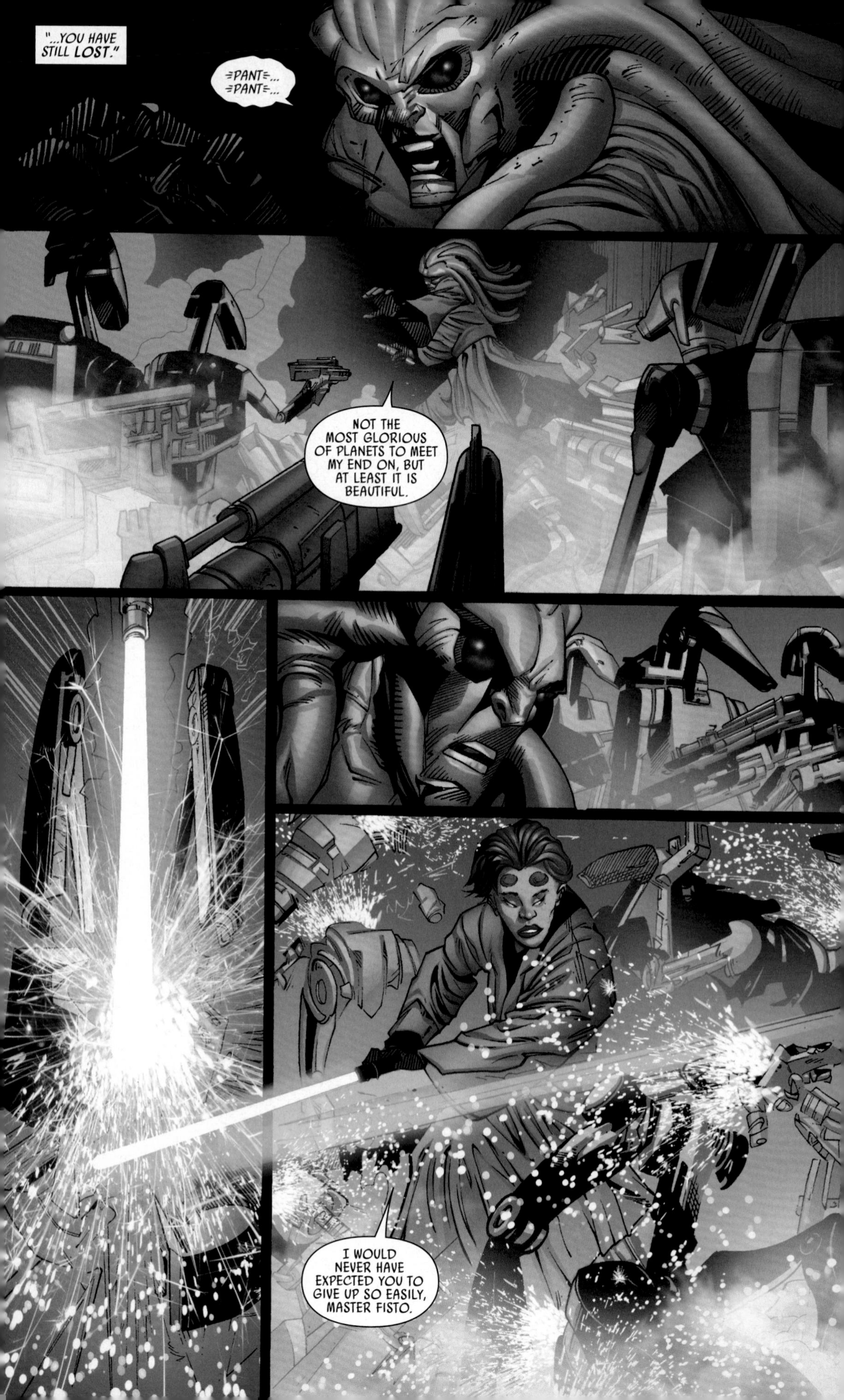
"...YOU HAVE STILL LOST."
=PANT=... =PANT=...
NOT THE MOST GLORIOUS OF PLANETS TO MEET MY END ON, BUT AT LEAST IT IS BEAUTIFUL.
I WOULD NEVER HAVE EXPECTED YOU TO GIVE UP SO EASILY, MASTER FISTO.

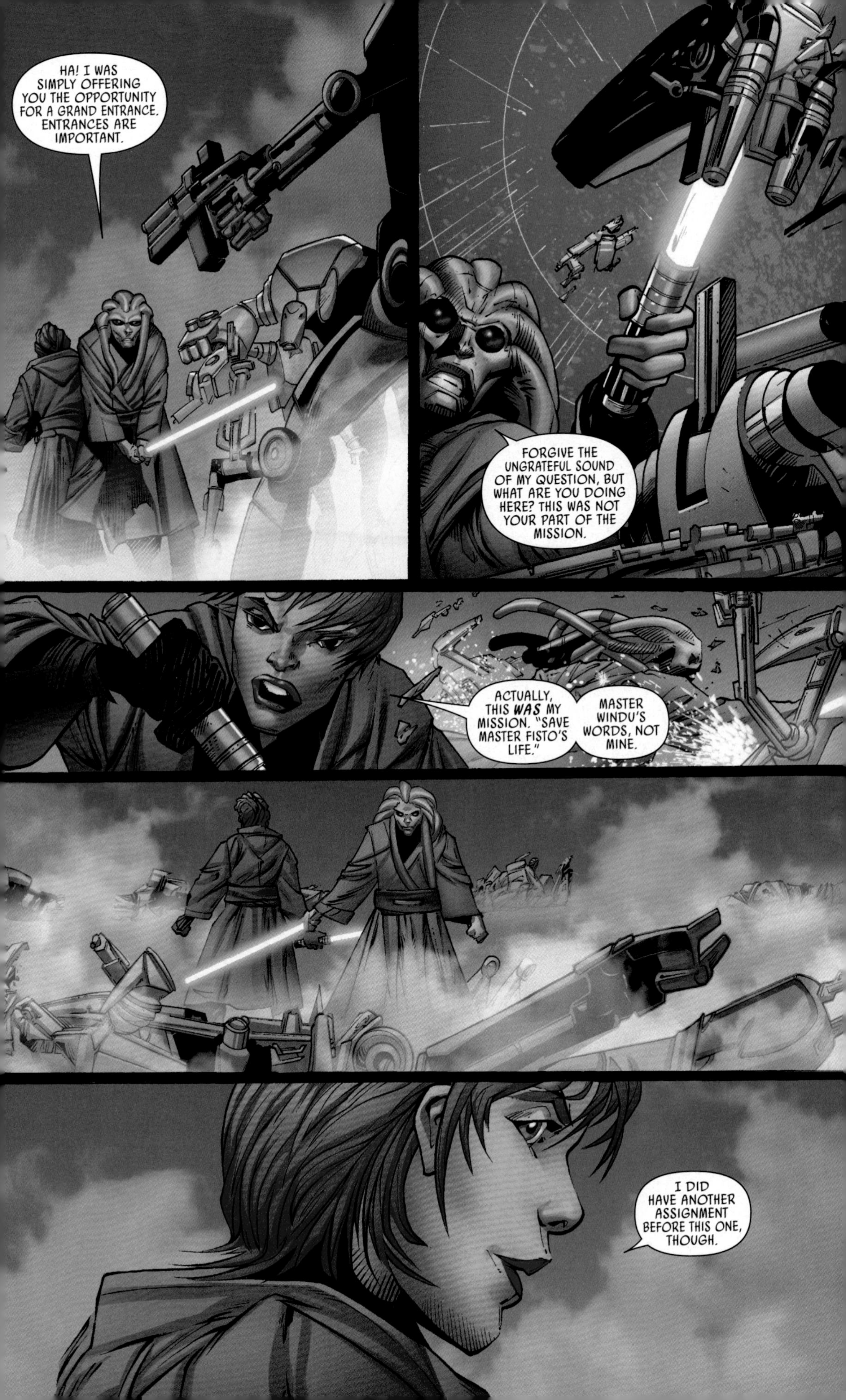
HA! I WAS SIMPLY OFFERING YOU THE OPPORTUNITY FOR A GRAND ENTRANCE. ENTRANCES ARE IMPORTANT.
FORGIVE THE UNGRATEFUL SOUND OF MY QUESTION, BUT WHAT ARE YOU DOING HERE? THIS WAS NOT YOUR PART OF THE MISSION.
ACTUALLY, THIS *WAS* MY MISSION. "SAVE MASTER FISTO'S LIFE."
MASTER WINDU'S WORDS, NOT MINE.
I DID HAVE ANOTHER ASSIGNMENT BEFORE THIS ONE, THOUGH.

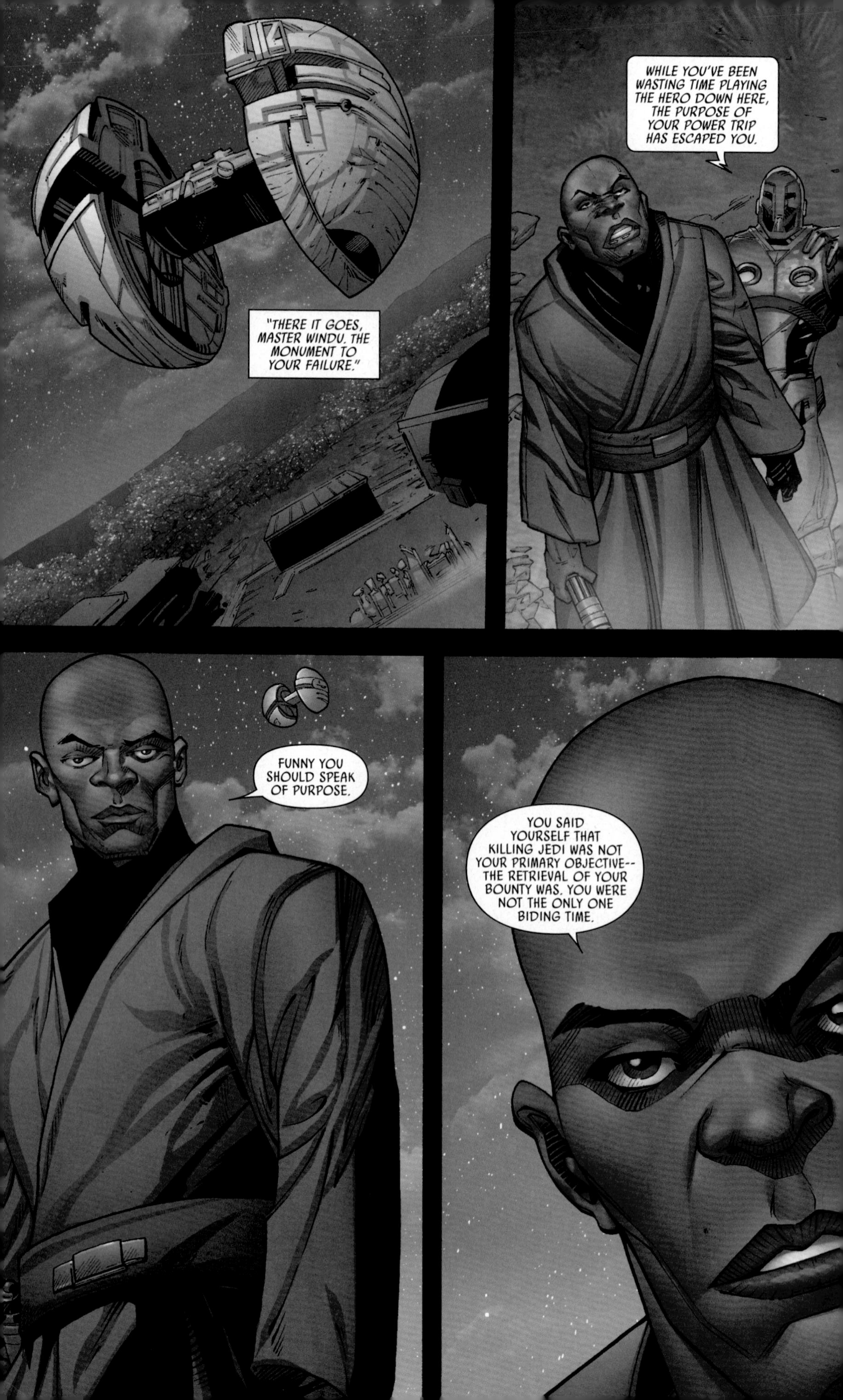
"THERE IT GOES, MASTER WINDU. THE MONUMENT TO YOUR FAILURE."
WHILE YOU'VE BEEN WASTING TIME PLAYING THE HERO DOWN HERE, THE PURPOSE OF YOUR POWER TRIP HAS ESCAPED YOU.
FUNNY YOU SHOULD SPEAK OF PURPOSE.
YOU SAID YOURSELF THAT KILLING JEDI WAS NOT YOUR PRIMARY OBJECTIVE-- THE RETRIEVAL OF YOUR BOUNTY WAS. YOU WERE NOT THE ONLY ONE BIDING TIME.

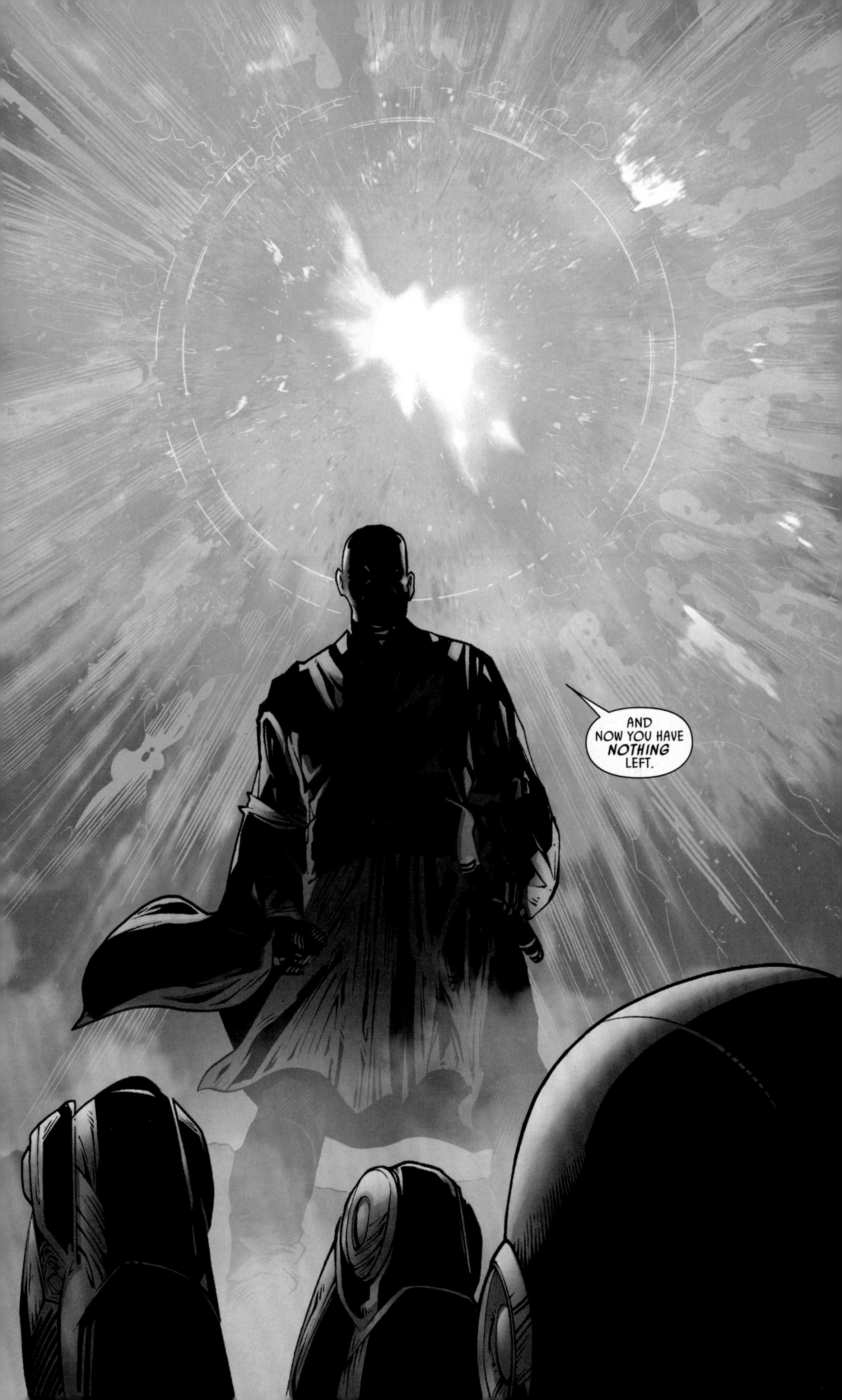
AND NOW YOU HAVE NOTHING LEFT.

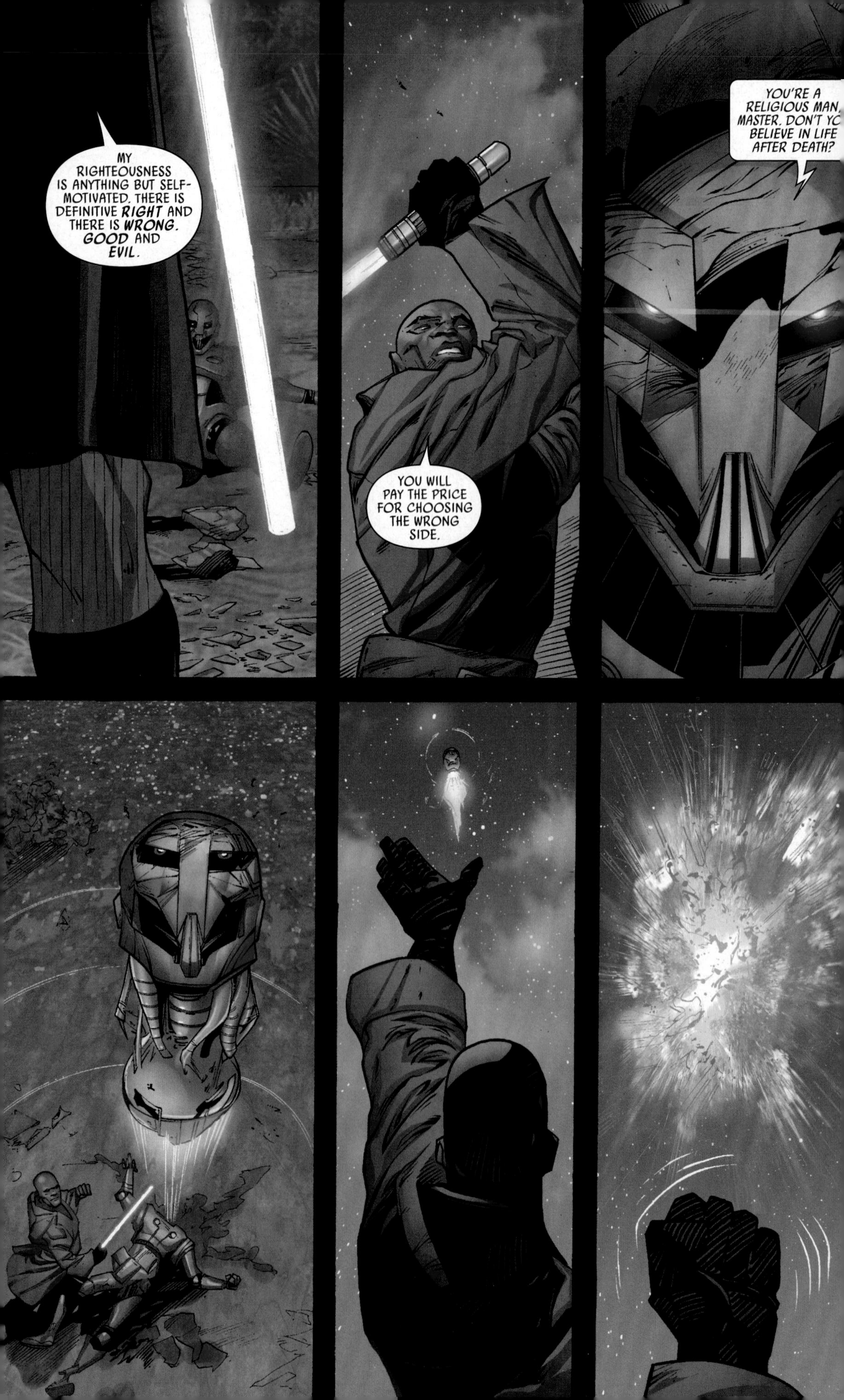
MY RIGHTEOUSNESS IS ANYTHING BUT SELF-MOTIVATED. THERE IS DEFINITIVE RIGHT AND THERE IS WRONG. GOOD AND EVIL.
YOU WILL PAY THE PRICE FOR CHOOSING THE WRONG SIDE.
YOU'RE A RELIGIOUS MAN, MASTER. DON'T YC BELIEVE IN LIFE AFTER DEATH?

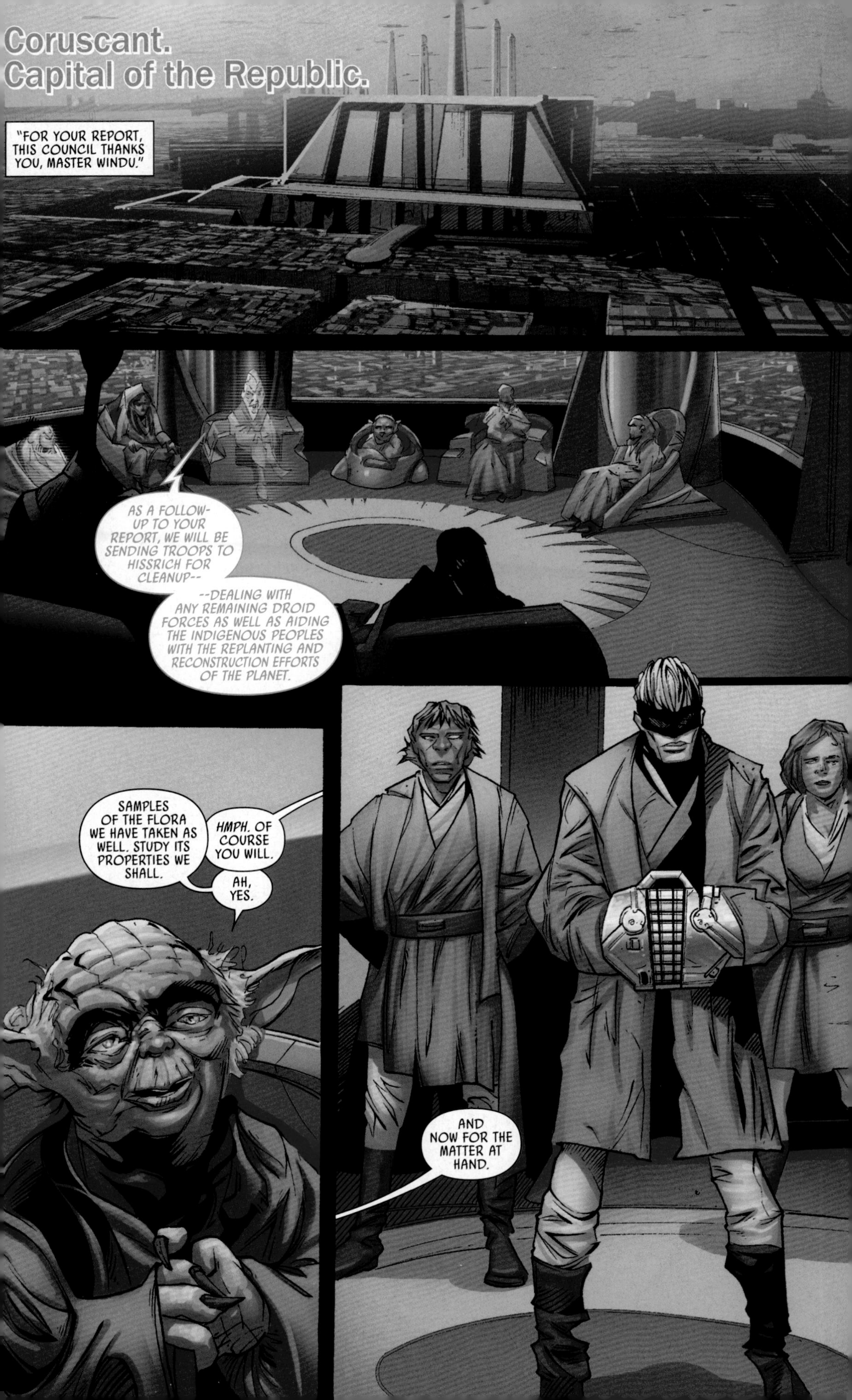
Coruscant.
Capital of the Republic.
"FOR YOUR REPORT, THIS COUNCIL THANKS YOU, MASTER WINDU."
AS A FOLLOW-UP TO YOUR REPORT, WE WILL BE SENDING TROOPS TO HISSRICH FOR CLEANUP--
--DEALING WITH ANY REMAINING DROID FORCES AS WELL AS AIDING THE INDIGENOUS PEOPLES WITH THE REPLANTING AND RECONSTRUCTION EFFORTS OF THE PLANET.
SAMPLES OF THE FLORA WE HAVE TAKEN AS WELL. STUDY ITS PROPERTIES WE SHALL.
HMPH. OF COURSE YOU WILL.
AH, YES.
AND NOW FOR THE MATTER AT HAND.

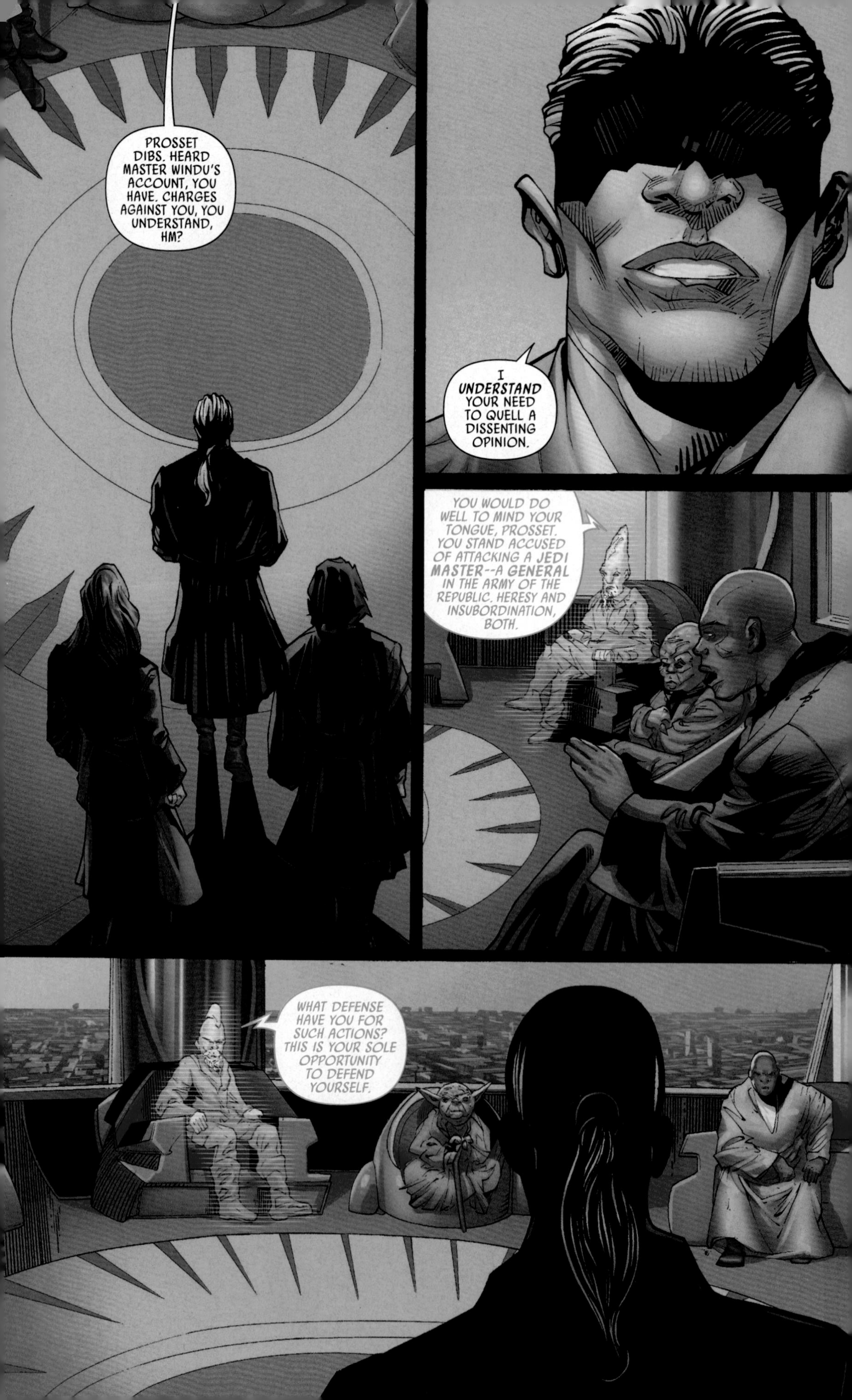
PROSSET DIBS. HEARD MASTER WINDU'S ACCOUNT, YOU HAVE. CHARGES AGAINST YOU, YOU UNDERSTAND, HM?
I UNDERSTAND YOUR NEED TO QUELL A DISSENTING OPINION.
YOU WOULD DO WELL TO MIND YOUR TONGUE, PROSSET. YOU STAND ACCUSED OF ATTACKING A JEDI MASTER--A GENERAL IN THE ARMY OF THE REPUBLIC. HERESY AND INSUBORDINATION, BOTH.
WHAT DEFENSE HAVE YOU FOR SUCH ACTIONS? THIS IS YOUR SOLE OPPORTUNITY TO DEFEND YOURSELF.

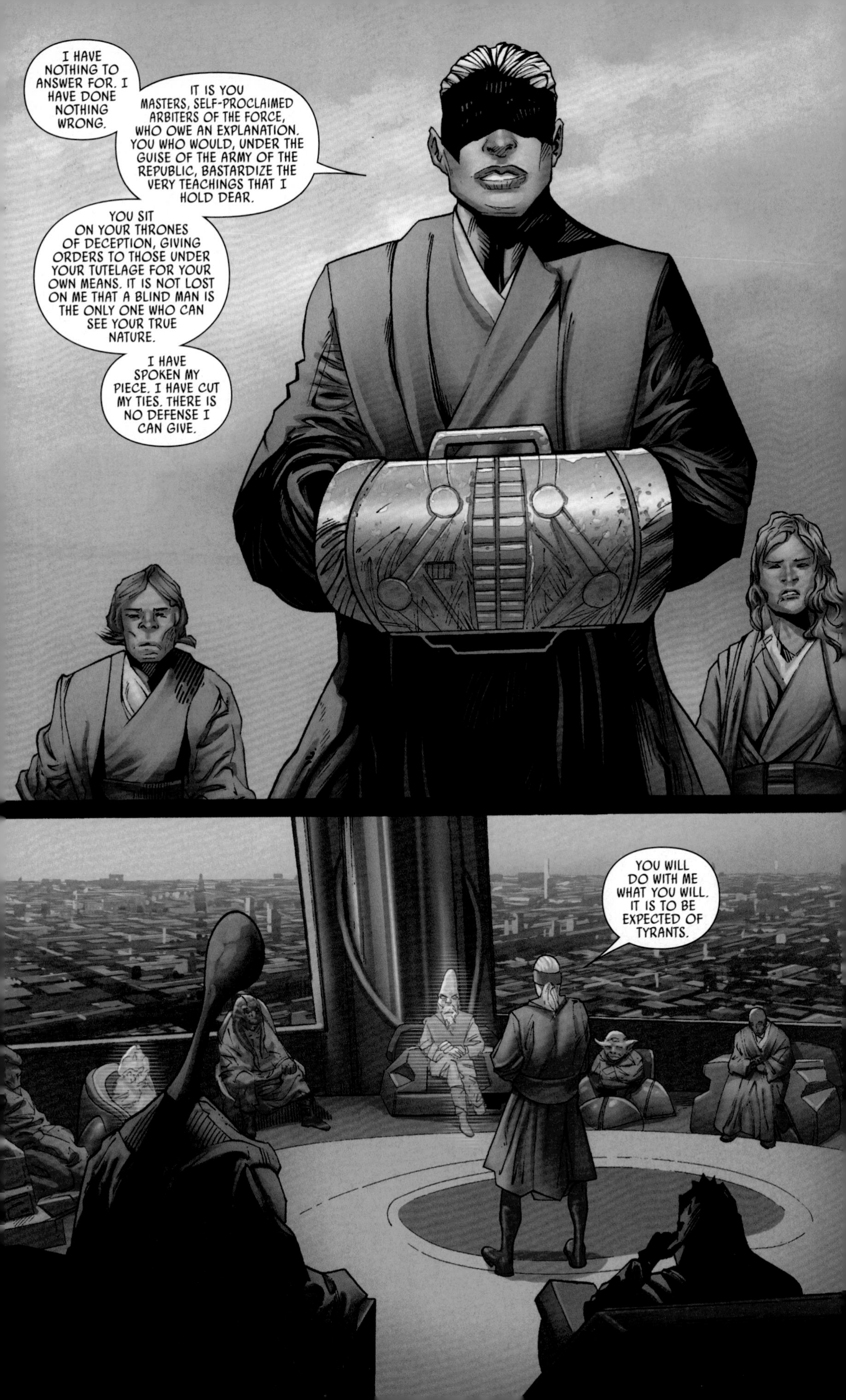
I HAVE NOTHING TO ANSWER FOR. I HAVE DONE NOTHING WRONG.
IT IS YOU MASTERS, SELF-PROCLAIMED ARBITERS OF THE FORCE, WHO OWE AN EXPLANATION. YOU WHO WOULD, UNDER THE GUISE OF THE ARMY OF THE REPUBLIC, BASTARDIZE THE VERY TEACHINGS THAT I HOLD DEAR.
YOU SIT ON YOUR THRONES OF DECEPTION, GIVING ORDERS TO THOSE UNDER YOUR TUTELAGE FOR YOUR OWN MEANS. IT IS NOT LOST ON ME THAT A BLIND MAN IS THE ONLY ONE WHO CAN SEE YOUR TRUE NATURE.
I HAVE SPOKEN MY PIECE. I HAVE CUT MY TIES. THERE IS NO DEFENSE I CAN GIVE.
YOU WILL DO WITH ME WHAT YOU WILL. IT IS TO BE EXPECTED OF TYRANTS.

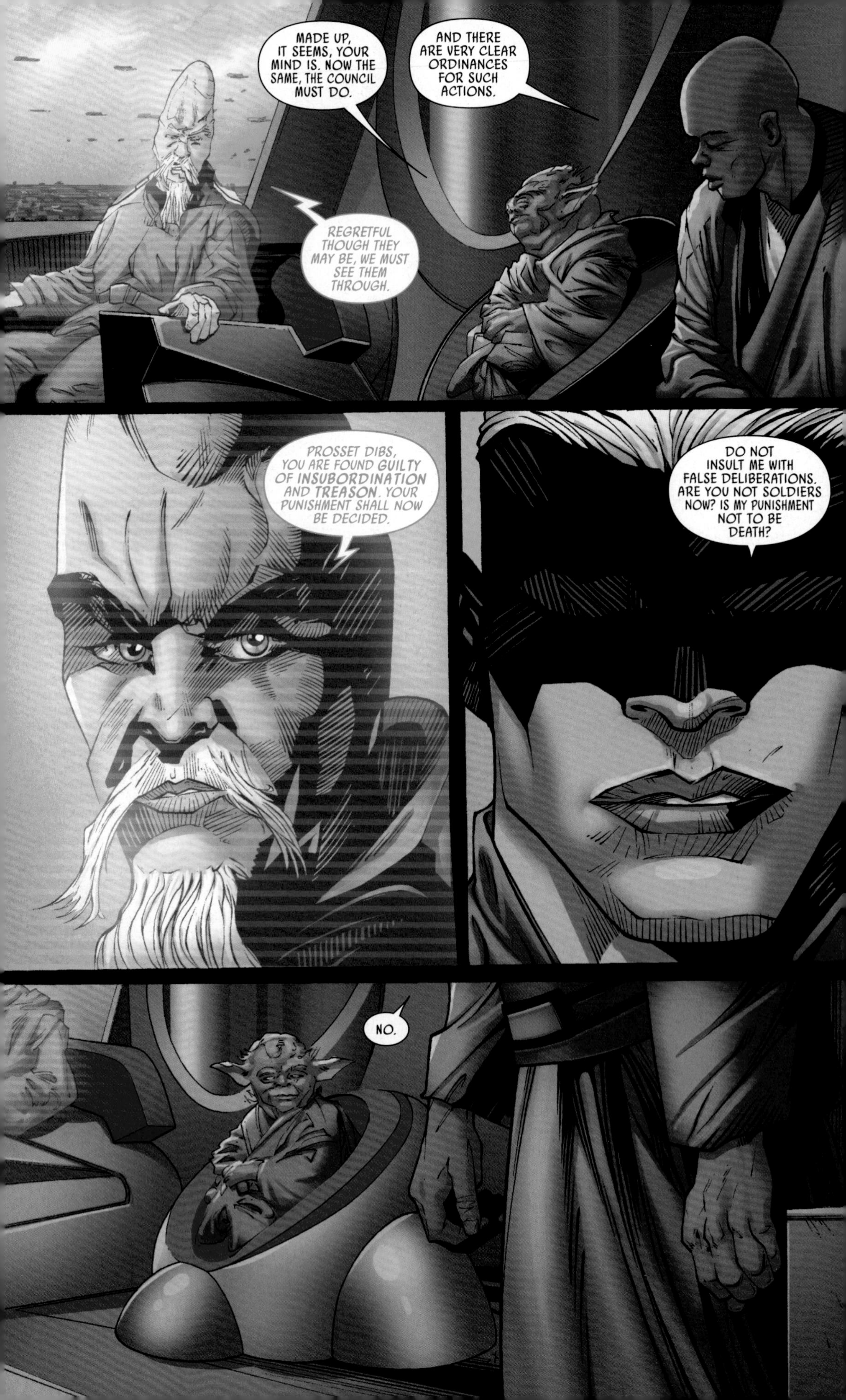
MADE UP, IT SEEMS, YOUR MIND IS. NOW THE SAME, THE COUNCIL MUST DO.
AND THERE ARE VERY CLEAR ORDINANCES FOR SUCH ACTIONS.
REGRETFUL THOUGH THEY MAY BE, WE MUST SEE THEM THROUGH.
PROSSET DIBS, YOU ARE FOUND GUILTY OF INSUBORDINATION AND TREASON. YOUR PUNISHMENT SHALL NOW BE DECIDED.
DO NOT INSULT ME WITH FALSE DELIBERATIONS. ARE YOU NOT SOLDIERS NOW? IS MY PUNISHMENT NOT TO BE DEATH?
NO.

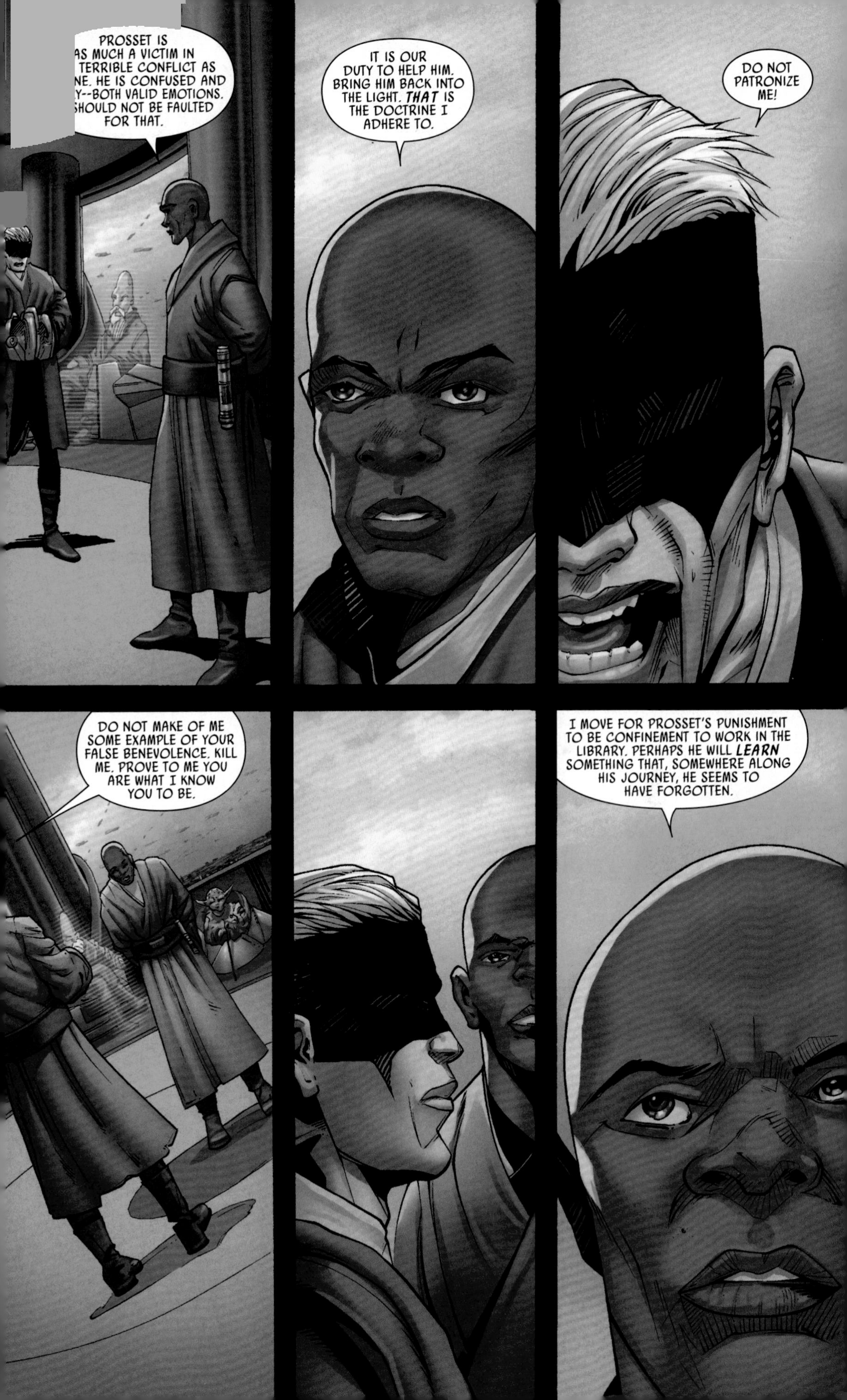

PROSSET IS AS MUCH A VICTIM IN TERRIBLE CONFLICT AS NE. HE IS CONFUSED AND Y--BOTH VALID EMOTIONS. SHOULD NOT BE FAULTED FOR THAT.
IT IS OUR DUTY TO HELP HIM. BRING HIM BACK INTO THE LIGHT. *THAT* IS THE DOCTRINE I ADHERE TO.
DO NOT PATRONIZE ME!
DO NOT MAKE OF ME SOME EXAMPLE OF YOUR FALSE BENEVOLENCE. KILL ME. PROVE TO ME YOU ARE WHAT I KNOW YOU TO BE.
I MOVE FOR PROSSET'S PUNISHMENT TO BE CONFINEMENT TO WORK IN THE LIBRARY. PERHAPS HE WILL *LEARN* SOMETHING THAT, SOMEWHERE ALONG HIS JOURNEY, HE SEEMS TO HAVE FORGOTTEN.

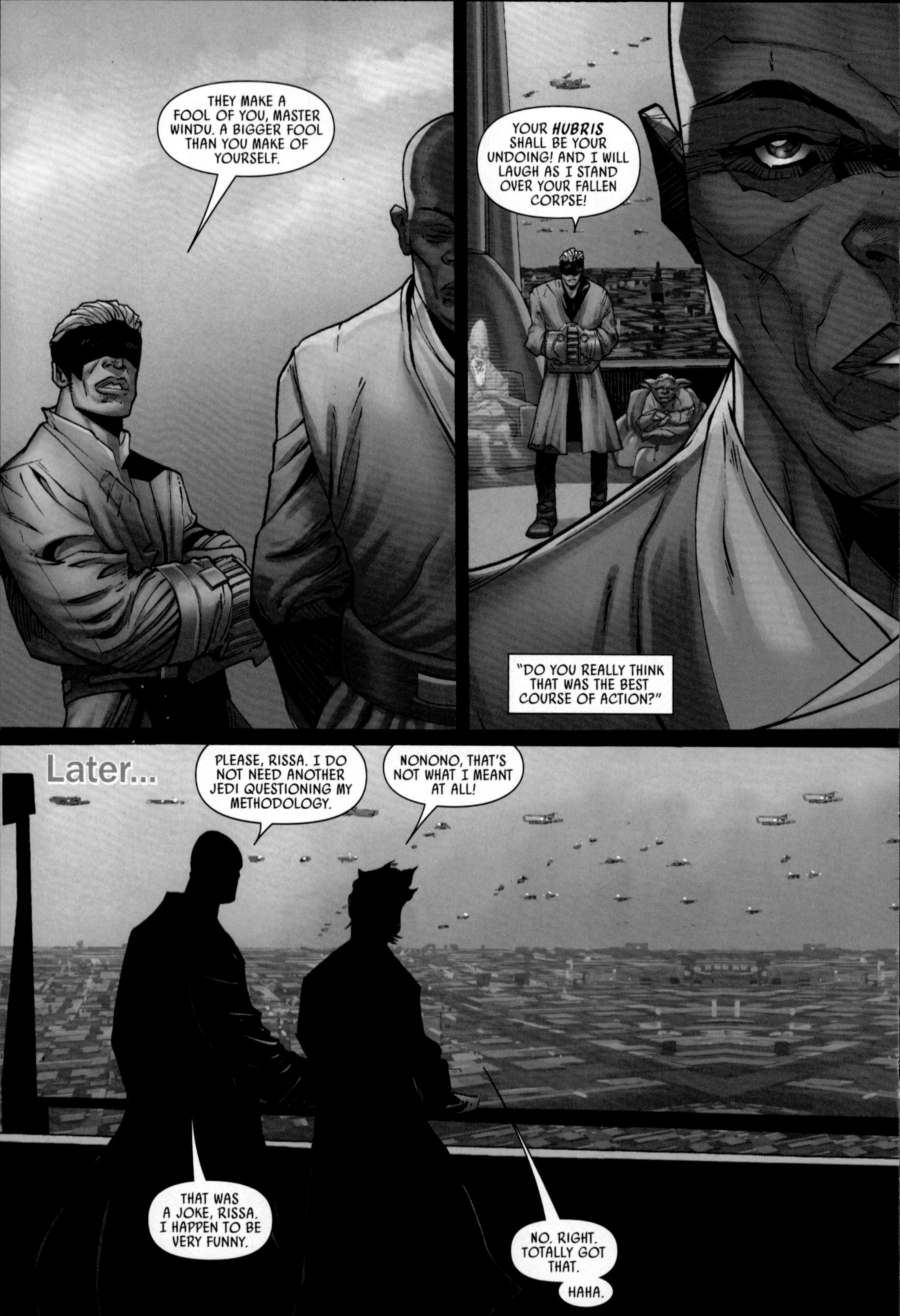
THEY MAKE A FOOL OF YOU, MASTER WINDU. A BIGGER FOOL THAN YOU MAKE OF YOURSELF.
YOUR HUBRIS SHALL BE YOUR UNDOING! AND I WILL LAUGH AS I STAND OVER YOUR FALLEN CORPSE!
"DO YOU REALLY THINK THAT WAS THE BEST COURSE OF ACTION?"
Later...
PLEASE, RISSA. I DO NOT NEED ANOTHER JEDI QUESTIONING MY METHODOLOGY.
NONONO, THAT'S NOT WHAT I MEANT AT ALL!
THAT WAS A JOKE, RISSA. I HAPPEN TO BE VERY FUNNY.
NO. RIGHT. TOTALLY GOT THAT.
HAHA.

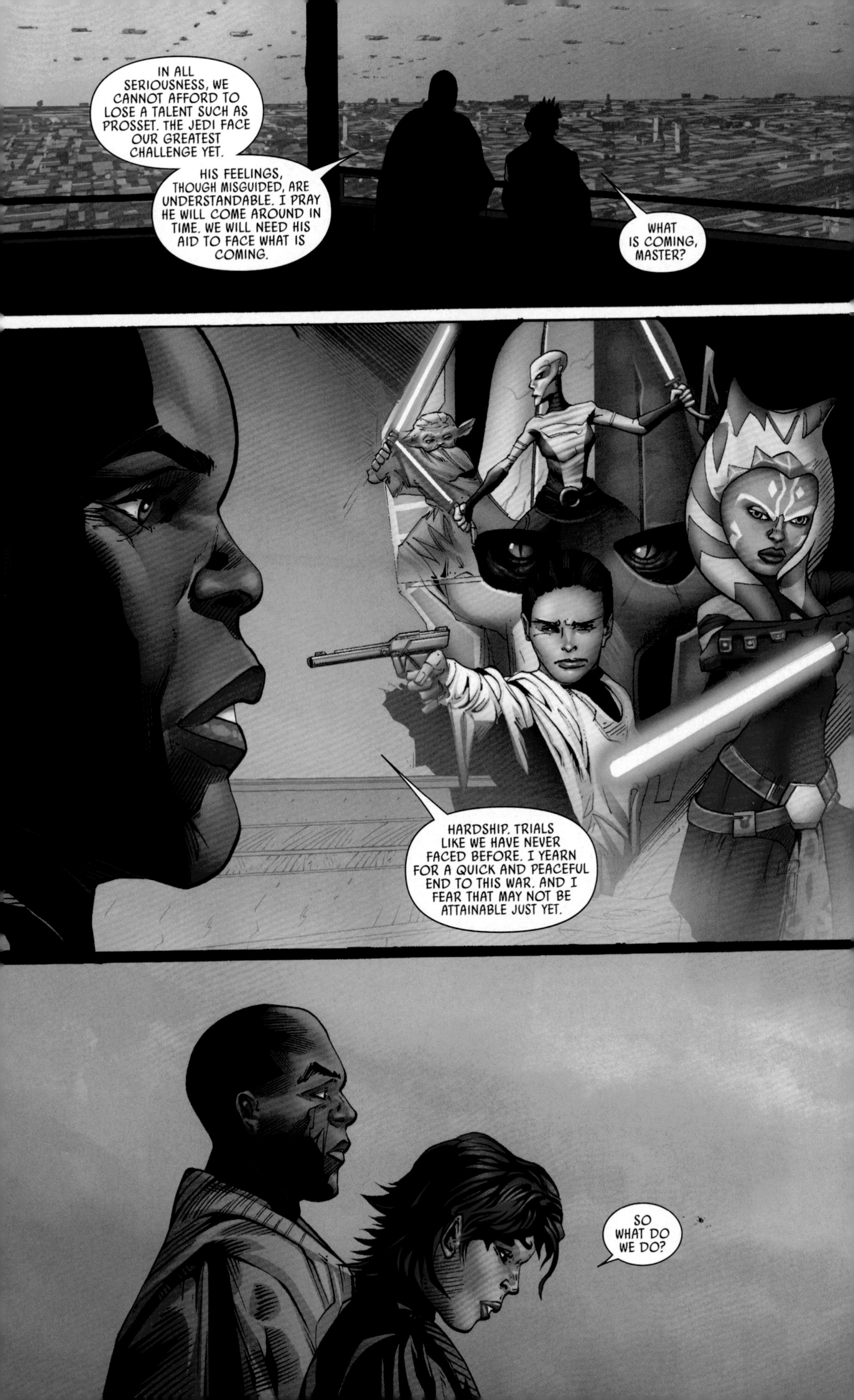
IN ALL SERIOUSNESS, WE CANNOT AFFORD TO LOSE A TALENT SUCH AS PROSSET. THE JEDI FACE OUR GREATEST CHALLENGE YET.
HIS FEELINGS, THOUGH MISGUIDED, ARE UNDERSTANDABLE. I PRAY HE WILL COME AROUND IN TIME. WE WILL NEED HIS AID TO FACE WHAT IS COMING.
WHAT IS COMING, MASTER?
HARDSHIP. TRIALS LIKE WE HAVE NEVER FACED BEFORE. I YEARN FOR A QUICK AND PEACEFUL END TO THIS WAR. AND I FEAR THAT MAY NOT BE ATTAINABLE JUST YET.
SO WHAT DO WE DO?

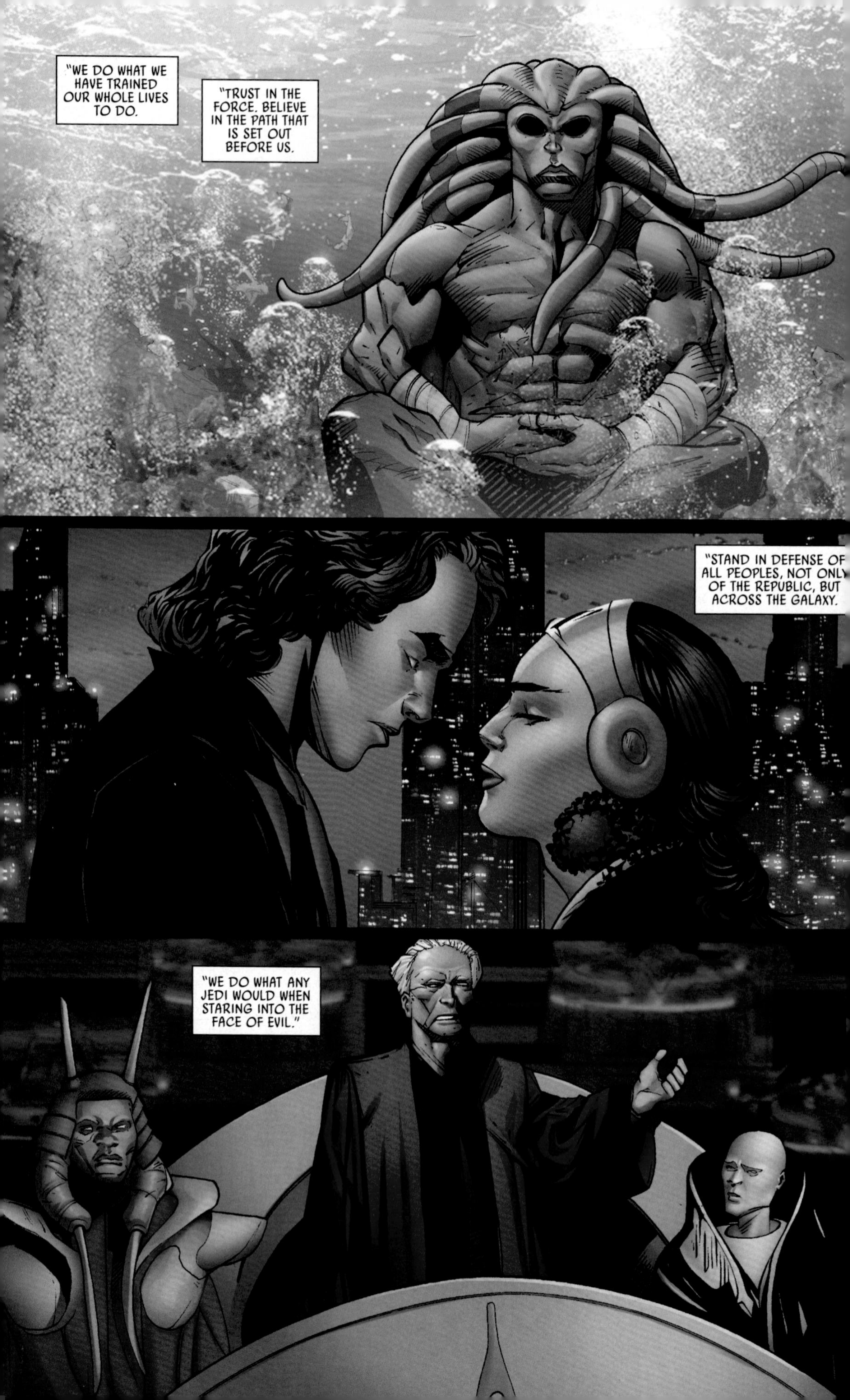
"WE DO WHAT WE HAVE TRAINED OUR WHOLE LIVES TO DO.
"TRUST IN THE FORCE. BELIEVE IN THE PATH THAT IS SET OUT BEFORE US.
"STAND IN DEFENSE OF ALL PEOPLES, NOT ONLY OF THE REPUBLIC, BUT ACROSS THE GALAXY.
"WE DO WHAT ANY JEDI WOULD WHEN STARING INTO THE FACE OF EVIL."

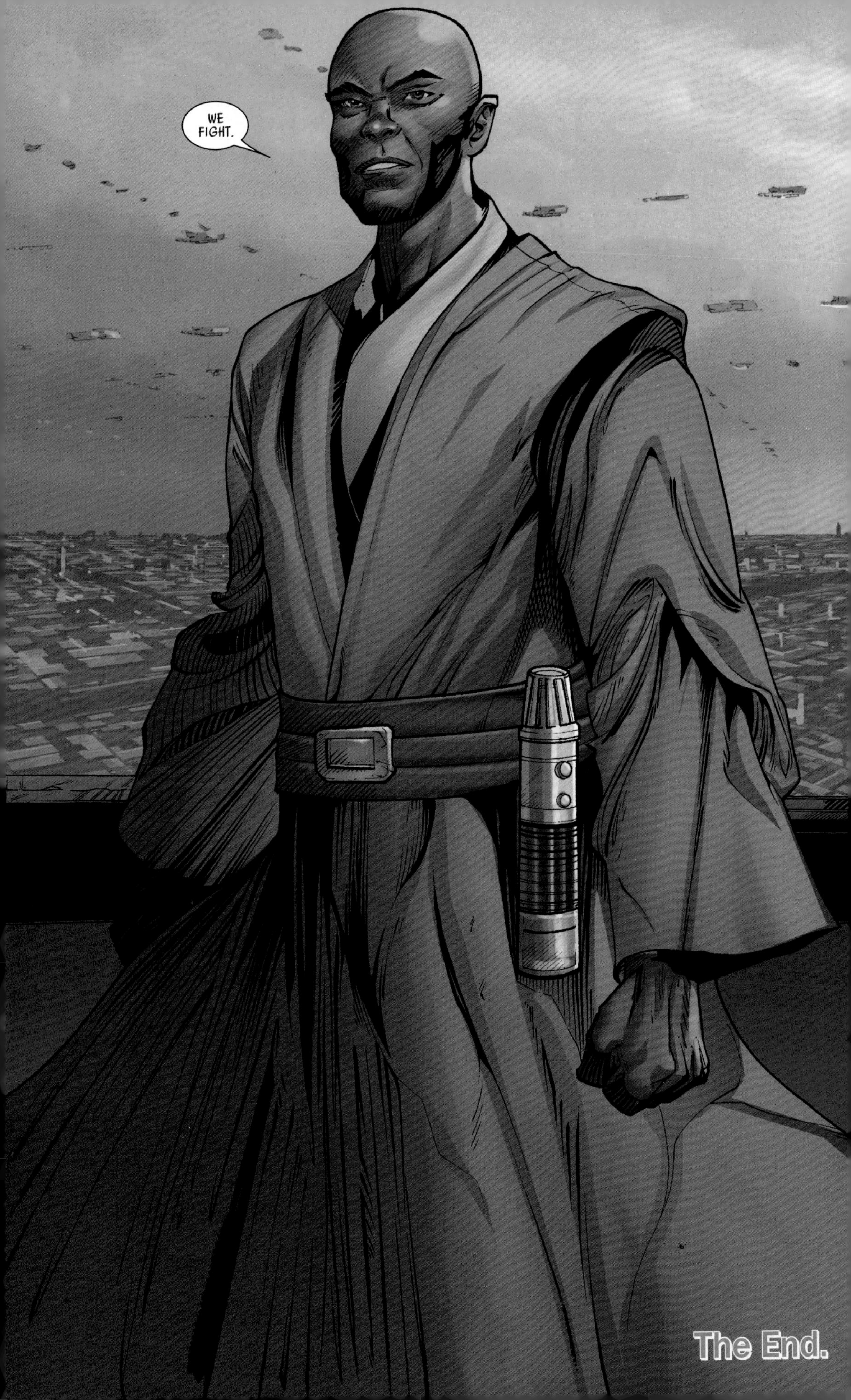
WE FIGHT.
The End.

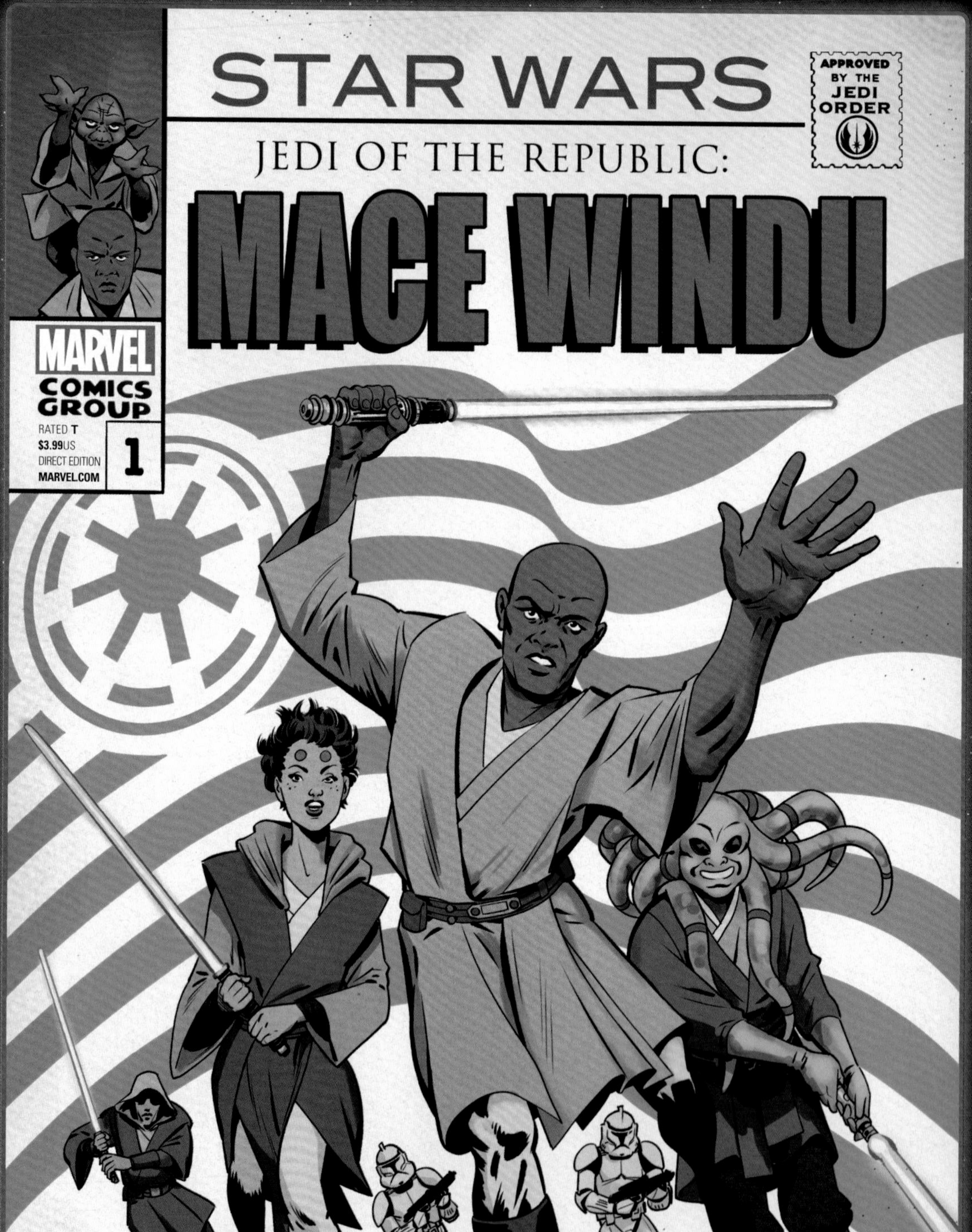
STAR WARS
APPROVED BY THE JEDI ORDER
JEDI OF THE REPUBLIC:
MACE WINDU
MARVEL COMICS GROUP
RATED T
$3.99US
DIRECT EDITION
MARVEL.COM
1

**STAR WARS: JEDI OF THE REPUBLIC — MACE WINDU 1**
**HOMAGE VARIANT BY JAVIER RODRÍGUEZ & ÁLVARO LÓPEZ**

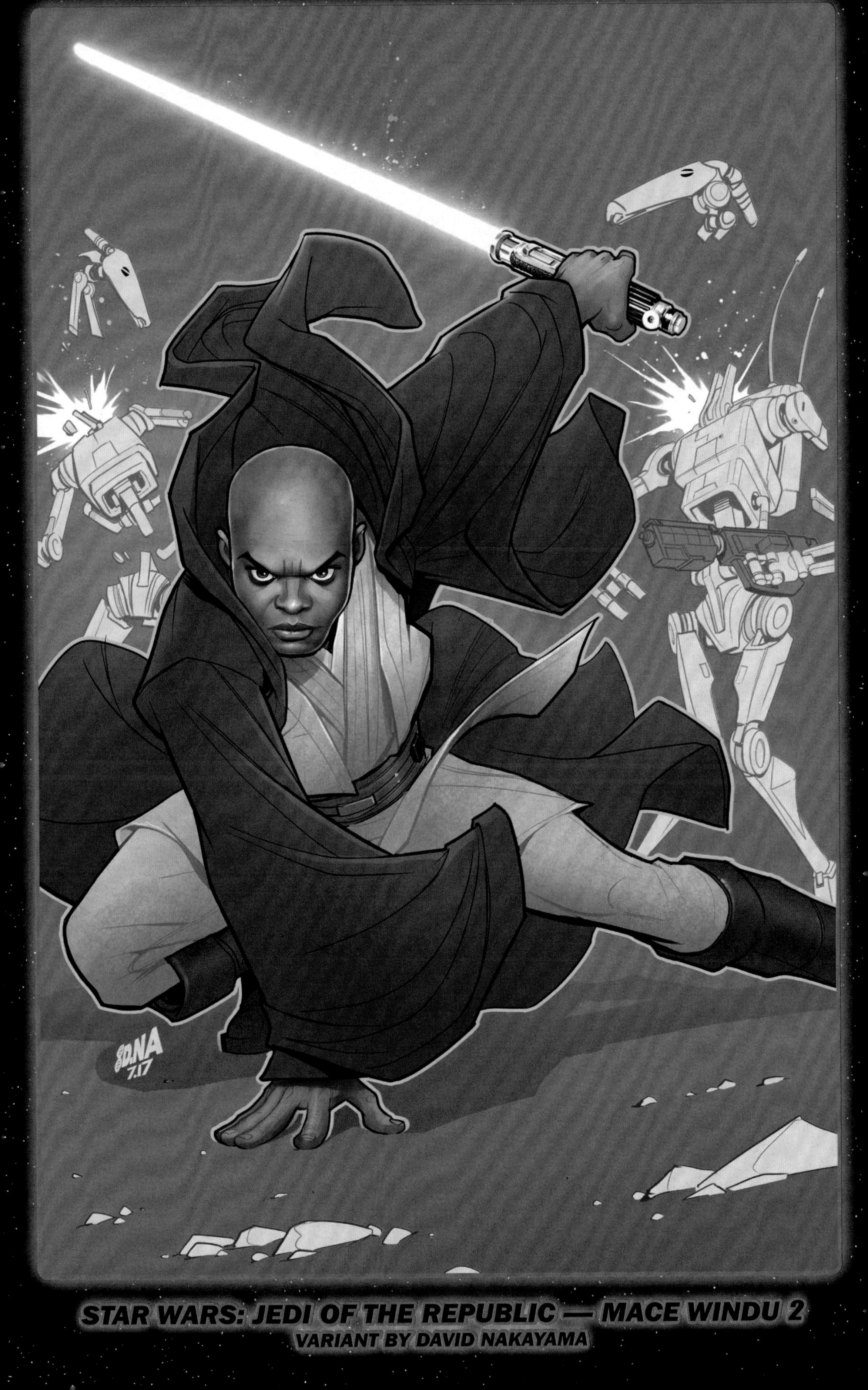

**STAR WARS: JEDI OF THE REPUBLIC — MACE WINDU 2**
**VARIANT BY DAVID NAKAYAMA**

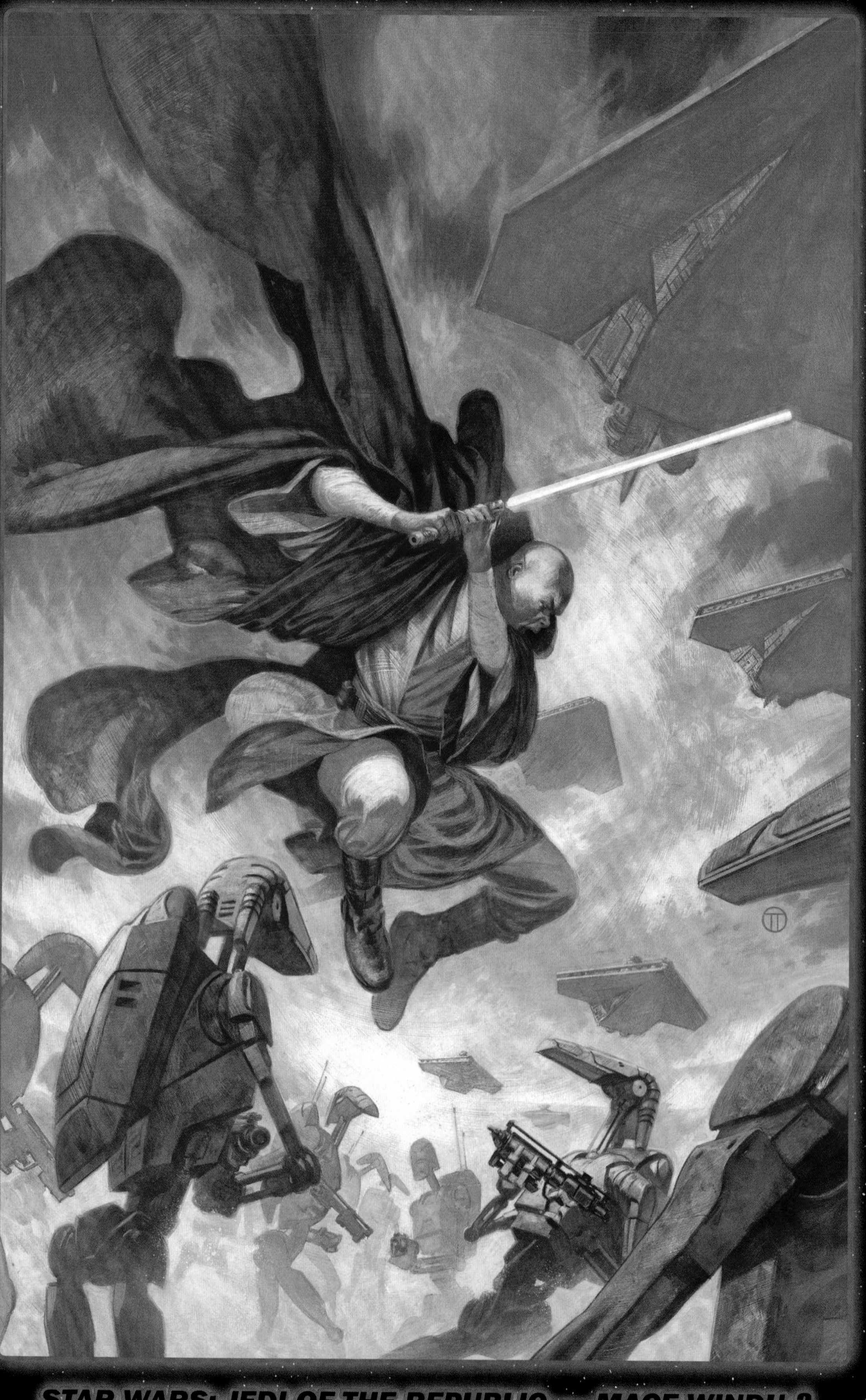

STAR WARS: JEDI OF THE REPUBLIC — MACE WINDU 3
VARIANT BY JULIAN TOTINO TEDESCO

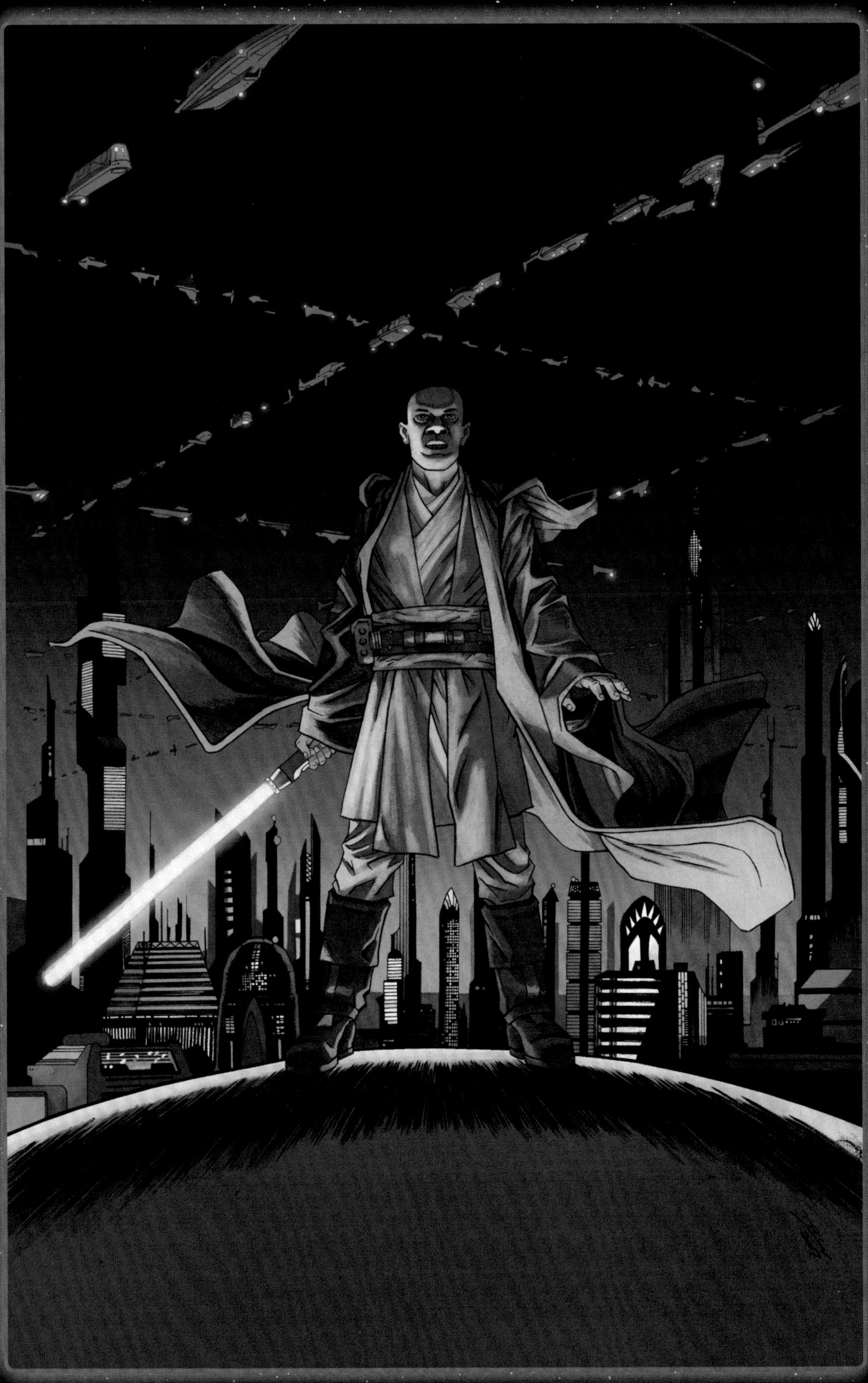

**STAR WARS: JEDI OF THE REPUBLIC — MACE WINDU 4**
**VARIANT BY DECLAN SHALVEY & JORDIE BELLAIRE**

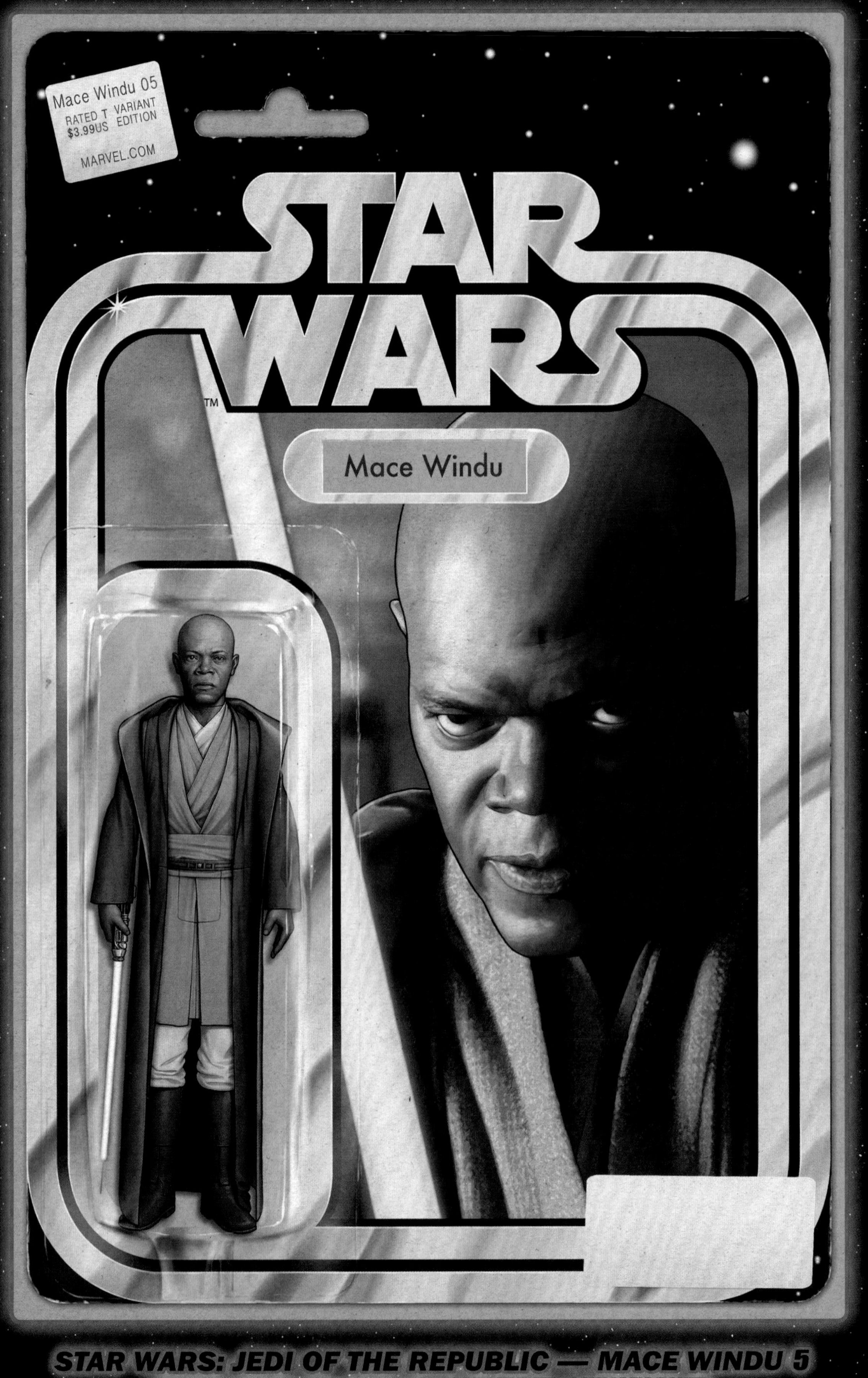
Mace Windu 05
RATED T
$3.99US
VARIANT EDITION
MARVEL.COM
STAR WARS
TM
Mace Windu

**STAR WARS: JEDI OF THE REPUBLIC — MACE WINDU 5**
**ACTION FIGURE VARIANT BY JOHN TYLER CHRISTOPHER**

# OFFICIAL GRAPHIC NOVEL ADAPTATION!

## STAR WARS: EPISODE I – THE PHANTOM MENACE HC
### 978-1-3029-0074-8

## AVAILABLE NOW WHEREVER BOOKS ARE SOLD

# BETRAYED BY HIS MASTER AND CRAVING VENGEANCE, MAUL STRIKES BACK!

**STAR WARS: DARTH MAUL - SON OF DATHOMIR**
978-1302908461

# ON SALE NOVEMBER 2017
## WHEREVER BOOKS ARE SOLD

TO FIND A COMIC SHOP NEAR YOU, VISIT COMICSHOPLOCATOR.COM

# FOR THE FULL STORY, READ

**STAR WARS: DARTH MAUL**
978-0785195894

# ON SALE NOW
## WHEREVER BOOKS ARE SOLD

# RETURN TO A GALAXY
# FAR, FAR AWAY!

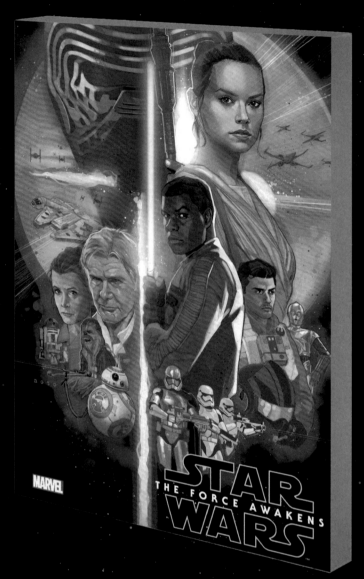

**STAR WARS: THE FORCE AWAKENS ADAPTATION TPB**
978-1302902032

# ON SALE NOVEMBER 2017
## WHEREVER BOOKS ARE SOLD

TO FIND A COMIC SHOP NEAR YOU, VISIT COMICSHOPLOCATOR.COM

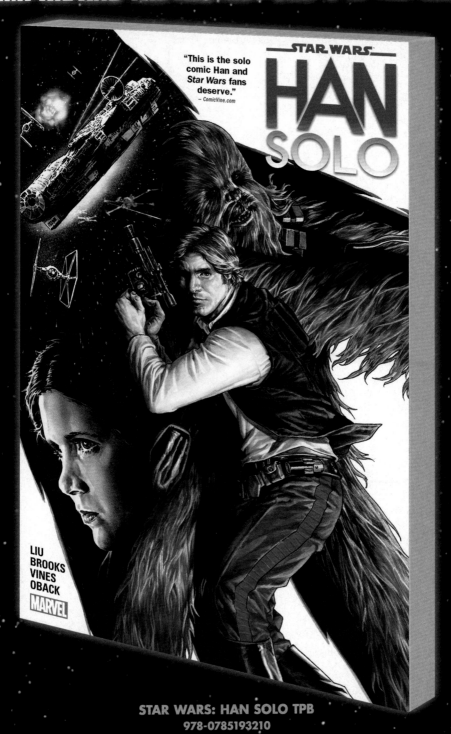

# THE DARK LORD OF THE SITH'S FIRST DEADLY MISSION

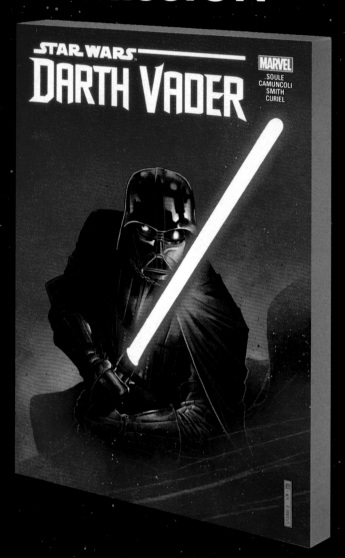

**STAR WARS: DARTH VADER: DARK LORD OF THE SITH
VOL. 1: IMPERIAL MACHINE TPB
978-1302907440**

# ON SALE NOVEMBER 2017
## WHEREVER BOOKS ARE SOLD

**TO FIND A COMIC SHOP NEAR YOU, VISIT COMICSHOPLOCATOR.COM**